WOMEN
AND THE *DICTIONARY OF NATIONAL BIOGRAPHY*

A GUIDE TO *DNB* VOLUMES 1885–1985
AND
MISSING PERSONS

WOMEN
and the *Dictionary of National Biography*

a guide to *DNB* volumes 1885–1985
and
Missing Persons

Gillian Fenwick

SCOLAR PRESS

Published by
SCOLAR PRESS
Gower House
Croft Road
Aldershot
Hants GU11 3HR
England

Ashgate Publishing Company
Old Post Road
Brookfield
Vermont 05036
USA

British Library Cataloguing in Publication Data

Fenwick, Gillian
  Women and the "Dictionary of National Biography": guide to DNB
  Volumes 1885–1985 and "Missing Persons"
  I. Title
  016.9207

Library of Congress Cataloging-in-Publication Data

Fenwick, Gillian.
  Women and the Dictionary of national biography: a Guide to DNB volumes
1885–1985 and Missing persons / Gillian Fenwick.
      p. cm.
  1. Dictionary of national biography–Bibliography.   2. Women – Great
Britain – Biography – Bibliography.   3. Women biographers – Great Britain –
Bibliography   4. Biography as a literary form – Bibliography.   5. Great
Britain – Biography – Bibliography.
  I. Title.
  DA28.D53F43   1994
  016.92072'0941-dc20   93-48315 CIP

ISBN 0-85967-914-4

Typeset by Poole Typesetting (Wessex) Ltd, Bournemouth, Dorset.
Printed in Great Britain by Hartnolls Ltd, Bodmin.

For
Miriam Patricia Cloak (1901–1988)
and
Margaret Edith Richardson (1887–1960)

Contents

Preface

This book on women subjects and contributors continues my work on the history of the *Dictionary of National Biography*.[1]

The *DNB* is alive and well, more than a century after its publication began. Supplements continue to be added, the *Missing Persons* volume was published in 1993, and a *New Dictionary of National Biography* is planned. From thorough but dull early supplements, ideas and editorial practice have changed so that the modern Dictionary is more as Leslie Stephen, the first editor, envisaged but was not always able to achieve. Today there is no room for what he termed 'names which are merely names'; articles are brief; and both personal recollection and scholarship are valued. *DNB* subjects have changed. There are fewer martyrs, saints, and heroines, but more astrophysicists and tennis players; fewer society hostesses and 'daughters of ...', and more trade unionists and entrepreneurs. Today, birth alone does not guarantee *DNB* entry. As one editor has suggested, most subjects select themselves for admission through their lives and work.

The *DNB* is more than a reference tool: it is a literary institution. Its health is, therefore, of concern to all who refer to it, write for it, 'select themselves' for it, or merely relish its existence and authority. As I waited for *Missing Persons* to be published in order to finish this book, the first series of the Dictionary, 1885–1900, seemed matchless not merely, in Lord Rosebery's words, 'the greatest literary monument of the Victorian age', but the best that the *DNB* could be. *Missing Persons* has made me think again, and think optimistically, about its future and the directions in which it may go. The Dictionary will never be finished, and my own work on its history and progress will require constant addenda. Even when it is up to date chronologically, the *DNB* will always require organizational revision. Now there is a desperate need for a single cumulative index. The *Index and Epitome* is an index to the first issue, 1885–1900, and the 1901 supplement; the most recent twentieth-century supple-

---

1. See Gillian Fenwick, *The Contributors' Index to the Dictionary of National Biography 1885–1901* (Winchester: St Paul's Bibliographies, 1989); '*The Athenaeum* and the *Dictionary of National Biography*', *Victorian Periodicals Review*, Vol. XXIII, No. 4 (Winter 1990), 180–188; and *Leslie Stephen's Life in Letters: A Bibliographical Study* (Aldershot: Scolar Press, 1993)

ment always contains an index from 1901 to the date of that volume; and *Missing Persons* has its own index. But to search for a subject it is necessary to consult all three sources. Even with a *New DNB* in prospect, the original will always be a valuable reference source, the usefulness of which will depend on its accessibility.

This book begins with a general overview of the *Dictionary of National Biography* from the 1880s to the present day, with particular reference to the role of women both as subjects and contributors. This is followed by Part 1, a comprehensive list of women subjects; Part 2, women contributors, beginning with lists of women contributors arranged by *DNB* volume, followed by an alphabetical index of women contributors and their *DNB* articles; Part 3, male contributors who have written about women; and Part 4, a summary occupation index of women subjects.

I am pleased to have the opportunity to thank the individuals and the institutions that have helped me as I worked on this project. For permission to quote from letters in their collections I thank the Trustees of the National Library of Scotland, and the University of Leeds. I appreciate the help and cooperation of John Murray Ltd and Oxford University Press. My thanks to John Bicknell, Mary Cross, Virginia Fenwick, David McKitterick, Virginia Murray, and the President and Fellows of Clare Hall, Cambridge, especially Mr John Garrod. My work was supported in part by two Northrop Frye Visiting Scholarships at Victoria University in the University of Toronto. I am most grateful to my friends and colleagues there for advice and encouragement, in particular President Eva Kushner, Dr Robert Brandeis and the staff of the E. J. Pratt Library, Professor Laure Riese, Professor Kenneth Thompson and Mrs Ann Lewis. I am especially grateful to Michael Collie, Professor Emeritus at York University, Toronto, who encouraged me to look at Leslie Stephen's career and whose searching questions led me into the publishing history of the *DNB* in 1984. His teaching and the example of his bibliographical work have been a profound influence and a source of inspiration. I thank Robert Cross of St Paul's Bibliographies for his enthusiastic support, and contacts made on my behalf. I am sad to record that my mother, Joyce Manning, who painstakingly checked all the references except those in *Missing Persons*, and who had become a *DNB* enthusiast, died before my work was completed. I am deeply grateful to Jane Millgate for her generous advice, support and time, and for her friendship.

Gillian Fenwick
Trinity College, University of Toronto
July 1994

Introduction

Anyone interested in women's history might take the *Dictionary of National Biography* as a starting point. In theory, here are the lives of all British women worthy of note from the beginnings of history until the late twentieth century, excluding the living. In practice, there are 1,518 women among 34,533 men. Here, too, are small but gradually increasing numbers of women writers working as *DNB* contributors from the late Victorian era to the present day. Despite the fact that the *DNB* has been, and to some extent still is, a male-dominated institution, its importance as a resource about and by women deserves recognition.

The Victorian Dictionary

There had been attempts at biographical dictionaries in Britain before the *DNB*. The *Biographia Britannica* was published in seven folios between 1747 and 1766. A second edition was planned, and appeared between 1778 and 1793, but publication stopped when only the letter F had been reached. The Society for the Diffusion of Useful Knowledge began a *Dictionary of Universal Biography* in 1814, but abandoned it after only seven of the proposed 32 volumes had been published and when only the letter A had been completed. Rose's *New General Biographical Dictionary*, published in 12 volumes between 1839 and 1847, aimed at universality but was inadequate in both national and international terms. The French *Biographie Universelle*, published in 40 volumes between 1843 and 1863, was an indication of what could be achieved, but in Britain the problems, chiefly of scale and finance, seemed insurmountable.

Scale was less of a problem where biographical collections specifically about women were concerned, and a few had been published. George Ballard of Magdalen College, Oxford, privately printed his *Memoirs of Several Ladies of Great Britain, who have been celebrated for their writings or skill in the learned languages, arts and sciences in 1752*, with another edition in 1775; and the *Biographium Fæmineum. The Female Worthies or Memoirs of the Most Illustrious Ladies of All Ages and Nations* was published in London in two volumes in 1766. In the nineteenth century Mary Hays's *Female Biography; or Memoirs of Illustrious and Celebrated Women* was published in London in six volumes in

1803, and in Philadelphia in three volumes in 1807; Julia Kavanagh published *Women in France in the Eighteenth Century* in 1850, *Women of Christianity* in 1852, *French Women of Letters* in 1862, and *English Women of Letters* in 1863. We know that there was a resource collection in the *DNB* offices, so, presumably, at least some of these works on women were available to the first editorial staff.

George Smith, of the publishers Smith, Elder & Co., recognized that a financial loss on a biographical dictionary was inevitable, but his commercial successes outside publishing, notably the purchase of the Apollinaris Table Water Company, were enough to finance the Dictionary and make the project practicable if not profitable; and he was keen to leave a lasting mark on literature and to make what he later described as a 'gift to English letters ... a fitting contribution on my part to English history.'[1] He took the previous failures as a challenge, and relished the idea of an individual and private enterprise undertaking a national project which, outside England, was only possible with state or institutional support.

The Victorian *DNB* was largely a male domain. Proprietor, editor, staff and the vast majority of contributors, to say nothing of Dictionary subjects, were men. By the autumn of 1882 Smith had appointed Leslie Stephen as editor. Stephen had been editing Smith's *Cornhill Magazine* since 1871, but its circulation was declining and Smith needed to make changes, beginning with a new editor. Offering Stephen the *DNB* was thus doubly to Smith's advantage. In October 1882 Stephen began setting up the *DNB* offices, soliciting suggestions for a sub-editor, and searching for contributors. That the staff would all be male was clearly taken for granted. Stephen told Edmund Gosse:

> I shall want a good sub-editor – a man of knowledge, good at abstracting, looking up authorities & the facts & an efficient whip in regard both to printers and contributors. If you happen to know of any such man, I should be much obliged by a suggestion.[2]

And later, in another letter to Gosse, he was undecided between his need for 'a man of business superiority or a man of antiquarian or other knowledge'.[3] Gosse suggested Thomas Hall Caine, who became a contributor but not a member of the permanent staff. Meanwhile, there were other candidates from Leslie Stephen's Oxford and Cambridge connections, including Frederick James Furnivall, an eminent scholar and editor of early English texts. Like Leslie Stephen he was an old Trinity Hall, Cambridge, man. He also became a contributor, but he was not offered the sub-editor's job. Leslie Stephen did, however, act on Furnivall's recommendation to approach Sidney Lee, a recent graduate of Balliol College, Oxford, and in March 1883 Lee became sub-editor. Between them, the editor and sub-editor knew enough Cambridge and Oxford men to establish what Leslie Stephen described as 'a good team at starting'.[4] Major contributions to the Dictionary were made by a number of contemporaries or near contemporaries of Leslie Stephen at Cambridge: Adolphus

William Ward was at Peterhouse, Cambridge, in the late 1850s; John Knox Laughton was at Caius College and, like Leslie Stephen, was a candidate in the mathematical tripos in the 1850s; Lionel Henry Cust was also a Cambridge man. Thompson Cooper, the compiler of Dictionary subject lists, was from Cambridge and, although he did not attend the university, his younger brother was at Trinity Hall during Leslie Stephen's period as a resident don and fellow in the early 1860s. Similarly, a number of Lee's Oxford contemporaries or near contemporaries became staff members or regular contributors. They included Charles Harding Firth, Charles Lethbridge Kingsford, Æneas James George Albert Mackay, Frederick Pollard, Reginald Lane Poole, James McMullen Rigg, John Horace Round, Thomas Seccombe, James Tait, and Thomas Frederick Tout. Between them, this group of men wrote more than a quarter of the Dictionary articles. There were 27,236 articles in the first series of the *DNB*, 1885–1900, written by 647 contributors. I classify about 70 article writers arbitrarily as major contributors, by which I mean that they each wrote more than 80 articles. Cooper wrote 1415 articles, Cust 759, Firth 222, Kingsford 375, Laughton 895, Mackay 126, Pollard 425, Poole 78, Rigg 605, Round 81, Seccombe 576, Tait 135, Tout 237, and Ward 58. Leslie Stephen wrote 281 and Sidney Lee 757.[5]

The importance of London clubs in the recruiting of *DNB* editorial staff and contributors is a subject beyond the scope of this work, but since Smith, Stephen and Lee all belonged to gentlemen's clubs – they were all, for example, members of the Athenaeum Club – it seems a fair assumption that this broadened the network of likely male contributors to the Dictionary, and, like the Universities, was another way in which women writers were excluded. The Dictionary offices were at 14 Waterloo Place in central London, just a stone's throw from the Athenaeum Club and within half a mile of most of the gentlemen's clubs in St James's. As C.H. Firth has described the *DNB* editorial office, there were evidently similarities between those club rooms and these on the top floor of 14 Waterloo Place:

> The small room at the back of the flat was the editor's sanctum. The large front room looking into Waterloo Place was the workshop; several large tables, many inkpots, piles of proofs and manuscripts on chairs and tables, a little pyramid of Stephen's pipes at one end of the chimney piece, a little pyramid of Lee's pipes at the other end. The narrow side room opening out of it held on its shelves a fine assortment of reference books, sets of the *Gentleman's Magazine* and of *Notes and Queries*, Wood, Le Neve, and other biographical collections.[6]

It was a setting in which women were, if not unwelcome, then at least out of place. Even when office routine was becoming too much of a drain on Leslie Stephen's physical and psychological health, and when the existing staff was proven to be incapable of coping with the work load, changes which included women were only reluctantly made. In late 1888 the clerical staff was increased from a single clerk, H. E. Murray, who worked at the Dictionary throughout the publication of the first issue, to include a young female typist. Leslie Stephen was less than sanguine about her arrival. He told Smith:

> I do not care to see the young lady beforehand – especially as we are to have a week's trial. I do not think that *we* shall be able to give her much to do beyond the typewriting. It remains to be seen how much time that will take. When she begins she had better come here and see me in the afternoon & I can give her some MSS to begin upon as soon as she likes. I shall want to explain many things.
>
> I fancy that our typewriter will want some grooming. It may be a little rusty and the blacking has to be done. But I suppose your young lady is up to that. Is she to be in the next room?[7]

By January 1883, the new editorial staff, Henry Tedder and Charles Keary, had drawn up the list of names for inclusion in the first volume of the Dictionary using existing lists and dictionaries, with additions. Thompson Cooper was then appointed compiler of lists, and on 9 June 1883 and every following October and April, lists of between 900 and 1000 names were printed in *The Athenaeum* for readers' suggestions, corrections, information on sources, and offers to undertake articles.[8] There were 555 names on the first list, including 15 women. When the *DNB* volumes in which these names appeared were published in April and June 1885, an additional eight women subjects had been added, presumably from *Athenaeum* readers' suggestions. It is likely that a reader's suggestions of additional subjects would often be accompanied by an offer to write *DNB* articles on those subjects. This is clearly the case in a number of instances where names omitted from the lists later appeared as Dictionary articles written by contributors with the same surname as the subject and, presumably, related to them. But it is interesting to note that of the 139 Dictionary articles on both male and female subjects not included in the first *Athenaeum* list, only two were written by women. This perhaps raises the question of how male-oriented a medium *The Athenaeum* was in which to seek contributors and suggestions for subjects. Certainly its literary, music, fine art and science gossip columns, its letters and its obituaries were dominated by male subjects and male writers. Seeking *DNB* subjects and contributors here was perhaps another way in which women were, albeit accidentally, excluded from the Dictionary.

The first volume of the *DNB* was published in January 1885. It included biographies of 505 subjects, 35 of them women. There were 87 contributors to the volume, four of whom were women.[9] There continued to be regular women contributors to this first series, and articles were written about women, but the numbers remained small and, with a few notable exceptions, articles on women tended to be shorter than those on men, or were merely appended to longer articles on male family members.[10] It is interesting, for example, to look at articles on eighteenth- and nineteenth-century women novelists and to compare their entries with similarly popular male novelists from the same periods. Leslie Stephen's article on Jane Austen is less than two pages in length, while his biography of Defoe covers 13 pages, and Swift 23. Similarly, while in a single article Stephen could cover Charlotte, Emily, Anne and Branwell Brontë in less than seven pages, he wrote 12 pages on Dickens and 16 on Thackeray. On numerous occasions, biographies of women are appended to the articles on their fathers, husbands and brothers, their entry in the supplementary index reading 'See under ...' and the name of the male relative, the tacit assumption being that the daughter, wife or sister merely squeezes into the Dictionary by virtue of her family connection. Other women go unmarked in the index, receiving only a cursory nod in the male relative's article. Such is the case, for example, with Leslie Stephen's second wife, Julia, now the subject of scholarly books and articles in her own right,[11] but only noted as unnamed 'wife' in Sidney Lee's article on Leslie Stephen. In a separate category, perhaps all her own, is George Eliot, who appears in the Dictionary under neither her original name, Mary Anne Evans or its variants, nor under her professional name, but under the married name she bore for less than a year and under which she died, Mary Ann Cross. The editorial policy behind this decision, whether moral or literary, is lost to us today, since no publication records or correspondence survive to throw light on it. It is even tempting to see such a move in purely pragmatic terms, which meant that a fairly dull volume of Cs could be enlivened by one of Leslie Stephen's articles, at least a year ahead of the time when it might otherwise have been published under E.

Women contributors, 1885–1901

By 1891 there were still, on average, only four or five women contributors to each volume. Or at least only four or five were named in the List of Writers at the start of each volume. But the evidence is suspicious in at least one case. These are the circumstances. Leslie Stephen's health continued to interfere with his ability to perform full time editorial duties, and in March 1890 Sidney Lee was named joint editor. Stephen hoped to regain his health, but he was ill again early in 1891 and resigned the editorship. Sidney Lee's name as editor appeared alone on the title page from June 1891. Two changes are then noticeable in the Lists of Writers for each volume. The first is that Sidney Lee's identifying initials, SLL, in the lists and at the end of articles he wrote, are changed to SL from Volume XXVII, published in June 1891. SLL stood for Solomon Lazarus Lee, the name under which his birth was registered and under which he grew up. But while he was at Oxford he began to style himself Sidney, and by 1880 he was anxious to drop the Lazarus altogether.[12] His appointment as full and sole editor of the Dictionary made it possible for him to make the change unobtrusively. The second change was that his sister's name, 'Miss Elizabeth Lee', appeared in the List of Writers of Volume XXXII of the Dictionary, published in October 1892. Lee was a lifelong bachelor and lived with his sister. From 1892 until the completion of the Dictionary she was a regular contributor. It is interesting to note that all but two of the 81 articles she wrote in the first series are on women subjects. This concentration on women was, in itself, unusual among women contributors. What makes Elizabeth Lee's case especially interesting, however, is what happened simultaneously to the breakdown of her brother's contributions. In the first 27 volumes, Sidney Lee had written 22 articles on women: in the subsequent 36 volumes of the first issue only six of his articles were on women. While the lack of documentary evidence to prove the case is disappointing, I suggest that Elizabeth Lee did not suddenly begin writing *DNB* articles on women in 1891, but that she had already been writing them, perhaps under her brother's guidance and under his name, for a number of years. Lee's new role as editor provided the opportunity to introduce his sister as a contributor in her own right.

The first series of the Dictionary and the three 1901 Supplements included biographies of 28,201 subjects, 998 of which were separate articles on women. There were 696 contributors, 45 of whom were women. Table 1 lists the women contributors, and indicates the number of articles they wrote and how many of those articles were on women subjects.

Eight of these 45 women may be considered major contributors, by which I mean that they wrote more than 80 articles. They were Mary Bateson, Agnes Mary Clerke, Jennett Humphreys, Elizabeth Lee, Lydia Miller Middleton, Bertha Porter, Mrs A. Murray Smith, and Charlotte Fell–Smith. Sidney Lee's table of major contributors in the Statistical Account in Volume LXIII of the first issue of the Dictionary is based on numbers of pages rather than numbers of articles written, and no women writers qualify. Lee goes as low as 58 contributions by a man in order to illustrate his point. In the modern *DNB*, editors insist on brevity. They realize how much work is required to encapsulate a person in 750–1000 words (only in exceptional cases are more allocated).[13] Lee's additional table of the longest articles in the first issue is further proof of the value accorded to length.

The eight are clearly the exceptions among the women contributors since, of the rest, 35 each wrote ten articles or less, and, of these, 14 wrote only one article each. The 45 women contributors wrote 1300 articles in total. What is perhaps surprising is that the proportion of their articles on women subjects is very low. They wrote only 179 articles on women, and, as shown, 79 of those were written by Elizabeth Lee. Taking out Lee and the other significant female contributor of articles on women, Jennett Humphreys, exactly half of whose 98 articles were on women, the other 43 women contributors wrote only 52 articles on women subjects.What this perhaps indicates is that the majority of women who wrote for the Dictionary did not do so because they felt passionately about women in history or about their female contemporaries. Most women contributors wrote only a few articles, and those articles were on men. It is

Table I.   Women contributors to the *Dictionary of National Biography*, 1885–1901

Contributor	Articles	
	Total	Women subjects
Mary Bateson	108	0
Rose Marian Bradley	2	0
Frances Bushby	4	0
Agnes Mary Clerke	150	1
Ellen Mary Clerke	6	3
Edith Coleridge	1	0
Alice Margaret Cooke	40	0
Cornelia Augusta Hewett Crosse	1	0
Anne Gilchrist	2	1
Jennett Humphreys	98	49
Alice Mary Humphry	1	0
Elizabeth Ingall	2	0
Catherine Rachel Jones	1	1
Elizabeth Lee	81	79
Margaret MacArthur	4	0
Agnes Macdonell	1	0
Alice Macdonell	5	0
Mrs S. L. May	1	1
Lydia Miller Middleton	207	14
Rosa Harriet Newmarch	7	0
Kate Norgate	44	9
Eliza Orme	3	0
Christabel Osborne	4	1
Bertha Porter	156	2
Eleanor Grace Powell	4	0
Emma Louise Radford	10	0
Anne Isabella Ritchie	1	1
Julia Anne Elizabeth Roundell	1	0
Ghetal Burdon-Sanderson	1	0
Lucy Maude Manson Scott	3	0
Eva Blantyre Simpson	1	0
Mrs A. Murray Smith	81	3
Charlotte Fell-Smith	231	10
Lucy Toulmin Smith	5	1
Caroline Emelia Stephen	1	1
Julia Prinsep Stephen	1	1
Charlotte Carmichael Stopes	2	0
Beatrix Marion Sturt	3	0
Emma Catharine Sutton	2	0
Elizabeth Marion Todd	2	0
Mary Tout	11	1
Louisa Charlotte Tyndall	1	0
Margaret Maria Verney	6	0
Ellen Williams	1	0
Sarah Wilson	3	0

interesting here to look at the lists of their contributions and to note that in 15 cases the contributor's surname is the same as that of her subject or subjects.[14] While it is not always possible to prove that they were writing about ancestors or relatives, the evidence does show that many minor women contributors did write biographies of family members. Leslie Stephen, for example, encouraged and helped Louisa Tyndall, widow of John Tyndall, to write about her husband;[15] and, although the surname gives no clue, Leslie Stephen's wife, Julia, wrote one Dictionary article, the life of her aunt, Julia Margaret Cameron.

Investigating the women contributors to the Victorian *DNB* is a frustrating business, and the resulting evidence is patchy. Only six of the 45 have qualified for admission to the *DNB*: Mary Bateson, Agnes Mary Clerke, Anne Gilchrist, Kate Norgate, Eliza Orme and Lucy Toulmin Smith. Biographical information on the rest is in some cases scattered in biographies of fathers, husbands and brothers, but in others is not available at all. Some published nothing but the one or two *DNB* articles they wrote on family members; while others clearly made something of a living from their regular Dictionary articles; and a few were respected specialists and academics who published, edited and translated on the scale of some Victorian men of letters. Table 2 is a list of the women contributors to the *DNB* 1885–1901 whose names are in the *British Library Catalogue* and the *Wellesley Index to Victorian Periodicals 1824–1900* showing the number of books they wrote, edited or translated, and the number of periodical articles they published. A few examples will indicate the range of writing experience and expertise among the first women contributors.

Mary Bateson's life, work and contributions to the *DNB* are little different from those of dozens of her male contemporaries. She was born in 1865, educated at home in Cambridge, at local schools, in Karlsruhe, and at Newnham College, Cambridge, which her parents had helped establish. In 1888 she began to lecture on history, and was still teaching at Newnham in 1906 when she died. She promoted reform of historical studies and teaching methods, and helped establish research fellowships at Newnham. In her early writings, she specialized in mediaeval studies, particularly monastic history. She contributed to *The English Historical Review* from 1890. In 1899 she began to study municipal history, editing papers from the Leicester city archives. In 1905 she was Warburton Lecturer at the University of Manchester, and in 1906 she was appointed one of three editors of the *Cambridge Mediaeval History*. According to the *DNB* article on her life, her ecclesiastical history professor at Cambridge, Mandell Creighton, 'checked a tendency to dissipate her energy in public agitation on the platform or in the press in the cause of political liberalism and women's enfranchisement, of which she was always a thorough-going advocate'. The *DNB* describes her as 'a scholar of the first rank, able to grapple with the hardest problems, and possessed of rare clearness and excellent method'.[16] She wrote and edited more than a dozen books and contributed 108 articles to the Dictionary.

Table 2.   Women contributors to the *DNB* 1885–1901 listed in the *British Library Catalogue* and the *Wellesley Index*

	BLC entries	*Wellesley Index* articles
Mary Bateson	16	
Rose Marian Bradley	3	
Frances Bushby	2	
Agnes Mary Clerke	9	52
Ellen Mary Clerke	4	66
Edith Coleridge	2	1
Alice Margaret Cooke	2	
Cornelia Augusta Hewett Crosse	2	21
Anne Gilchrist	4	3
Jennett Humphreys	13	4
Elizabeth Ingall	3	
Catherine Rachel Jones	3	2
Elizabeth Lee	34	3
Margaret MacArthur	1	1
Agnes Macdonell		5
Lydia Miller Middleton	3	
Rosa Harriet Newmarch	32	
Kate Norgate	6	
Eliza Orme	2	3
Bertha Porter	1	
Emma Louise Radford	1	
Anne Isabella Ritchie	39	56
Julia Anne Elizabeth Roundell	6	1
Eva Blantyre Simpson	7	
Mrs A. Murray Smith	7	3
Charlotte Fell-Smith	12	
Lucy Toulmin Smith	14	1
Caroline Emelia Stephen	5	6
Julia Prinsep Stephen	2	
Charlotte Carmichael Stopes	21	
Mary Tout	1	
Louisa Charlotte Tyndall	1	
Margaret Maria Verney	8	4
Ellen Williams	4	
Sarah Wilson	2	8

Agnes Mary Clerke wrote even more articles for the Dictionary – 150. She was born in Ireland in 1842, and also educated at home. She became interested in astronomy as a child, and from 1867 to 1877 she lived in Italy, studying astronomy in libraries and writing articles on the subject published in British journals, as well as books on the history of astronomy and modern developments which quickly became standard reference works. She was a regular contributor to *The Edinburgh Review* on both astronomy and classical literature.

She also wrote articles for *The Observatory Magazine* and *Encyclopaedia Britannica*, and contributed almost all the lives of astronomers to the *DNB* up to 1901. In 1892 she was awarded the Actonian prize at the Royal Institution, and in 1903 was elected an honorary member of the Royal Astronomical Society.

Rosa Harriet Newmarch wrote only seven *DNB* articles, although she was otherwise a voluminous writer and an expert in her field of libretto translation. She helped to introduce the works of Tchaikovsky, and later Czech and Slavonic composers, to English audiences. She was official programme writer to the Queen's Hall Orchestra from 1908 to the late 1920s. The British Library Catalogue lists more than 30 works written, edited and translated by her.

Agnes Macdonell is perhaps more typical of the first *DNB* women writers. She wrote only one *DNB* article, the life of her husband's brother, James Macdonell, the journalist. The little it is possible to discover about her is in the Dictionary article on her husband, John Macdonell (1845–1921). He was a classics scholar, journalist and barrister, knighted in 1903. According to the *DNB* article, 'Lady Macdonell was herself a gifted writer and a constant helper of her husband in all his work'.

Margaret Verney is another example of a woman who contributed articles only on family members. She was an heiress and wife of an MP, and actively involved in health care and education. Her mother-in-law, Lady Frances Parthenope Verney, the sister of Florence Nightingale, had begun collecting documents in the 1850s for a history of the Verney family, but died before its publication. Margaret, the new Lady Verney, completed the work in hand and finished the series as well as writing about the Verneys in magazines and six articles for the *DNB*.

Kate Norgate was born in 1853. She was largely self-taught, although the historian John Richard Green encouraged her writing. According to the *DNB*, her *England under the Angevin Kings* 'revealed a new historian. Miss Norgate's mastery of the original sources showed critical power and found expression in good, clear narrative … [Her work] made the distinction between men and women historians an anachronism'. She wrote 44 *DNB* articles and six books of history

Others wrote only a few articles for the Dictionary and yet were regular contributors to contemporary literary magazines. Ellen Mary Clerke, Agnes's elder sister, was fluent in Italian and Arabic. She wrote poetry and fiction, and for 20 years contributed a weekly leading article to *The Tablet*. Anne Isabella Ritchie wrote only the life of Elizabeth Barrett Browning for the *DNB* and yet she was a voluminous writer of both books and magazine articles. She was Thackeray's elder daughter, and Leslie Stephen's sister-in-law. Her work appeared in *The Cornhill Magazine* which Thackeray and Stephen both edited in their time, although she is chiefly remembered for her novels and her biographical edition of Thackeray's works. It is impossible to determine how many early women contributors were personally recruited by the Dictionary staff. Anne Ritchie is an obvious example, and the others from Leslie Stephen's and Sidney Lee's immediate families suggest that it may not have been uncommon. As well as Anne Ritchie and Julia Stephen, Caroline Emelia Stephen, Leslie's sister, also wrote an article, and Sidney Lee's sister, Elizabeth, wrote 81 for the first series and 29 for the 1901–1911 supplement, as well as undertaking the editorial work described below.

The overwhelming majority of articles on women in the first series of the *DNB* were written by men. Table 3 lists the 140 male contributors who wrote on women subjects, indicating the total number of articles they wrote and how many of those articles were on women. Applying the arbitrary classification used to identify major contributors to the *DNB* 1885–1901 as a whole – more than 80 articles – the only major writer on women was Joseph Knight, with 104 articles. Only nine men wrote more than 20 articles on women: George Clement Boase, Thompson Cooper, Richard Garnett, Gordon Goodwin, William Hunt, Joseph Knight, Sidney Lee, Thomas Seccombe and Leslie Stephen. Of this group, five – Cooper, Hunt, Lee, Seccombe and Stephen – were members of the permanent *DNB* staff. This seems to suggest that in-house writing was often the only way to secure contributions on women for the Dictionary, aside from the regular, specialist contributors, and contributors writing the odd article or two about family members. From the four significant outside writers, Boase and Garnett specialized in women writers and Knight actresses. Twenty of Boase's 36 articles and 25 of Garnett's 30 are on writers. All but five of Knight's 104 contributions on women are on actresses, and of the remainder three are dramatists, one an opera singer, and one a courtesan. Knight's case is perhaps especially worthy of note, since, aside from royalty and aristocrats, writers account for by far the single largest group of women subjects.

Into the twentieth century

The first series of the *DNB* was completed in 63 volumes in 1900, and the project might have ended there. Leslie Stephen, still involved in the Dictionary as a contributor and as a sometimes unwelcome adviser to Sidney Lee, certainly disapproved of the plan for supplementary volumes of subjects who had died too late for their inclusion in the alphabetical sequence 1885–1900 or who had been accidentally omitted. He did, somewhat reluctantly, agree to write the lives of two of his friends, James Payn and Henry Sidgwick, but rejected the offer to write on Gladstone. The three supplementary volumes produced in 1901 marked the end of an era. Queen Victoria herself was dead, and, chronologically, the last subject in the Dictionary. George Smith died in 1901, Leslie Stephen in 1904, and by then the Dictionary offices were closed, the organization broken up, and its papers destroyed.

Table 3.   Male contributors of articles on women to the *Dictionary of National Biography*, 1885–1901

Contributor	Articles	
	Women subjects	Total
Osmund Airy	2	20
George Atherton Aitkin	5	46
John Goldworth Alger	9	87
William Arthur Jobson Archbold	5	350
Thomas Andrew Archer	7	126
Walter Armstrong	1	33
John Ashton	1	7
William Edward Armytage Axon	4	56
George Fisher Russell Barker	8	300
Percy Arthur Barnett	1	1
Ronald Bayne	3	131
Thomas Wilson Bayne	12	158
Charles Raymond Beazley	1	21
Dalrymple James Belgrave	1	1
George Vere Benson	1	18
George Thomas Bettany	3	206
Augustus Charles Bickley	5	86
Bever Harry Blacker	1	54
William Garden Blaikie	5	105
George Clement Boase	36	714
George Simonds Boulger	3	182
Robert Henry Brodie	1	11
Arthur Aikin Brodribb	2	7
Richard Charles Browne	1	13
Arthur Henry Bullen	2	181
Edwin Cannan	2	29
Edward Irving Carlyle	6	669
Henry Manners Chichester	2	498
Richard Copley Christie	1	8
Edward Dutton Cook	3	17
Thompson Cooper	25	1423
James Sutherland Cotton	2	23
William Prideaux Courtney	12	607
Mandell Creighton	3	59
Lionel Henry Cust	15	765
James Caxton Dibdin	1	3
Richard Watson Dixon	1	14
Austin Dobson	4	41
John Andrew Doyle	1	31
George Thorn-Drury	1	15
Edward Gordon Duff	1	11
John Woodfall Ebsworth	2	26
Alexander Charles Ewald	1	2
Louis Alexander Fagan	2	92

Table 3 continued

Contributor	Articles	
	Women subjects	Total
Caesar Litton Falkiner	1	44
Charles Harding Firth	3	228
James Gairdner	13	77
Samuel Rawson Gardiner	2	25
Richard Garnett	30	196
John Westby-Gibson	2	58
John Thomas Gilbert	2	106
Herbert Harlakenden Gilchrist	1	2
Gordon Goodwin	23	1164
Alexander Gordon	10	699
Edmund Gosse	2	16
Arthur Henry Grant	3	65
Robert Edmund Graves	6	209
William Alexander Greenhill	1	49
Henry Riversdale Grenfell	1	1
Francis Hindes Groome	1	15
Alexander Balloch Grosart	4	136
James Cuthbert Hadden	9	97
John Andrew Hamilton	3	286
Robert Harrison	1	90
Thomas Finlayson Henderson	18	870
Charles Ernest Hughes	1	5
William Hunt	37	582
Benjamin Daydon Jackson	1	94
Augustus Jessopp	1	45
Rees M. Jenkin Jones	1	59
Thomas Edward Kebbel	1	9
Charles Kent	3	59
Charles Lethbridge Kingsford	8	375
Joseph Knight	104	375
John Knox Laughton	7	915
Sidney Lee	32	764
Robin Humphrey Legge	5	46
William Boswell Lowther	2	20
Joseph Hirst Lupton	1	44
Norman MacColl	2	8
Michael MacDonagh	1	11
James Ramsay Macdonald	1	59
John Macdonell	1	6
Aeneas James George Mackay	4	127
William Dunn Macray	2	20
John Alexander Fuller-Maitland	3	71
Edward Henry Marshall	1	8
Charles Trice Martin	1	37

Table 3 continued

Contributor	Articles	
	Women subjects	Total
Theodore Martin	2	8
Frank Thomas Marzials	1	14
Charles Herbert Mayo	1	9
Alexander Hastie Millar	2	78
Arthur Miller	1	21
William Cosmo Monkhouse	4	140
Norman Moore	5	459
Albert Nicholson	48	80
Edmund Toulmin Nicolle	1	3
Pierce Laurence Nolan	1	10
Gerald Le Grys Norgate	4	248
David James O'Donoghue	2	66
Freeman Marius O'Donoghue	7	249
Thomas Olden	3	68
John Henry Overton	4	74
William George Bernard Page	1	1
Henry Paton	2	78
Albert Frederick Pollard	5	501
Ernest Radford	2	104
William Fraser Rae	4	31
James McMullen Rigg	18	641
William Roberts	1	3
George Croom Robertson	1	6
Charles John Robinson	1	41
John Horace Round	3	81
Lloyd Charles Sanders	2	37
James Moffat Scott	1	28
Thomas Seccombe	41	654
Robert Farquharson Sharp	1	35
Evelyn Shirley Shuckburgh	3	19
George Barnett Smith	1	77
William Barclay Squire	13	164
Leslie Stephen	22	283
Henry Morse Stephens	1	227
George Stronach	2	68
Charles William Sutton	11	312
James Tait	5	135
Henry Richard Tedder	2	185
Daniel Lleufer Thomas	1	152
Henry Avray Tipping	1	5
Thomas Frederick Tout	6	237
Walter Hawken Tregellas	2	26
Edmund Venables	6	125
Alsager Vian	12	114

Table 3 concluded

Contributor	Articles	
	Women subjects	Total
Adolphus William Ward	15	61
Robert Avery Ward	1	1
Morgan George Watkins	5	51
Francis Watt	4	128
Charles Welch	1	74
Stephen Wheeler	1	20
Charles Harold Evelyn White	1	2
Bernard Barham Woodward	2	91
Unsigned Contributions	10	320

With the end of his full-time employment as editor of the Dictionary, Lee 'suffered financially', according to Edward Irving Carlyle.[17] He was in an awkward position. Unlike his chief associates, Smith and Stephen, he was still a relatively young man, only 41, when the last volume of the 1901 supplement was published in October 1901. For nearly 20 years, the Dictionary had been his life. He had come to it almost directly from his undergraduate studies at Balliol College, Oxford, in 1883, and although he had developed a reputation as a Shakespeare scholar, it was the Dictionary which provided his livelihood.

Before his death, Smith had outlined a proposal for Lee to produce 'a summary guide to the vast and varied contents of the Dictionary and its Supplement',[18] the *Index and Epitome*. This single, condensed volume was produced under Lee's direction by a team of ten editors, each responsible for a volume or volumes of the original 66-volume issue, the main Dictionary and its three 1901 supplements. The *Index and Epitome* was published in March 1903. The summarizers are listed in Table 4:

As shown, Lee's sister Elizabeth was now given an official editorial staff position as summarizer of Volumes XXXI–XXXV. Her summary work, covering subjects between Basil Kennett and William Maltby in the alphabetical sequence, pages 718–832, is unremarkable as editorial work and indistinguishable from that of the other summarizers, but the fact that she was given the task at all is noteworthy. Given Lee's financial position it is perhaps understandable that he should have sought a way to increase his household income by allocating part of the summary to Elizabeth.

George Smith's widow, Elizabeth, to whom he had bequeathed the Dictionary, determined to fulfil his wishes by continuing it into the twentieth century. But when Lee was called upon to edit a 1901–1911 Supplement there was little organizational continuity. He had none of the resources of the old Dictionary and he found the work arduous. The staff had been dismissed, the office library

Table 4. *Index and Epitome* summarizers

Volumes	Editor
I–VI	Charles Ernest Hughes
VII–XII	Andrew Clark
XIII–XVIII	Richard Greentree
XIX–XXX	Gerald le Grys Norgate
XXXI–XXXV	Elizabeth Lee
XXXVI	P. C. Yorke
XXXVII–XLI	Albert Frederick Pollard
XLII	Gerald le Grys Norgate
XLIII–XLVIII	Edward Irving Carlyle
XLIX–LI	Charles Ernest Hughes
LII	Gerald le Grys Norgate
LIII	Thomas Seccombe
LIV	Gerald le Grys Norgate
LV–LVII	P. C. Yorke
LVIII–LX	Andrew Clark
LXI–LXIII	Charles Ernest Hughes
Supplements I–III	Charles Ernest Hughes

dispersed, and many of the old core of regular contributors and specialists lost. New staff had to be found and trained. Nevertheless, the work was quickly done between October 1910 and December 1912. The three volumes of the supplement were reviewed in *The Athenaeum* as they were published. A review of the first volume points to a circumstance beyond the control of the editor and writers, that 'on the whole the men and women of letters in this volume are not of exceptional interest'.[19] For the first time, the *DNB* could only record the lives of the recently deceased and, as the reviewer notes, there were, for example, no great artists in the volume. Without a foundation of in-house writers, it was increasingly colleagues and friends who wrote about those they had known. Information was sometimes more readily available to them and appreciations could be personal, but this increased the possibility of bias and insufficient historical perspective. The review notes that biographers have a duty 'to make the record fit the man, and to suppress the well-meant eulogies of friends and relations as well as the desire to fuel old controversies over again'. *DNB* contributors were not writing obituaries for daily newspaper readers, but writing articles which must stand the test of time and be of use to future researchers, historians and biographers. The Dictionary had to aim for the brief definitive life. The review concludes that 'There is, in fact, much fine, confused interest in this volume, and if some may question the propriety of including a patent medicine vendor in its scope, whereas not a single plumber or pastry cook is to be discovered, still the hoardings are always with us, and act as passports to fame of a sort'. The reviewer would have to wait for *Missing Persons* to fill those gaps.

Yet, if the first volume was dull, a review of the second says it 'falls short of its predecessor in interest',[20] noting that diplomatists, colonial administrators and politicians abound. Even William Holman Hunt's life is written about 'a little tamely'. *Athenaeum* readers were quick to draw attention to errors and omissions in the supplement, but to the reviewer of the third volume they were of less note than that certain articles, such as Archbishop Temple's, read 'rather tamely; the facts are all right, but they are unrelieved by a single story'.[21]

None of the reviewers seems to have noticed that there were few women subjects and even fewer women writers in the new supplement. Although the percentage of women subjects in the Dictionary had risen from the 1885–1901 figure of 3.5 per cent to 4.6 per cent, the mere 76 articles on women in the new supplement and the shortness of the articles makes the women inconspicuous. The 45 women writers from the first series had all but vanished; only two now wrote for the 1901–1911 supplement, Elizabeth Lee, and the formerly voluminous Charlotte Fell-Smith. The 6.4 per cent of women contributors to the first issue now became only 4.8 per cent, eight women among 158 men.

In 1917 the Dictionary was presented to Oxford University Press and the Lees' involvement with it was at an end. The 1912–1921 supplement, edited by H. W. C. Davis and John Reginald Homer Weaver, was not published until 1927. The percentages of women subjects and writers were both down, to 4.5 per cent and 4 per cent respectively. In the preface the editors note that the new volume was 'planned on less ample lines' than the previous supplement because to continue its scale throughout the twentieth century 'would be beyond the means of most of those for whose use such a work is primarily intended'. Article lengths and numbers of articles were therefore restricted. This and the 1914–1918 war with its huge loss of male lives perhaps explain why only 15 women subjects appear in the volume, but not why of the 273 contributors, only 11 were women. They were all new writers for the Dictionary, and none of them ever wrote for it again. The twentieth-century editors were clearly not concerned to build a core of regular contributors, at least among its women contributors. In the preface, the editors note that they 'have had the advantage of the assistance of Miss Margaret Toynbee, B.A., formerly exhibitioner of St. Hugh's College, Oxford', and she did go on to write for the Dictionary in the 1920s and 1930s. But in their acknowledgements of 'valuable criticisms and suggestions' they recognize 39 men and no women.

The progress of the Dictionary supplements through the next 60 years or so can, for the present purpose, conveniently be summarized in Tables 5–7 which also include the earlier volumes. As the figures suggest, nothing very remarkable happened in terms of women and the *DNB* for 50 years. Numbers of articles of both men and women increased volume by volume; the articles were shorter, so that two pages became the standard for even the most eminent, and a page or even a column the norm for others; most contributors now wrote

Table 5.   *DNB* editors

Volumes	Editor
1885–1890	Leslie Stephen
1890–1891	Leslie Stephen and Sidney Lee
1891–1900	Sidney Lee
1901	Sidney Lee
1901–1911	Sidney Lee
1912–1921	H. W. C. Davis and J. R. H. Weaver
1922–1930	J. R. H. Weaver
1931–1940	L. G. Wickham Legg
1941–1950	L. G. Wickham Legg and Edgar Trevor Williams
1951–1960	Edgar Trevor Williams and Helen M. Palmer
1961–1970	Edgar Trevor Williams and C. S. Nicholls
1971–1980	Lord Blake and C. S. Nicholls
1981–1985	Lord Blake and C. S. Nicholls
Missing Persons	C. S. Nicholls

Table 6.   *DNB* subjects

Volumes	Women/Total	% of women subjects
1885–1901	998/28,201	3.5
1901–1911	76/ 1,660	4.6
1912–1921	15/ 450	4.5
1922–1930	23/ 569	4.0
1931–1940	37/ 730	5.1
1941–1950	42/ 725	5.8
1951–1960	60/ 760	7.9
1961–1970	45/ 745	6.0
1971–1980	50/ 748	6.7
1981–1985	45/ 380	11.8
Missing Persons	130/ 1,086	12.0
TOTAL	1521/36,054	4.2

only one article per volume, so the numbers of writers increased overall. But men were still predominant. As late as the 1951–1960 supplement, not published until 1971, it was still possible for the editor to use headings in his new 'Facts and Figures' preface such as 'Public men', 'Schoolmasters', and 'Business men'; although he did mention in the Prefatory Note that 'The cause of women was perhaps one of the few to achieve its assured victory when the war ended', and he goes on to list several women's 'firsts' and achievements, not least of which is the appearance of assistant editor Helen Palmer's name on the title page of the volume. It is impossible to explain why there were not significantly more women contributors through the 1960s, 70s, and 80s, as women assumed

Table 7.   *DNB* writers

Volumes	Women/Total	% of women writers
1885–1901	45/696	6.4
1901–1911	8/166	4.8
1912–1921	11/273	4.0
1922–1930	14/345	4.0
1931–1940	35/479	7.3
1941–1950	43/564	7.6
1951–1960	38/603	6.3
1961–1970	45/611	7.4
1971–1980	55/636	8.6
1981–1985	28/344	8.1
Missing Persons	125/639	19.6

new status in society and moved into the workplace in large numbers. I can only offer the suggestion that the *DNB* organization was still largely run by men, and that little had changed for many years. Edgar Williams had been with the Dictionary since 1949 when he began editing the 1941–1950 volume. In the 1961–1970 Prefatory Note he says that since this is the third volume he has edited 'it will scarcely be surprising that it follows the pattern of its predecessors'. And he acknowledges the contribution of 22 advisers, all men, many of whom he had listed in the acknowledgements to the 1951–1960 volume. Continuity began to imply stagnation.

A new era

Williams's successor as editor, Lord Blake, had been a contributor to the Dictionary since the 1951–1960 supplement, but it was under his editorial leadership that, I suggest, the *DNB* took a leap forward. With national biographical dictionaries in both Australia and Canada now being published, Commonwealth numbers were reduced, making the Dictionary increasingly British, although not dogmatically so, with exceptions such as Eamon de Valera, Alfred Hitchcock, Jomo Kenyatta, Kwame Nkrumah, Archbishop Makarios and Robert Menzies. Including lives of those whose careers were, in Lord Blake's view, so deeply involved in British life that to omit them 'would have been to disappoint a legitimate expectation', was a recognition of readers' needs and wishes and a deliberate strategy. The *DNB*, for perhaps the first time in its history, was aiming to be interesting as well as informative. Any *DNB* editor would have relished Winston Churchill as subject, and in addition the 1971–1980 volume included Montgomery, Mountbatten, Mosley, Auden, Britten, Lennon, Chaplin, Coward, Wodehouse and Edward VIII. The list of memorable subjects is long enough to be unquotable in such a summary, but the point is that, by chance, the new editor found himself with exciting subjects which he cleverly matched with interesting contributors. To mention a few of the better-known may illustrate the point – John Arlott, Alan Bell, Chris Bonington, Asa Briggs, David Cecil, Tam Dalyell, Derek Ezra, Michael Foot, Jo Grimmond, Edward Heath, Eric Hobsbawm, Alec Douglas-Home, Brian Inglis, Roy Jenkins, Frank Kermode, Philip Larkin, Bernard Lovell, Harold Macmillan, Norris McWhirter, Spike Milligan, Sheridan Morley, Malcolm Muggeridge, Nigel Nicolson, Derek Nimmo, Enoch Powell, Auberon Waugh, and Woodrow Wyatt – but this is to overlook literally dozens of other eminent contributors. And, although only 50 of the 748 subjects, 6.7 per cent, were women, there too there was a sense of change. Sculptor Barbara Hepworth, nutritionist Harriette Chick, novelist Agatha Christie, and actress Cicely Courtneidge were not just eminent women in their fields, but among the most eminent people in their fields. The same holds true of the women contributors, up to 8.6 per cent in this volume, but including names likely to be recognized, whose accounts would attract attention – Lettice Cooper, Frances Donaldson, Margot Fonteyn, Victoria Glendinning, Jenny Lee, Elizabeth Longford and Dilys Powell. A woman as assistant editor was not new, and Christine Nicholls's name had appeared on the title page of the 1961–1970 volume; but now she became associate editor and Lord Blake spoke for them both in the Prefatory Note when he described their policy:

> The choice of both entries and authors lies with the editors. Some entrants choose themselves for inclusion, indeed most do; but there is a borderline where opinions may well differ. The editors hope that they have not omitted anyone who ought to be in, but they cannot expect that the 'fringe' will be other than controversial. They recognize too that fame may surface later than the date of the publication of the volume. Gerard Manley Hopkins and Wilfrid Owen omitted from earlier volumes are famous examples, but it would be hard to blame the editors of the day.

Here was a hint of the work being planned, and the new direction the *DNB* was to take under Christine Nicholls. And it is a nice touch that, according to Lord Blake, it was at her suggestion that to mark the Dictionary's centenary in 1985 a commemorative lecture on Leslie Stephen was held, to which all the contributors to the 1971–1980 volume were invited.

The 1971–1980 volume was published in 1986. Immediately, Lord Blake and Christine Nicholls began work on the next supplement, and by 1990 a new volume was already prepared and published. For the first time, it covered a five-year period, 1981–1985. The editors describe it as an experiment, tried 'because there was public pressure for the Supplements to appear more frequently and new technology made the prospect feasible'. It was easier for the editorial staff to handle only half the number of articles of earlier supplements and fewer contributors, although proportionately there were more contributors for the number of articles as, increasingly, most wrote only one. A further advantage was that, as they wryly note, 'a five-year period makes it possible to capture the personal knowledge of colleagues who under the ten-year rule might already themselves have joined the entrants as candidates for inclusion'. *DNB* articles must now be short and crisp, with no room for work on the scale of Sidney Lee's 111 pages on Queen Victoria, making the Dictionary more as Leslie Stephen envisaged – pithy, condensed, strictly biographical. The editors' increased awareness of *DNB* readers led them to efforts not merely to satisfy needs but to please in the process, in their words to 'inform, delight, and sometimes startle the reader'. The contributors are politicians, academics, professional writers, actors, and television celebrities. They are given free rein, liberally sprinkling their articles with anecdotes and sounding their own trumpets if they choose. Edward Heath, for example, writes that Boyle 'had a great love of music which he shared with Edward Heath'. The percentage of women subjects was up to 11.8 in the volume, 45 lives from a total of 380, although women contributors actually dropped to 8.1 per cent. The Prefatory Note ends with the news that the editors have 'embarked upon a volume which contains biographies of those people who have inadvertently been omitted from the DNB in the past', and a call for candidates. *Missing Persons* was underway.

The word had already gone out in British broadsheet newspapers, as well as magazines, the literary press and scholarly journals, and the suggestions began to pour in. Two basic rules of the *DNB* had always applied: subjects must be dead, and, since 1901, they must have died in the decade covered by the supplementary volume. Aside from straightforward oversight this meant that subjects who achieved posthumous fame missed their *DNB* opportunity. Gerard Manley Hopkins was a much-cited example. He had been ambivalent to publication, and even destroyed much of his work, although he sent copies to Robert Bridges who waited until 1918 before publishing. Wilfred Owen was another. As a review in the *TLS* was to point out 'it is reassuring that so many have a favourite Missing Person for whom they are prepared to campaign. This shows both a respect for the *DNB*, and a healthy interest in the past'.[22] One hundred thousand suggestions were pruned to a thousand on the basis of Sidney Lee's criterion for including a subject, 'the probability that his [or her] career would be the subject of intelligent enquiry on the part of an appreciable number of persons a generation or more hence'. Christine Nicholls, as editor, was assisted by a consultant editor for each of the four period divisions: up to 1500, 1501–1700, 1701–1850 and 1851–1985. Many of the omissions had been among occupations new at the time of the original issue, 1885–1901. Notable are the numbers in commerce, finance, industry, and, most particularly, the sciences – hydrography, surveying, mineralogy, geology, physics, meteorology, mathematics, botany, soil science, conservation, chemistry and metallurgy. There are engineers, instrument-makers, clock-makers, architects. There are pioneers, firsts, inventors, entrepreneurs, self-made men and women so under-represented in the early volumes. Clearly, as the editor notes, 'The passage of time was necessary to establish their claims'.

Women subjects account for 12 per cent of the articles in *Missing Persons*, 130 of 1,086 articles.There are the founders, the firsts and the forgotten, such as Margaret Llewelyn Davies, general secretary of the Woman's Co–operative Guild, and first woman president of the Co–operative Congress; Eliza Orme, first woman LLB in Britain, and Frances Mary Buss, founder of North London Collegiate School for Ladies. Much lauded in reviews of the new volume was the inclusion of Isabella Mary Beeton of *Beeton's Book of Household Management* fame. She was at school in Heidelberg, and talented in music and languages, but preferred pastry-making which her family thought 'ultra modern and not quite nice'. It emerges that she was not the stereotypical middle-aged housewife, and that she died at the age of 28 after a short career in magazines publishing, editing and fashion patterns. Writer Winifred Holtby was probably not included immediately after her death because her books and journalism were not a tremendous success in her own lifetime, and the issues about which she felt passionately – world peace, feminism and race – not as high-profile as they are today. Her books have had more recent attention than at the time of publication. Flora Thompson falls into the same category. Radclyffe Hall published *The Well of Loneliness* in 1928, but it was prosecuted under the Obscene Publications Act of 1857 and not republished in Britain until 1949, and she was not included in the 1940s supplement. Royal mistresses, illegitimacy and lesbianism are now admissible, as indicated by lives of Lillie Langtry and Alice Keppel, with a nod in the direction of Violet Trefussis. Even more spectacular than the number of women subjects is the rise in the number of women contributors, up to 19.6 per cent and more than double even the recent percentages. This, presumably, is a sign of the way content as well as contributors will move in the future. Altogether, *Missing Persons* is probably the most interesting single volume of the *DNB* to date; but then so it should be, since the editor was drawing on a residual pool from the beginnings of time up to 1985, and picking the plums from occupations, skills, and ways of life now valued which were dismissed or overlooked by earlier editors. But even when *DNB* publication returns to five- or ten-year supplements, the tone established by *Missing Persons* should have set new standards: its occupational index is detailed and extensive, and, though its numbers may still be weighted towards men, its language is not.

The future of the *DNB* looks bright. There are plans for a large-scale revision to reflect modern research and scholarship. The Dictionary is being transferred to CD-ROM which will make ongoing revision simple and the material available in either hard copy or on disk. There is a greater openness, a broader definition of achievement and value, and appreciation beyond the confines of long-enduring Victorian respectability. Future editors will have to ensure that the categories listed in the *Missing Persons* occupation index do not become the controlling yardstick for future subjects. *Missing Persons* is proof that values change. The lesson to be learned from it is that they will go on changing. As recently as 1985, Lord Blake wrote in the Prefatory Note to the 1971–1980 volume that 'The choice of both entries and authors lies with the editors'. Ultimately, this will remain the case, although Christine Nicholls writes that *Missing Persons* 'reflects the public's view of who should appear in a work of biographical reference'. Colin Matthew promises to preserve that openness. He will edit the *New Dictionary of National Biography*, which he says 'involves the revision/rewriting of entries in the old, plus further entries'. His recent circular and questionnaire to members of British and North American societies, associations, universities, libraries, and other institutions is in part an announcement and in part a call for cooperation and assistance. Leslie Stephen began the Dictionary with a similar openness in 1882 with his announcement in *The Athenaeum* followed by the printed lists of likely subjects and calls for contributors and further suggestions.

What has happened in the century between their calls is a revolution in women's lives and in ways of thinking about women. Victorian women were not expected to achieve the sort of recognition which *DNB* entry requires. Scholarship, creativity, pre-eminence and fame were not the realm of the angel in the house, and personal qualities, the feminine ideal, were not the stuff of a work of reference. In the circumstances, it is small wonder that the early editors, even into the twentieth century, did not feel the need to search too strenuously for the women of talent and achievement revealed by *Missing Persons*. I suggest that the same holds true today, but for the very different reason that women are now so much a part of public life that they, in Lord Blake's phrase, 'choose themselves for inclusion'. What this means is that their lives appear in the *DNB* on the basis not only of their achievements but also of the ideological standards of the day. In late Victorian England these factors would admit a 'society hostess', 'famous beauty', or 'daughter of Lord —' to the Dictionary, but would exclude Anna Atkins, botanist, or Eleanor Coade, manufacturer of artificial stone.

Part 4 of this book is an occupational index of all the women subjects in the *DNB* 1885–1985 and *Missing Persons*. I have based the categories on those of the 'Occupational Index of Entrants' in *Missing Persons*, merging some of its categories together, such as mathematics with sciences, where there were few entries, and adding new categories not represented in *Missing Persons* but common in the earlier *DNB*, such as society women, mistresses, prostitutes, famous beauties, heiresses, and eccentrics, a catch-all group, not strictly of occupations. By far the largest group is authors, historians, scholars, librarians, and journalists. I have chosen not to make subdivisions within it because it is not always clear on the evidence of the *DNB* exactly what a subject's writing was about, or in what field she was considered scholarly. This does not, of course, preclude names appearing in more than one category if, for example, a woman was a writer and an astronomer, or a princess and a poet. It is interesting that the next largest group is theatre, cinema, dance, music, song, and broadcasting. In the early *DNB* especially, women in public life who were not writers or scholars of one sort or another were more likely to be involved in the dubious world of public performance than in any other single occupational group. I have left as a single group business, industry, finance, printing, and publishing, not merging it with a larger group, in order to draw attention to the fact that there are so few entries. This undoubtedly will be an expanding category in future volumes of the Dictionary. Similarly, I have made a separate category of domestic servants and shop keepers, a group with only four entries despite the fact that these have been major fields of occupation for women for centuries. The *DNB* shows that there are some areas in which it is nearly impossible to achieve public distinction. Religion, saints, martyrs, hymn writers, fanatics, recluses, and missionaries is a category with dozens of entries in the first series of the *DNB* but few in recent years. This group will presumably also expand in future volumes with new laws on ordination, although the numbers of martyrs and recluses, as with heroines and famous beauties, are not what they once were.

Despite the fact that women subjects are outnumbered by men almost 23 to 1, the *DNB* draws attention to women's achievements. Despite the fact that the Dictionary was founded, shaped and run by Victorian men whose standards of womanhood prevailed well into the twentieth century, it is an affirmation of women's presence in history. The early *DNB* remains a monument to Victorian male society: the modern *DNB* has shifted its position but is no doubt just as much a product of its time. The Victorian Dictionary was largely written by men and women 'of letters': the *New DNB* promises to 'draw on the scholarly expertise of the vast expansion of the academic world which has occurred since the 1880s'. That expansion happens to include women.

Notes

1. Leonard Huxley, *The House of Smith, Elder* (printed in London for private circulation, 1923), 181–182.
2. Letter from Leslie Stephen to Edmund Gosse, 14 November 1882. Brotherton Library, University of Leeds.
3. Letter from Leslie Stephen to Edmund Gosse, 13 December 1882. Brotherton Library, University of Leeds.
4. Letter from Leslie Stephen to James Cotter Morison, 23 November 1882. Library of the University of Newcastle upon Tyne.
5. For a complete account of individual contributions to the first series of the *DNB* and the 1901 Supplements, see Gillian Fenwick, *The Contributors' Index to the Dictionary of National Biography, 1885–1901* (Winchester: St Paul's Bibliographies, 1989).
6. C. H. Firth, 'Memoir of Sidney Lee', *DNB* 1912–1921, xix.

7. Letter from Leslie Stephen to George Smith, 19 December 1888. Smith Papers, National Library of Scotland.
8. For a more detailed study of the role of *The Athenaeum* in the publishing history of the first issue of the *DNB*, see Gillian Fenwick, '*The Athenaeum* and the *Dictionary of National Biography*, 1885–1901', *Victorian Periodicals Review*, Vol. XXIII, No. 4 (Winter 1990), 180–188.
9. The four women contributors were Agnes Mary Clerke, Ellen Mary Clerke, Jennett Humphreys, and Caroline Emelia Stephen. Agnes Clerke wrote six articles in this volume, Ellen Clerke two, Jennett Humphreys four, and Caroline Emelia Stephen one. See *The Contributors' Index*.
10. Among the exceptions were the long articles on British queens, including Augustus Jessop's 30-page article on Queen Elizabeth, and Sidney Lee's monumental article on Queen Victoria, which filled 111 pages of the 1901 Supplement and became the basis of his 1902 book, *Queen Victoria A Biography* (London: Smith, Elder & Co.).
11. For a bibliography of recent works on Julia Stephen, see Diane F. Gillespie and Elizabeth Steele (eds), *Julia Duckworth Stephen: Stories for Children, Essays for Adults* (Syracuse, NY: Syracuse University Press, 1987).
12. This incidentally leads to a confusing anomaly in the 1908 reprinting of the Dictionary – the one on which subsequent reprintings of the 22-volume set of the first issue have been based – where the initials SLL do not appear in the List of Contributors, while some articles still bear those initials. From this List of Contributors, it is, therefore, impossible to identify the author of those articles as Sidney Lee.
13. Prefatory Note to the *DNB* 1981–1985 v.
14. Edith Coleridge's single article, for example, is on Herbert Coleridge; Alice Mary Humphry's on William Gilson Humphry; Catherine Rachel Jones's on Charlotte Jones; Elizabeth Lee wrote on Harriet and Sophia Lee; Agnes Macdonnell on James Macdonnell; Emma Louise Radford on John Radford; Eva Blantyre Simpson on Sir James Young Simpson; Charlotte Fell-Smith on Humphrey, Stephen and William Smith; Lucy Toulmin Smith on Joshua Toulmin Smith; Charlotte Carmichael Stopes on Leonard and Richard Stopes; Beatrix Marion Sturt on Charles Sturt; Elizabeth Marion Todd on James and Robert Todd; Louisa Charlotte Tyndall on John Tyndall; Margaret Verney on two Sir Edmund Verneys, Sir Francis, Sir Harry and Sir Ralph Verney and Ralph, second Earl Verney; and Ellen Williams on Rowland Williams.
15. See *Sir Leslie Stephen's Mausoleum Book* (Oxford: Clarendon Press, 1977), 100 and 110.
16. *Dictionary of National Biography* 1901–1911, 110–112.
17. Edward Irving Carlyle, 'Lee, Sidney', *DNB* 1922–1930, 500.
18. *Dictionary of National Biography Index and Epitome*, v.
19. *The Athenaeum*, No. 4416 (15 June 1912), 674–675.
20. *The Athenaeum*, No. 4432 (5 October 1912), 367–368.
21. *The Athenaeum*, No. 4442 (14 December 1912), 719–720.
22. Violet Powell, 'Late Entries', *The Times Literary Supplement*, 5 February 1993, 21.

Part 1

WOMEN SUBJECTS

Women subjects 1885-1985 and *Missing Persons*

This section is arranged alphabetically. Each entry consists of four lines of information as follows:

First line: subject's surname, followed by given name, or given name only in the case of queens, princesses, saints, etc. Names are followed by birth and death dates where known or *b*, *d* or *fl* if only the birth, death or period of their flourishing is known. The details are given as printed in the *DNB*: I have made no attempt to correct errors or omissions.

second line: occupation, role or reason for fame, usually taken verbatim from the *DNB* article.

third line: contributor's name. In a very few cases, articles are unsigned, indicating in-house editorial writing.

fourth line: *DNB* volume and page reference. For articles in the first issue, 1885-1900, two references are given: the first is to the 63 volume issue, the second to the 21 volume reissue. For the three volumes of the 1901 supplement, the individual volume number is given as *1901 I, II,* or *III,* followed by the reference to Volume XXII of the 22 volume reissue. For articles in the subsequent ten-year, and later five-year supplements, the years covered by the volumes are indicated: *1951-1960, 1981-1985* etc. *Missing Persons* is also included.

Abdy, Maria *d*1867
    poet
    John Horace Round
    I 31; *I* 31

Abington, Frances 1737–1815
    actress
    Edward Dutton Cook
    I 52–54; *I* 52–54

Acland, Christian Henrietta Caroline
1750–1815
    daughter of Earl of Ilchester
    William Prideaux Courtney
    I 59–60; *I* 59–60

Acton, Eliza 1799–1859
    author
    Jennett Humphreys
    I 66–67; *I* 66–67

Adam, Jean 1710–1765
    poet
    John Westby–Gibson
    I 86–87; *I* 86–87

Adams, Mary Grace Agnes 1898–1984
    broadcasting pioneer
    Sally Adams
    1981–1985 5–6

Adams, Sarah Flower 1805–1848
    poet
    Richard Garnett
    I 101; *I* 101

Addison, Laura *d*1852
    actress
    Edward Dutton Cook
    I 133; *I* 133

Adela 1062–1137
    mother of King Stephen
    Sidney Lee
    I 134–136; *I* 134–136

Adelaide 1792–1849
    wife of William IV
    Ellen Mary Clerke
    I 136–137; *I* 136–137

Adeliza *d*1066?
    daughter of William I
    John Horace Round
    I 137; *I* 137

Adeliza of Louvain *d*1151
    second wife of Henry I
    John Horace Round
    I 137–138; *I* 137–138

Ælfgifu *fl*956
    wife of King Eadwig
    William Hunt
    I 149–150; *I* 149–150

Ælfgifu *fl*1030
    perhaps mistress of Olaf the 'Saint'
    William Hunt
    I 150; *I* 150

Ælfthryth *d*929
    daughter of King Alfred
    William Hunt
    I 167; *I* 167

Ælfthryth, or Elfrida 945–1000
    wife of King Eadgar
    William Hunt
    I 167–168; *I* 167–168

Aguilar, Grace 1816–1847
    novelist
    Sidney Lee
    I 179–180; *I* 179–180

Aikenhead, Mary 1787–1858
    founder of Irish Sisters of Charity
    Caroline Emelia Stephen
    I 183; *I* 183

Aikin, Lucy 1781–1864
    compiler of historical memoirs
    Arthur Aikin Brodribb
    I 186–187; *I* 186–187

Albani, Marie Louise Cécilie Emma
1852–1930
    singer
    John Mewburn Levien
    1922–1930 8–10

Albany, Louisa Maximiliana Carolina
Emanuel 1753–1824
  wife of the Young Pretender
  Alexander Charles Ewald
  I 216–217; *I* 216–217

Albertazzi, Emma 1813–1847
  singer
  Ellen Mary Clerke
  I 231–232; *I* 231–232

Aldgyth *fl* 1063
  daughter of Ælfred
  William Hunt
  I 245; *I* 245

Aldrich-Blake, Louisa Brandreth
1865–1925
  surgeon
  Ray Strachey
  1922–1930 11

Alexander, Cecil Frances 1818–1895
  poet
  Edward Irving Carlyle
  1901 I 30–31; *XXII* 30–31

Alexander, Helen 1654–1729
  heroine
  Alexander Balloch Grosart
  I 272–273; *I* 272–273

Alexandra 1844–1925
  Queen–consort of Edward VII
  George Compton Archibald Arthur
  1922–1930 12–17

Alexandra Victoria Alberta Edwina
Louise Duff 1891–1959
  wife of Queen Victoria's grandson
  John Wheeler-Bennett
  1951–1960 12–13

Alford, Marianne Margaret 1817–1888
  artist, art patron, author
  Lionel Henry Cust
  1901 I 33–34; *XXII* 33–34

Alice Mary Victoria Augusta Pauline
1883–1981
  granddaughter of Queen Victoria
  Kenneth Rose
  1981–1985 8–9

Alice Maud Mary 1843–1878
  daughter of Queen Victoria
  Arthur Henry Grant
  I 285–286; *I* 285–286

Allingham, Margery Louise 1904–1966
  novelist
  Henry Reymond Fitzwalter Keating
  1961–1970 27–28

Amelia 1783–1810
  daughter of George III
  Jennett Humphreys
  I 352; *I* 352

Anderson, Adelaide Mary 1863–1936
  civil servant
  Meta Zimmeck
  Missing Persons 15–16

Anderson, Elizabeth Garrett 1836–1917
  physician
  Fanny Cecilia Johnson
  1912–1921 6–7

Anderson, Kitty 1903–1979
  educationist
  Mary Warnock
  1971–1980 13–14

Anderson, Lucy 1790–1878
  pianist
  William Barclay Squire
  I 388–389; *I* 388–389

Anderson, Mary Reid 1880–1921
  women's labour organizer
  James Joseph Mallon
  1912–1921 7–8

Anderson, Stella 1892–1933
  Stella Benson, novelist
  Georgina Battiscombe
  1931–1940 13–14

Anne of Bohemia 1366–1394
  wife of Richard II
  James Gairdner
  I 420–423; *I* 420–423

Anne 1456–1485
  wife of Richard III
  James Gairdner
  I 423–425; *I* 423–425

Anne 1507–1536
  Anne Boleyn, wife of Henry VIII
  James Gairdner
  I 425–429; *I* 425–429

Anne of Cleves 1515–1557
  wife of Henry VIII
  James Gairdner
  I 429–431; *I* 429–431

Anne of Denmark 1574–1619
  wife of James I
  Adolphus William Ward
  I 431–441; *I* 431–441

Anne 1665–1714
  Queen of Great Britain and Ireland
  Adolphus William Ward
  I 441–474; *I* 441–474

Anning, Mary 1799–1847
  discoverer of Lyme icthyosaurus
  Bernard Barham Woodward
  1901 I 51–52; *XXII* 51–52

Anspach, Elizabeth, Margravine of
1750–1828
  dramatist
  Edward Dutton Cook
  II 36–37; *I* 508–509

Arabella Stuart 1575–1615
  daughter of Earl of Lennox
  Samuel Rawson Gardiner
  II 53; *I* 525

Arber, Agnes 1879–1960
  botanist
  Hugh Hamshaw Thomas
  1951–1960 28–30

Arblay, Frances, Madame d' 1752–1840
  Fanny Burney, novelist
  Leslie Stephen
  II 55–58; *I* 527–528

Arbuthnot, Harriet 1793–1834
  diarist
  Elizabeth Longford
  Missing Persons 21–22

Arendrup, Edith 1846–1934
  artist
  Richard Millward
  Missing Persons 22–23

Armine or Armyne, Mary *d*1675–6
  philanthropist
  Sidney Lee
  II 87; *I* 559

Armitage, Ella Sophia 1841–1931
  historian, archaeologist, author
  Joan Counihan
  Missing Persons 23

Arne, Cecilia 1711–1789
  singer
  William Barclay Squire
  II 103–104; *I* 575–576

Arundell, Blanche 1583–1649
  defender of Wardour Castle
  Richard Charles Browne
  II 143; *I* 615

Arundell, Mary *d*1691
  Latin translator
  Walter Hawken Tregellas
  II 147–148; *I* 619–620

Ashford, Margaret Mary Julia 1881–1972
  Daisy Ashford, author
  Hugo Brunner
  1971–1980 21–22

Ashley, Laura 1925–1985
  dress designer, interior decorator,
  entrepreneur
  Emlyn Hooson
  1981–1985 12–13

Ashton, Winifred 1888–1965
  Clemence Dane, playwright and
  novelist
  William Aubrey Darlington
  1961–1970 38–40

Ashwell, Lena Margaret 1872–1957
  actress
  Ivor Brown
  1951–1960 36–37

Askew, Anne 1521–1546
  martyr
  James Gairdner
  II 190–192; *I* 662–664

Asquith, Cynthia Mary Evelyn 1887–1960
  writer
  David Cecil
  1951–1960 39

Asquith, Emma Alice Margaret 1864–1945
  Margot, Countess of Oxford and
  Asquith
  Leslie Poles Hartley
  1941–1950 23–24

Astell, Mary 1668–1731
  author
  John Henry Overton
  II 201–202; *I* 673–674

Astor, Nancy Witcher 1879–1964
  politician, hostess
  John Grigg
  1961–1970 43–44

Atkins, Anna 1799–1871
  botanist, publisher, photographic
  artist
  Larry J. Schaaf
  Missing Persons 28

Attwell, Mabel Lucie 1879–1964
  illustrator
  Brian Alderson
  1961–1970 55–57

Augusta Sophia 1768–1840
  daughter of George III
  Jennett Humphreys
  II 255; *I* 727

Aust, Sarah 1744–1811
  topographical writer
  Sidney Lee
  II 258; *I* 730

Austen, Jane 1775–1817
  novelist
  Leslie Stephen
  259–260; *I* 731–732

Austin, Sarah 1793–1867
  translator
  John Macdonell
  II 270–271; *I* 742–743

Aylward, Gladys May 1902–1970
  missionary
  John Pollock
  1961–1970 57–58

Ayrton, Hertha 1854–1923
  physicist
  Willem D. Hackmann
  Missing Persons 30–31

Ayrton, Matilda Chaplin 1846–1883
  doctor
  Sidney Lee
  II 292–293; *I* 764–765

Bache, Sarah 1771?–1844
  hymn writer
  Alexander Gordon
  II 318; *I* 790

Bacon, Ann 1528–1610
  governess to Edward VI
  Alexander Balloch Grosart
  II 323–324; *I* 795–796

Baddeley, Sophia 1745–1786
  actress, singer
  Joseph Knight
  II 383–384; *I* 855–856

Baden-Powell, Olave St Clair 1889–1977
  Girl Guide leader
  Sheila Walker
  1971–1980 31–32

Bagnold, Enid Algerine 1889–1981
  novelist, playwright
  Nigel Nicolson
  1981–1985 21–22

Bailey, Mary 1890–1960
aviator
Oliver Stewart
1951–1960 52

Baillie, Isobel 1895–1983
singer
Keith Falkner
1981–1985 22–23

Baillie, Grizel 1665–1746
heroine, poet
Alexander Balloch Grosart
II 413–414; *I* 805–806

Baillie, Joanna 1762–1851
dramatist
George Barnett Smith
II 414–417; *I* 886–889

Baillie, Marianne 1795?–1830
traveller, poet
Arthur Henry Grant
II 418–419; *I* 890–891

Baker, Anne Elizabeth 1786–1861
philologist
Thompson Cooper
III 1; *I* 921

Balfour, Clara Lucas 1808–1878
lecturer, author
Jennett Humphreys
III 49–50; *I* 969–970

Balfour, Frances 1858–1931
churchwoman, suffragist, author
Norman Maclean
1931–1940 34–35

Ball, Frances 1794–1861
Frances Mother Theresa, founder of
convents
Thompson Cooper
III 72–73; *I* 992–993

Ball, Hannah 1734–1792
Wesleyan Methodist
William Edward Armytage Axon
III 73; *I* 993

Bankes, Mary *d*1661
heroine
George Vere Benson
III 123–124; *I* 1043–1044

Banks, Isabella 1821–1897
novelist
Elizabeth Lee
1901 I 123; *XXII* 123

Banks, Sarah Sophia 1744–1818
virtuoso, collector
Benjamin Daydon Jackson
III 133; *I* 1053

Bannerman, Anne *d*1829
poet
Thompson Cooper
III 139; *I* 1059

Barbauld, Anna Letitia 1743–1825
writer
Arthur Aikin Brodribb
III 144–146; *I* 1064–1066

Barber, Mary 1690?–1757
poet
Jennett Humphreys
III 148–149; *I* 1068–1069

Barker, Jane 1652–1727?
poet, novelist
Alison Shell
Missing Persons 43

Barker, Lilian Charlotte 1874–1955
assistant prison commissioner
Harold Scott
1951–1960 64–65

Barnard, Anne 1750–1825
author
Alexander Balloch Grosart
III 236–237; *I* 1156–1057

Barnard, Charlotte Alington 1830–1869
Claribel, ballad writer
William Barclay Squire
III 237; *I* 1157

Barnett, Henrietta Octavia Weston
1851–1936
  social reformer
  Lionel Frederic Ellis
  1931–1940 44–45

Barry, Ann Spranger 1734–1801
  actress
  Joseph Knight
  III 309–310; *I* 1229–1230

Barry, Elizabeth 1658–1713
  actress
  Joseph Knight
  III 317–319; *I* 1237–1239

Bartholomew, Ann Charlotte *d*1862
  painter, author
  Ernest Radford
  III 332–333; *I* 1252–1253

Bartley, Sarah 1783–1850
  actress
  Joseph Knight
  III 336–337; *I* 1256–1257

Barton, Elizabeth 1506?–1534
  fanatic
  Sidney Lee
  III 343–346; *I* 1263–1266

Barwell, Louisa Mary 1800–1885
  musician, writer
  Alexander Gordon
  III 349–350; *I* 1269–1270

Bates, Sarah *d*1811
  singer
  John Alexander Fuller Maitland
  III 399; *I* 1319

Bateson, Mary 1865–1906
  historian
  T. F. Tout
  1901–1911 I 110–112

Bather, Lucy Elizabeth 1836–1864
  children's writer
  Arthur Henry Grant
  III 404; *I* 1324

Bathilda, Baltechildis, Baldechild, or
Baldhild *d*678?
  wife of Clovis II
  Thomas Andrew Archer
  III 404–406; *I* 1324–1326

Batten, Edith Mary 1905–1985
  social work pioneer, educationist
  Simon Wilton Phipps
  1981–1985 30–31

Baxter, Lucy 1837–1902
  Leader Scott, art writer
  Paul Waterhouse
  1901–1911 I 113

Baylis, Lilian Mary 1874–1937
  theatre manager
  Edward J. Dent
  1931–1940 53–54

Bayly, Ada Ellen 1857–1903
  Edna Lyall, novelist
  Elizabeth Lee
  1901–1911 I 114–116

Baynard, Ann 1672–1697
  noted for learning and piety
  Sidney Lee
  III 452–453; *I* 1372–1373

Beale, Dorothea 1831–1906
  educationist
  Elizabeth Lee
  1901–1911 I 116–118

Beale, Mary 1632–1697
  portrait painter
  Robert Edmund Graves
  IV 2–3; *II* 2–3

Beatrice Mary Victoria Feodore
1857–1944
  daughter of Queen Victoria
  Cecil Faber Aspinall-Oglander
  1941–1950 67–68

Beauclerk, Diana 1734–1808
  artist
  Austin Dobson
  IV 35–36; *II* 35–36

Beaufort, Margaret 1443–1509
daughter of Duke of Somerset
Henry Avray Tipping
IV 48–49; *II* 48–49

Beaumont, Agnes 1652–1720
religious autobiographer
William Robert Owens
Missing Persons 52

Becher, Eliza 1791–1872
actress
Joseph Knight
IV 74–75; *II* 74–75

Becker, Lydia Ernestine 1827–1890
advocate of women's suffrage
Charles William Sutton
1901 I 159–160; *XXII* 159–160

Beeton, Isabella Mary 1836–1865
journalist, author
Margaret Beetham
Missing Persons 54–55

Behn, Afra, Aphra, or Ayfara 1640–1689
dramatist, novelist
Edmund Gosse
IV 129–131; *II* 129–131

Bell, Gertrude Margaret Lowthian
1868–1926
traveller, archaeologist, government
servant
William David Hogarth
1922–1930 74–76

Bell, Maria *d*1825
painter
Robert Edmund Graves
IV 171; *II* 171

Bell, Vanessa 1879–1961
painter
Anne Olivier Bell
1961–1970 92–94

Bellamy, George Anne 1731?–1788
actress
Joseph Knight
IV 178–179; *II* 178–179

Bendish, Bridget 1650–1726
granddaughter of Oliver Cromwell
Sidney Lee
IV 212–213; *II* 212–213

Benger, Elizabeth Ogilvy 1778–1827
author
Jennett Humphreys
IV 221–222; *II* 221–222

Bennett, Agnes Maria *d*1808
novelist
Jennett Humphreys
IV 240–241; *II* 240–241

Bentley, Phyllis Eleanor 1894–1977
novelist
Lettice Cooper
1971–1980 50

Benwell, Mary *fl*1761–1800
painter
Robert Edmund Graves
IV 319; *II* 319

Berengaria *d* after 1230
wife of Richard I
William Hunt
IV 325–326; *II* 325–326

Berkeley, Eliza 1734–1800
author
Jennett Humphreys
IV 344–345; *II* 344–345

Berners, Bernes, or Barnes, Juliana *b*1388?
writer
Morgan George Watkins
IV 390–392; *II* 390–392

Berry, Mary 1763–1852
author
Charles Kent
IV 399–401; *II* 399–401

Bertha, Bercta, or Adilberga *d* before 616
daughter of Haribert, King of
the Franks
William Hunt
IV 402; *II* 402

Bertie, Catharine 1520–1580
relative of Catherine of Aragon
Thompson Cooper
IV 403; *II* 403

Besant, Annie 1847–1933
theosophist, educationist,
Indian politician
Sackville Hatton Harrington Lovett
and Patrick Cadell
1931–1940 72–74

Betham, Mary Matilda 1776–1852
writer, painter
Anne Gilchrist
IV 423; *II* 423

Bewick, Jane 1787–1881
writer
Austin Dobson
IV 452–453; *II* 452–453

Bicknell, M. [Margaret?] 1695?–1723
actress
Joseph Knight
V 11; *II* 473

Biffin or Beffin, Sarah 1784–1850
painter
Jennett Humphreys
V 19; *II* 481

Billington, Elizabeth 1768–1818
singer
William Barclay Squire
V 37–39; *II* 499–501

Bing, Gertrud 1892–1964
scholar
Enriqueta Frankfort
1961–1970 108–109

Bingham, Margaret *d*1814
painter
Ernest Radford
V 50–51; *II* 512–513

Bishop, Ann 1814–1884
singer
William Barclay Squire
V 89–90; *II* 551–552

Bishop, Isabella Lucy 1831–1904
traveller, author
Charles P. Lucas
1901–1911 I 166–168

Black, Clementina Maria 1853–1922
suffragist, writer
Janet E. Grenier
Missing Persons 69–70

Blackburn, Helen 1842–1903
women's suffragist
Charlotte Fell-Smith
1901–1911 I 168–169

Blackburne, Anna *d*1794
botanist
George Thomas Bettany
V 121; *II* 583

Blackwell, Elizabeth *fl*1737
botanist
Richard Garnett
V 144; *II* 606

Blackwell, Elizabeth 1821–1910
first woman doctor
Charlotte Fell-Smith
1901–1911 I 170–171

Blamire, Susanna 1747–1794
poet
Mandell Creighton
V 191–192; *II* 653–654

Bland, Edith 1858–1924
E. Nesbit, children's writer
Frederick Joseph Harvey
1922–1930 84

Bland, Elizabeth *fl*1681–1712
Hebrew scholar
Robert Henry Brodie
V 196; *II* 658

Bland, Maria Theresa 1769–1838
singer
William Barclay Squire
V 198–199; *II* 660–661

Blandy, Mary *d*1752
  murderer
  Leslie Stephen
  V 202; *II* 664

Blaugdone, Blagdone, Blagdown, or
Blaugdon, Barbara *c*1609–1704
  Quaker preacher
  Bridget Hill
  Missing Persons 72–7

Blessington, Marguerite 1789–1849
  author
  Charles Kent
  V 213–215; *II* 675–677

Blind, Mathilde 1841–1896
  poet
  Richard Garnett
  1901 I 219–220; *XXII* 219–220

Bloomfield, Georgiana 1822–1905
  author
  Elizabeth Lee
  1901–1911 I 183

Blount, Martha 1690–1762
  friend of Alexander Pope
  Jennett Humphreys
  V 248–249; *II* 710–711

Blyton, Enid Mary 1897–1968
  children's writer
  George Greenfield
  1961–1970 115–117

Boadicea *d*62
  Queen of the Iceni
  Arthur Miller
  V 279–280; *II* 741–742

Bocher, Boucher, or Butcher, Joan *d*1550
  martyr
  Sidney Lee
  V 286–287; *II* 748–749

Bodda Pyne, Louisa Fanny 1832–1904
  singer
  Frederick Corder
  1901–1911 I 186–187

Bodichon, Barbara Leigh Smith
1827–1891
  benefactress of Girton College,
  Cambridge
  Norman Moore
  1901 I 229; *XXII* 229

Bonaventure, Thomasine *d*1510?
  benefactress
  Walter Hawken Tregellas
  V 336–337; *II* 798–799

Bondfield, Margaret Grace 1873–1953
  trade-union leader, MP
  Mary Agnes Hamilton
  1951–1960 122–123

Bonham Carter, Helen Violet 1887–1969
  Baroness Asquith, political figure
  William Haley
  1961–1970 120–121

Bonhote, Elizabeth 1744–1818
  author
  Jennett Humphreys
  V 345–346; *II* 807–808

Booth, Catherine 1829–1890
  'Mother of the Salvation Army'
  Ronald Bayne
  1901 I 233–235; *XXII* 233–235

Booth, Sarah 1793–1867
  actress
  Joseph Knight
  V 389–390; *II* 851–852

Boothby, Miss Hill 1708–1756
  friend of Dr Johnson
  Evelyn Shirley Shuckburgh
  V 391–392; *II* 853–854

Bosanquet, Helen 1860–1925
  social reformer
  Jose Ferial Harris
  Missing Persons 78–79

Boucherett, Emilia Jessie 1825–1905
  advocate of women's progress
  Charlotte Fell-Smith
  1901–1911 I 196–197

Boughton, Joan *d*1494
  martyr
  William Hunt
  VI 6; *II* 914

Boutel, Mrs *fl*1663–1696
  actress
  Joseph Knight
  VI 35; *II* 943

Bovey or Boevey, Catharina 1669–1726
  philanthropist
  Jennett Humphreys
  VI 37–38; *II* 945–946

Bowdler, Henrietta Maria 1754–1830
  writer
  Sidney Lee
  VI 43; *II* 951

Bowdler, Jane 1743–1784
  author
  Sidney Lee
  VI 43; *II* 951

Bowen, Elizabeth Dorothea Cole
1899–1973
  writer
  Victoria Glendinning
  1971–1980 73–74

Bowes, Elizabeth 1502?–1568
  disciple of John Knox
  Mandell Creighton
  VI 55; *II* 963

Bowes, Mary Eleanor 1749–1800
  writer
  William Edward Armytage Axon
  VI 60–61; *II* 968–969

Boyle, Constance Antonina 1865–1943
  women's rights campaigner
  Kathryn Fuller
  Missing Persons 81–88

Bracegirdle, Anne 1663?–1748
  actress
  Joseph Knight
  VI 141–142; *II* 1049–1050

Braddock, Elizabeth Margaret 1899–1970
  trade union activist, MP
  Elizabeth Vallance
  Missing Persons 82–83

Bradshaw, Ann Maria 1801–1862
  actress
  Joseph Knight
  VI 174; *II* 1120

Bradstreet, Anne 1612–1672
  poet
  Jennett Humphreys
  VI 186–187; *II* 1094–1095

Brahms, Caryl 1901–1982
  novelist, critic, journalist,
  songwriter
  Ned Sherrin
  1981–1985 51–52

Brand, Barbarina 1768–1854
  poet, dramatist
  Thompson Cooper
  VI 212; *II* 1120

Brand, Hannah *d*1821
  actress, dramatist
  Joseph Knight
  VI 212–213; *II* 1120–1121

Brassey, Anna or Annie 1839–1887
  traveller, author
  Edward Henry Marshall
  1901 I 261–262; *XXII* 261–262

Braithwaite, Florence Lilian 1873–1948
  actress
  Diana Morgan
  1941–1950 102–103

Bray, Anna Eliza 1790–1883
  novelist
  William Prideaux Courtney
  VI 234–235; *II* 1142–1143

Bray, Caroline 1814–1905
  author
  Elizabeth Lee
  1901–1911 I 218–219

Brazil, Angela 1868–1947
writer
Arthur Marshall
1941–1950 104–105

Brent, Charlotte *d*1802
singer
William Barclay Squire
VI 261; *II* 1169

Brettargh, Katharine 1579–1601
puritan
William Edward Armytage Axon
VI 286–287; *II* 1194–1195

Brightwell, Cecilia Lucy 1811–1875
etcher, author
Alexander Gordon
VI 340; *II* 1248

Brightwen, Eliza 1830–1906
naturalist
Edmund Gosse
1901–1911 I 225–226

Brigit 453–523
saint
Thomas Olden
VI 340–342; *II* 1248–1250

Brittain, Vera Mary 1893–1970
writer, pacifist, feminist
Eirene White
1961–1970 139–140

Broderip, Frances Freeling 1830–1878
author
George Clement Boase
VI 375–376; *II* 1283–1284

Brontë, Charlotte 1816–1855
novelist
Leslie Stephen
VI 406–413; *II* 1314–1321

Brooke, Charlotte *d*1793
author
John Thomas Gilbert
VI 418–419; *II* 1326–1327

Brooke, Elizabeth 1601–1683
writer
Jennett Humphreys
VI 420; *II* 1328

Brooke, Frances 1724–1789
author
Jennett Humphreys
VI 420–421; *II* 1328–1329

Broughton, Rhoda 1840–1920
novelist
Myra Curtis
1912–1921 69–70

Browne, Frances 1816–1879
writer
Gillian Avery
Missing Persons 95

Browning, Elizabeth Barrett 1806–1861
poet
Anne Isabella Ritchie
VII 78–82; *III* 78–82

Brownrigg, Elizabeth, *d*1767
murderer
George Fisher Russell Barker
VII 84; *III* 84

Brunton, Mary 1778–1818
novelist
William Edward Armytage Axon
VII 148; *III* 148

Bryan, Margaret *fl*1815
schoolmistress, writer
Jennett Humphreys
VII 154; *III* 154

Bryant, Sophie 1850–1922
educationist, Irish patriot,
suffragist
Sheila Fletcher
Missing Persons 97–98

Buchan or Simpson, Elspeth 1738–1791
founder of Buchanite sect
Thomas Finlayson Henderson
VII 178–179; *III* 178–179

Bufton, Eleanor 1840?–1893
actress
Joseph Knight
1901 I 332; *XXII* 332

Bulkeley, Sophia *fl*1688
Jacobite, court beauty
Jennett Humphreys
VII 233–234; *III* 233–234

Bulmer, Agnes 1775–1836
poet
Richard Watson Dixon
VII 258; *III* 258

Bunn, Margaret Agnes 1799–1883
actress
Joseph Knight
VII 269–270; *III* 269–270

Bunsen, Frances 1791–1876
heiress
George Clement Boase
VII 272; *III* 272

Burdett-Coutts, Angela Georgina
1814–1906
philanthropist
J. P. Anderson
1901–1911 I 259–266

Burges, Mary Anne 1763–1813
author, linguist, naturalist
Jennett Humphreys
VII 307; *III* 307

Burnet, Elizabeth 1661–1709
writer
Jennett Humphreys
VII 393–394; *III* 393–394

Burnet, Margaret 1630?–1685?
presbyterian
Osmund Airy
VII 407–408; *III* 407–408

Burnett, Frances Eliza Hodgson
1849–1924
author
Gillian Avery
Missing Persons 105–106

Burney, Sarah Harriet 1770?–1844
novelist
Jennett Humphreys
VII 419–420; *III* 419–420

Burrell, Sophia 1750?–1802
poet, dramatist
Jennett Humphreys
VII 442; *III* 442

Burrows, Christine Mary Elizabeth
1872–1959
educationist
Ruth Florence Butler
1951–1960 163–164

Burton, Catharine 1668–1714
Carmelite nun
Thompson Cooper
VIII 1; *III* 453

Burton, Isabel 1831–1896
traveller, writer
James Sutherland Cotton
1901 I 348–349; *XXII* 348–349

Bury, Charlotte Susan Maria 1775–1861
novelist
George Clement Boase
VIII 22–23; *III* 474–475

Bury, Elizabeth 1644–1720
nonconformist, diarist
Jennett Humphreys
VIII 24–25; *III* 476–25

Busk, Rachel Harriette 1831–1907
writer
Elizabeth Lee
1901–1911 I 276

Buss, Frances Mary 1827–1894
educator
Janet Gough
Missing Persons 107

Butler, Christina Violet 1884–1982
pioneer of social–work training
Brian Harrison
Missing Persons 107–108

Butler, Eleanor 1745?–1829
recluse
Sidney Lee
VIII 48–49; *III* 500–501

Butler, Elizabeth Southerden 1846–1933
painter
John Black Atkins
1931–1940 127–128

Butler, Josephine Elizabeth 1828–1906
social reformer
Edith S. Hooper
1901–1911 I 282–283

Butt, Clara Ellen 1872–1936
singer
John Mewburn Levien
1931–1940 130–131

Buxton, Bertha H. 1844–1881
novelist
George Clement Boase
VIII 105; *III* 557

Byrne, Anne Frances 1775–1837
painter
Jennett Humphreys
VIII 127; *III* 579

Byrne, Julia Clara 1819–1894
author
Elizabeth Lee
1901 I 364–365; *XXII* 364–365

Byrne, Letitia 1779–1849
engraver
Jennett Humphreys
VIII 127; *III* 579

Byron, Augusta Ada 1815–1852
mathematician
Anthony Hyman
Missing Persons 110

Cable, Alice Mildred 1878–1952
missionary
William James Platt
1951–1960 170–171

Cadell, Jessie 1844–1884
novelist, Persian scholar
Richard Garnett
VIII 177–178; *III* 629–630

Calderwood, Margaret 1715–1774
diarist
Charles John Robinson
VIII 246; *III* 698

Callcott, Maria 1785–1842
traveller, author
Sidney Lee
VIII 258; *III* 710

Calvert, Caroline Louisa Waring
1834–1872
Louisa Atkinson, author
John Westby Gibson
VIII 265–266; *III* 717–718

Cam, Helen Maud 1885–1968
historian
Kathleen Major
1961–1970 166–167

Cameron, Julia Margaret 1815–1879
photographer
Julia Prinsep Stephen
VIII 300; *III* 752

Cameron, Lucy Lyttelton 1781–1858
children's writer
Edmund Venables
VIII 300–301; *III* 752–753

Camm, Anne 1627–1705
Quaker
Augustus Charles Bickley
VIII 303–304; *III* 755–756

Campbell, Anna Mackenzie 1621?–1706?
royalist
Osmund Airy
VIII 311–312; *III* 763–764

Campbell, Beatrice Stella 1865–1940
Mrs Patrick Campbell, actress
John Courtenay Trewin
1931–1940 138–141

Campbell, Harriette 1817–1841
 novelist
 Jennett Humphreys
 VIII 359; *III* 811

Campbell, Janet Mary 1877–1954
 medical officer
 Margaret Hogarth
 1951–1960 181–182

Campbell, Willielma 1741–1786
 religious zealot
 William Garden Blaikie
 VIII 397–398; *III* 849–850

Candler, Ann 1740–1814
 poet
 Jennett Humphreys
 VIII 405; *III* 857

Cannera or Cainner *d*530?
 saint
 Thomas Andrew Archer
 VIII 413–414; *III* 865–866

Canning, Elizabeth 1734–1773
 impostor
 Austin Dobson
 VIII 418–420; *III* 870–872

Caradori–Allan, Maria Caterina
Rosalbina 1800–1865
 singer
 William Barclay Squire
 IX 30–31; *III* 939–940

Carey or Carew, Elizabeth *fl*1590
 patron of poets
 unsigned
 IX 64–65; *III* 973–974

Carey, Rosa Nouchette 1840–1909
 novelist
 Elizabeth Lee
 1901–1911 I 314–315

Cargill, Ann 1748?–1784
 Miss Brown, actress, singer
 Joseph Knight
 IX 79; *III* 988

Carleton, Mary 1642?–1673
 criminal
 Jennett Humphreys
 IX 95–96; *III* 1004–1005

Carlile or Carlisle, Anne *d*1680?
 painter
 Jennett Humphreys
 IX 99; *III* 1008

Carmylyon, Alice or Ellys *fl*1527–1531
 painter
 Charles Trice Martin
 IX 132; *III* 1041

Carne, Elizabeth Catherine Thomas
1817–1873
 author
 George Clement Boase
 IX 135; *III* 1044

Caroline 1683–1737
 Queen of Great Britain and
 Ireland
 Adolphus William Ward
 IX 139–145; *III* 1048–1054

Caroline Mathilda 1751–1775
 Queen of Denmark and Norway
 Adolphus William Ward
 IX 145–150; *III* 1054–1059

Caroline Amelia Elizabeth 1868–1821
 wife of George IV
 John Ashton
 IX 150–153; *III* 1059–1062

Carpenter, Margaret Sarah 1793–1872
 painter
 William Cosmo Monkhouse
 IX 159; *III* 1068

Carpenter, Mary 1807–1877
 philanthropist
 Alexander Gordon
 IX 159–161; *III* 1068–1070

Carrington, Dora de Houghton 1893–1932
 painter
 Frances Partridge
 Missing Persons 116

Carter, Elizabeth 1717–1806
poet, writer
George Fisher Russell Barker
IX 194–196; *III* 1103–1105

Carter, Ellen 1762–1815
artist
Lionel Henry Cust
IX 196–197; *III* 1105–1106

Cartwright, Frances Dorothy 1780–1863
poet, biographer
Jennett Humphreys
IX 223; *III* 1132

Carus-Wilson, Eleanora Mary 1897–1977
economic historian
Peter Mathias
1971–1980 125–126

Carwardine, Penelope 1730?–1800?
painter
Jennett Humphreys
IX 239; *III* 1148

Cary, Mary *c*1621–*post*1653
writer
Bernard Capp
Missing Persons 118–119

Casali, Andrea 1720?–1763?
painter
Lionel Henry Cust
IX 256; *III* 1165

Catchpole, Margaret 1773–1841
adventuress
Morgan George Watkins
IX 278; *III* 1187

Catherine of Valois 1401–1437
wife of Henry V
Sidney Lee
IX 289–290; *III* 1198–1199

Catherine of Aragon 1485–1536
wife of Henry VIII
James Gairdner
IX 290–303; *III* 1199–1212

Catherine Howard *d*1542
wife of Henry VIII
James Gairdner
IX 303–308; *III* 1212–1217

Catherine Parr 1512–1548
wife of Henry VIII
James Gairdner
IX 308–312; *III* 1217–1221

Catherine of Braganza 1638–1705
wife of Charles II
Thomas Frederick Tout
IX 312–319; *III* 1221–1228

Catley, Ann 1745–1789
singer
Jennett Humphreys
IX 319–320; *III* 1228–1229

Caton-Thompson, Gertrude 1888–1985
archaeologist, prehistorian
Archibald Laurence Patrick Kirwan
1981–1985 77–78

Cavell, Edith 1865–1915
nurse
Benedict William Ginsburg
1912–1921 100–101

Cavendish, Ada 1839–1895
actress
Joseph Knight
1901 I 398–399; *XXII* 398–399

Cavendish, Christiana *d*1675
supporter of Charles II
Thomas Finlayson Henderson
IX 343–344; *III* 1252–1253

Cavendish, Elizabeth 1758–1824
patron of arts
Thomas Finlayson Henderson
IX 344; *III* 1253

Cavendish, Georgiana 1757–1806
daughter of Earl Spencer
Thomas Finlayson Henderson
IX 347–348; *III* 1256–1257

Cavendish, Margaret 1624?–1674
  writer
  Joseph Knight
  IX 355–357; *III* 1264–1266

Cecilia or Cecily 1469–1507
  daughter of Edward IV
  Thomas Andrew Archer
  IX 412–413; *III* 1321–1322

Celesia, Dorothea 1738–1790
  poet, dramatist
  Gordon Goodwin
  IX 414; *III* 1323

Celeste, Madame 1814?–1882
  actress
  Joseph Knight
  IX 415; *III* 1324

Cellier, Elizabeth *fl*1680
  midwife
  Thompson Cooper
  IX 417; *III* 1326

Centlivre, Susannah 1667?–1723
  actress, dramatist
  Joseph Knight
  IX 420–422; *III* 1329–1331

Challans, Eileen Mary 1905–1983
  Mary Renault, writer
  Brian Alderson
  1981–1985 80

Chambers, Dorothea Katharine
1878–1960
  tennis champion
  John George Smyth
  1951–1960 203–204

Chandler, Johanna 1820–1875
  philanthropist
  Jennett Humphreys
  X 38–39; *IV* 38–39

Chandler, Mary 1687–1745
  poet
  Jennett Humphreys
  X 39; *IV* 39

Chapman, Mary Francis 1838–1884
  novelist
  Norman MacColl
  X 56–57; *IV* 56–57

Chapone, Hester 1727–1801
  essayist
  Jennett Humphreys
  X 58–59; *IV* 58–59

Charke, Charlotte *d*1760?
  actress, writer
  Joseph Knight
  X 65–67; *IV* 65–67

Charles, Elizabeth 1828–1896
  author
  Elizabeth Lee
  1901 I 417–419; *XXII* 417–419

Charlesworth, Maria Louisa 1819–1880
  author
  George Clement Boase
  X 115; *IV* 115

Charlotte Augusta 1796–1817
  daughter of George IV
  Austin Dobson
  X 120–122; *IV* 120–122

Charlotte Augusta Matilda 1766–1828
  daughter of George III
  Adolphus William Ward
  X 122–123; *IV* 122–123

Charlotte Sophia 1744–1818
  wife of George III
  Francis Watt
  X 123; *IV* 123

Charretie, Anna Maria 1819–1875
  painter
  Louis Alexander Fagan
  X 135; *IV* 135

Chase, Marian Emma 1844–1905
  painter
  B. S. Long
  1901–1911 I 356

Chatelain, Clara de 1807–1876
    composer, author
    George Clement Boase
    X 140–141; *IV* 140–141

Chatterton, Henrietta Georgiana Marcia
Lascelles 1806–1876
    writer
    George Clement Boase
    X 143; *IV* 143

Chessar, Jane Agnes 1835–1880
    teacher
    William Hunt
    X 200; *IV* 200

Cheyne, Jane 1621–1669
    poet, dramatist
    Jennett Humphreys
    X 220; *IV* 220

Chick, Harriette 1875–1977
    nutritionist
    Hugh Macdonald Sinclair
    1971–1980 142–143

Chidley, Katherine *fl*1641–1653
    radical pamphleteer, religious
    separatist
    Ian J. Gentles
    Missing Persons 127–128

Chisholm, Caroline 1808–1877
    emigrants' friend
    George Clement Boase
    X 260–261; *IV* 260–261

Cholmondeley, Mary 1563–1626
    litigant
    Jennett Humphreys
    X 272; *IV* 272

Christie, Agatha Mary Clarissa 1890–1976
    novelist, playwright
    Henry Reymond Fitzwalter Keating
    1971–1980 144–145

Christina *fl*1086
    nun
    Thomas Frederick Tout
    X 289–290; *IV* 289–290

Christina of Markyate *b c*1096
    recluse, prioress
    Charles Holwell Talbot
    Missing Persons 129–130

Chudleigh, Elizabeth 1720–1788
    mistress of Duke of Kingston
    William Hunt
    X 298–301; *IV* 298–301

Chudleigh, Mary 1656–1710
    poet
    Jennett Humphreys
    X 303; *IV* 303

Churchill, Arabella 1648–1730
    mistress of James II
    Evelyn Shirley Shuckburgh
    X 307; *IV* 307

Churchill, Clementine Ogilvy Spencer-
1885–1977
    Baroness Spencer-Churchill
    Mary Soames
    1971–1980 147–149

Churchill, Jeanette 1854–1921
    society hostess, writer
    Godfrey Hugh Lancelot Le May
    Missing Persons 130–131

Cibber, Susannah Maria 1714–1766
    actress
    Theodore Martin
    X 359–362; *IV* 359–362

Clairmont, Clara Mary Jane 1798–1879
    friend of Byron and Shelley
    Richard Garnett
    X 369–370; *IV* 369–370

Clare, Elizabeth de *d*1360
    founder of Clare College,
    Cambridge
    Evelyn Shirley Shuckburgh
    X 376–377; *IV* 376–377

Clark, Esther 1716–1794
    poet
    Richard Greene
    Missing Persons 135

Clarke, Harriet Ludlow *d*1866
   artist, engraver
   Lionel Henry Cust
   X 426; *IV* 426

Clarke, Mary Anne 1776–1852
   mistress of Duke of York
   Henry Morse Stephens
   X 436–437; *IV* 436–437

Clarke, Mary Victoria Cowden 1809–1898
   writer
   Charles Ernest Hughes
   1901 II 28–29; *XII* 453–454

Clarke, Maude Violet 1892–1935
   historian
   Vivian Hunter Galbraith
   1931–1940 182–183

Claypoole or Claypole, Elizabeth
1629–1658
   daughter of Oliver Cromwell
   Charles Harding Firth
   XI 11–12; *IV* 467–468

Clement or Clements, Margaret
1508–1570
   learned lady
   Jennett Humphreys
   XI 33; *IV* 489

Clerke, Agnes Mary 1842–1907
   astronomy historian
   H. P. Hollis
   1901–1911 I 371–72

Clifford, Anne 1590–1676
   Countess of Dorset
   George Fisher Russell Barker
   XI 56–57; *IV* 512–513

Clifford, Margaret 1560?–1616
   Countess of Cumberland
   Thomas Andrew Archer
   XI 68; *IV* 524

Clifford, Rosamond *d*1176?
   mistress of Henry II
   Thomas Andrew Archer
   XI 75–77; *IV* 531–533

Clitherow, Margaret *d*1586
   martyr
   Thompson Cooper
   XI 103; *IV* 554

Clive, Caroline 1801–1873
   author
   George Fisher Russell Barker
   XI 103–104; *IV* 559–560

Clive, Catherine 1711–1785
   Kitty Clive, actress
   Theodore Martin
   XI 104–107; *IV* 560–563

Clough, Anne Jemima 1820–1892
   first principal of Newnham College,
   Cambridge
   Elizabeth Lee
   1901 II 35–36; *XXII* 460–461

Coade, Eleanor 1733–1821
   manufacturer of artificial stone
   Alison Kelly
   Missing Persons 140–141

Cobbold, Elizabeth 1767–1824
   poet
   Jennett Humphreys
   XI 145–146; *IV* 601–602

Cobbe, Frances Power 1822–1904
   philanthropist, religious writer
   Alexander Gordon
   1901–1911 I 377–379

Cockburn, Alicia or Alison 1712?–1794
   author
   Thomas Finlayson Henderson
   XI 181–183; *IV* 637–639

Cockburn, Catharine 1679–1749
   dramatist, writer
   Leslie Stephen
   XI 183–184; *IV* 639–640

Cohen, Harriet 1896–1967
   pianist
   Ivor Newton
   1961–1970 229–230

Cole, Margaret Isabel 1893–1980
  writer, political activist
  John Saville
  1971–1980 165–167

Coleridge, Mary Elizabeth 1861–1907
  poet, novelist, essayist
  Edith Sichel
  1901–1911 I 382–383

Coleridge, Sara 1802–1852
  writer
  Richard Garnett
  XI 317; *IV* 773

Collier, Jane 1710–1754/5
  novelist
  Isobel Grundy
  Missing Persons 144

Collier, Mary 1688–*c*1762
  poet
  Richard Greene
  Missing Persons 144–145

Collignon, Catherine 1755–1832
  translator
  Thompson Cooper
  XI 355; *IV* 811

Collins, Josephine 1887–1958
  actress, singer
  John Courtenay Trewin
  1951–1960 241–243

Collyer, Mary *d*1763
  author
  Thompson Cooper
  XI 386; *IV* 842

Colquhoun, Janet 1781–1846
  writer
  John Alexander Fuller Maitland
  XI 401–402; *IV* 857–858

Colville, Elizabeth
  poet
  James McMullen Rigg
  XI 419–420; *IV* 875–876

Compton, Fay 1894–1978
  actress
  John Courtenay Trewin
  1971–1980 168–169

Compton-Burnett, Ivy 1884–1969
  novelist
  Julian Mitchell
  1961–1970 236–237

Cons, Emma 1838–1912
  evangelist, philanthropist, theatre
  manager
  Sheridan Morley
  Missing Persons 149–150

Conway, Anne *d*1679
  metaphysician
  Thompson Cooper
  XII 50; *IV* 975

Cook, Eliza 1818–1889
  poet
  Gerald le Grys Norgate
  1901 II 53–54; *XXII* 478–479

Cooper, Elizabeth *fl*1737
  author
  Arthur Henry Bullen
  XII 143–144; *IV* 1068–1069

Cooper, Gladys Constance 1888–1971
  actress, theatre manager
  Sheridan Morley
  1971–1980 175–177

Corbaux, Marie Françoise Catherine
Doetter 1812–1883
  painter, critic
  Thompson Cooper
  XII 195; *IV* 1120

Corbett Ashby, Margery Irene 1882–1981
  feminist, internationalist
  Jenifer Hart
  1981–1985 98–99

Cornelys, Theresa 1723–1797
  singer, theatre director
  Henry Richard Tedder
  XII 223–225; *IV* 1148–1150

Corner, Julia 1798–1875
children's writer
Elizabeth Lee
1901 II 62; *XXII* 487

Cornford, Frances Crofts 1886–1960
poet
Geoffrey Keynes
1951–1960 256–257

Cornwallis, Caroline Frances 1786–1858
author
Mrs S. L. May
XII 233–234; *IV* 1158–1159

Cornwallis, Jane 1581–1659
writer
Thompson Cooper
XII 242; *IV* 1167

Costello, Louisa Stuart 1799–1870
painter, author
George Clement Boase
XII 277; *IV* 1202

Cosway, Maria Cecilia Louisa *fl*1820
painter
Louis Alexander Fagan
XII 278–279; *IV* 1203–1204

Courtneidge, Esmeralda Cicely 1893–1980
actress
Derek Pepys-Whiteley
1971–1980 184–185

Courtney, Kathleen D'Olier 1878–1974
suffragist, campaigner for world
peace
Janet E. Grenier
Missing Persons 153–154

Cousin, Anne Ross 1824–1906
hymn writer
J. Cuthbert Hadden
1901–1911 I 426–427

Coventry, Anne 1673–1763
writer
Sidney Lee
XII 357; *IV* 1282

Coventry, Maria, Countess 1733–1760
famous beauty
William Hunt
XII 359; *IV* 1284

Cowley, Hannah 1743–1809
dramatist, poet
Joseph Knight
XII 382–383; *IV* 1307–1308

Cowper, Mary 1685–1724
Lady of the Bedchamber
James McMullen Rigg
XII 386; *IV* 1311

Craigie, Pearl Mary Teresa 1867–1906
John Oliver Hobbs, novelist and
dramatist
Sidney Lee
1901–1911 I 435–437

Crampton, Victoire 1837–1871
singer
George Clement Boase
XIII 7; *V* 7

Crane, Lucy 1842–1882
art critic
Albert Nicholson
XIII 10–11; *V* 10–11

Craven, Louisa, Countess of 1785?–1860
actress
Joseph Knight
XIII 43; *V* 43

Craven, Pauline Marie Armande Aglaé
1808–1891
author
Elizabeth Lee
1901 II 79–80; *XXII* 504–505

Creed, Elizabeth 1644?–1728
philanthropist
Gordon Goodwin
XIII 68–69; *V* 68–69

Cresswell, Madam *fl*1670–1684
courtesan
John Woodfall Ebsworth
XIII 72; *V* 72

Crewdson, Jane 1808–1863
poet
Charles William Sutton
XIII 84; *V* 84

Crewe, Frances Anne *d*1818
famous beauty
James McMullen Rigg
XIII 84; *V* 84

Cripps, Isobel 1891–1977
Dame Isobel Cripps
Colin Watson
1971–1980 192–193

Cristall, Anne Batten *b*1769
poet
Richard Greene
Missing Persons 158–159

Crofts or Croft, Elizabeth *fl*1554
impostor
Sidney Lee
XIII 115; *V* 115

Cross, Mary Ann 1819–1880
George Eliot, novelist
Leslie Stephen
XIII 216–222; *V* 216–222

Crouch, Anna Maria 1763–1805
singer
William Barclay Squire
XIII 232–233; *V* 232–233

Crowdy, Rachel Eleanor 1884–1964
social reformer
Alice Prochaska
1961–1970 250–251

Crowe, Catherine 1800?–1876
novelist, writer
Richard Garnett
XIII 237; *V* 237

Cullis, Winifred Clara 1875–1956
physiologist
Ruth Elizabeth Mary Bowden
1951–1960 276–278

Currer, Frances Mary Richardson
1785–1861
book collector
Henry Richard Tedder
XIII 340; *V* 340

Currie, Mary Montgomerie 1843–1905
Violet Fane, author
Elizabeth Lee
1901–1911 I 454–455

Cuthburh or Cuthburga *fl*700
saint
William Hunt
XIII 363; *V* 363

Damer, Anne Seymour 1749–1828
sculptor
Leslie Stephen
XIII 450–451; *V* 450–451

Darbishire, Helen 1881–1961
scholar, critic, educationist
Kathleen Tillotson
1961–1970 270–271

Darling, Grace Horsley 1815–1842
heroine
unsigned
XIV 57–58; *V* 507–508

Darlugdach *d*522
saint
Thomas Olden
XIV 63; *V* 513

Darusmont, Frances 1795–1852
philanthropist
Richard Garnett
XIV 70–72; *V* 520–522

Dashwood, Edmée Elizabeth Monica
1890–1943
E. M. Delafield, author
Margaret Bellasis
1941–1950 197–198

Davenport, Mary Ann 1765?–1843
actress
Joseph Knight
XIV 111–112; *V* 561–562

Davidson, Frances Joan 1894–1985
   Baroness Northchurch, politician
   Katharine Elliot
   1981–1985 109–110

Davidson, Harriet Miller 1839–1883
   author
   William Garden Blaikie
   XIV 124–125; *V* 574–575

Davies, Catherine 1773–1841?
   author
   William Roberts
   XIV 131; *V* 581

Davies, Cecilia 1750?–1836
   singer
   William Barclay Squire
   XIV 131–132; *V* 581–582

Davies, Christian 1667–1739
   Mother Ross, soldier
   Alsager Vian
   XIV 132–133; *V* 582–583

Davies, Lucy Clementina 1795–1879
   author
   George Clement Boase
   XIV 147; *V* 597

Davies, Marianne 1744–1816?
   musician
   William Barclay Squire
   XIV 147–148; *V* 597–598

Davies, Sarah Emily 1830–1921
   educationist
   Margaret Thyra Barbara Stephen
   1912–1921 148–149

Davis or Davies, Mary *fl*1663–1669
   actress
   Joseph Knight
   XIV 169–170; *V* 619–620

Davison, Emily Wilding 1972–1913
   feminist
   Liz Stanley
   Missing Persons 176

Davison, Maria Rebecca 1780?–1858
   actress
   Joseph Knight
   XIV 178–179; *V* 628–629

Davy, Jane 1780–1855
   society figure
   William Prideaux Courtney
   XIV 193–194; *V* 643–644

Davys, Mary *fl*1756
   dramatist, novelist
   Thompson Cooper
   XIV 209; *V* 659

Dawes or Daw, Sophia 1790–1840
   adventuress
   John Goldworth Alger
   XIV 214–215; *V* 664–665

Dawson, Nancy 1730?–1767
   dancer
   Alsager Vian
   XIV 227–228; *V* 677–678

Delany, Mary 1700–1788
   biographer
   Leslie Stephen
   XIV 308–310; *V* 758–760

De la Ramée, Marie Louise 1839–1908
   Ouida, novelist
   Elizabeth Lee
   1901–1911 *I* 487–488

Denman, Gertrude Mary 1884–1954
   public servant
   Elizabeth Brunner
   1951–1960 295–296

Despard, Charlotte 1844–1939
   feminist, social reformer
   Margaret Frances Mulvihill
   Missing Persons 182–183

Dick, Anne *d*1741
   poet
   Jennett Humphreys
   XV 14; *V* 919

Dickons, Maria 1770?–1833
  singer
  William Barclay Squire
  XV 37–38; *V* 942–943

Dickson, Elizabeth 1793?–1862
  philanthropist
  Jennett Humphreys
  XV 43–44; *V* 948–949

Digby, Lettice 1588?–1658
  heiress
  John Knox Laughton
  XV 67–68; *V* 972–973

Dilke, Emilia Frances 1840–1904
  art historian
  Sidney Lee
  1901–1911 I 507–508

Dillwyn, Elizabeth Amy 1845–1935
  novelist, feminist, industrialist
  David Painting
  Missing Persons 184–185

Dixie, Florence Caroline 1857–1905
  author, traveller
  O. J. R. Howarth
  1901–1911 I 510

Dixon, Sarah 1672–1765
  poet
  Richard Greene
  Missing Persons 186

Dobson, Susannah *d*1795
  translator
  Charles William Sutton
  XV 137; *V* 1042

Dod, Charlotte 1871–1960
  sportswoman
  John Barrett
  Missing Persons 187–188

Dodgson, Frances Catharine 1883–1954
  artist
  James Byam Shaw
  1951–1960 303–304

Dormer, Jane 1538–1612
  companion of Queen Mary
  Alsager Vian
  XV 245–247; *V* 1150–1152

Dors, Diana 1931–1984
  actress
  Peter Waymark
  1981–1985 119–120

Dorset, Catherine Anne 1750?–1817?
  poet
  Jennett Humphreys
  XV 253; *V* 1158

Douglas, Jane 1698–1753
  daughter of Marquis of Douglas
  Henry Paton
  XV 334–335; *V* 1239–1240

Douglas, Janet *d*1537
  conspirator
  Henry Paton
  XV 335–336; *V* 1240–1241

Douglas, Margaret 1515–1578
  mother of Lord Darnley
  Thomas Finlayson Henderson
  XV 339–343; *V* 1244–1248

Dove, Jane Frances 1847–1942
  educationist
  Elsie Edith Bowerman
  1941–1950 219–220

Dowriche, Anne *fl*1589
  poet
  Sidney Lee
  XV 405–406; *V* 1310–1311

D'Oyly Carte, Bridget 1908–1985
  theatre manager
  Hugh Wontner
  1981–1985 122–122

Drake, Judith *fl*1696
  writer, feminist, medical practitioner
  Bridget Hill
  Missing Persons 192

Drane, Augusta Theodosia 1823–1894
historian, biographer, poet
Thompson Cooper
1901 II 155–156; *XXII* 580–581

Drummond, Annabella 1350?–1402
wife of Robert III of Scotland
Aeneas James George Mackay
XVI 22–25; *VI* 22–25

Drummond, Margaret 1472?–1501
mistress of James IV of Scotland
Alsager Vian
XVI 37–38; *VI* 37–38

Du Bois, Dorothea 1728–1774
author
Jennett Humphreys
XVI 77–78; *VI* 77–78

Dudley, Jane 1537–1554
Greek scholar, humanist
Sidney Lee
XVI 105–107; *VI* 105–107

Dunbar, Agnes 1312?–1369
defender of Dunbar Castle
Alsager Vian
XVI 150–151; *VI* 150–151

Duncombe, Susanna 1730?–1812
poet, artist
Jennett Humphreys
XVI 178; *VI* 178

Dunlop, Frances Anne Wallace
1730–1815
friend of Robert Burns
Thomas Finlayson Henderson
XVI 205; *VI* 205

Durham, Mary Edith 1863–1944
traveller, writer, anthropologist
Harry Hodgkinson
Missing Persons 197–198

Dussek, Sophia 1775–1830?
musician, composer
William Barclay Squire
XVI 268; *VI* 268

Eadburga, Eadburh, Bugga, or Bugge
*d*751
saint
William Hunt
XVI 305–306; *VI* 305–306

Eadburge, Eadburgh, or Eadburh *fl*802
Queen of West Saxons
William Hunt
XVI 306; *VI* 306

Eanflaed *b*626
Queen of Northumbria
William Hunt
XVI 315–316; *VI* 315–316

Eastlake, Elizabeth 1809–1893
author
Thomas Seccombe
1901 II 173–175; *XXII* 598–600

Ebba or Æbba *d*679
saint
William Hunt
XVI 341–342; *VI* 341–342

Ebsworth, Mary Emma 1794–1881
dramatist
John Woodfall Ebsworth
XVI 347; *VI* 347

Eden, Emily 1797–1869
novelist, traveller
George Clement Boase
XVI 356; *VI* 356

Edgeworth, Maria 1767–1849
novelist
Leslie Stephen
XVI 380–382; *VI* 380–382

Edith or Eadgyth 962?–984
saint
William Hunt
XVI 387; *VI* 387

Edith or Eadgyth *d*1075
wife of Edward the Confessor
William Hunt
XVI 387–389; *VI* 387–389

Edwards, Amelia Ann Blanford
1831–1892
    novelist, journalist, Egyptologist
    James Sutherland Cotton
    1901 II 176–178; *XXII* 601–603

Edwards, Matilda Barbara Betham-
1836–1919
    novelist
    Hilda Johnstone
    1912–1921 169–170

Edwin, Elizabeth Rebecca 1771?–1854
    actress
    Joseph Knight
    XVII 134–135; *VI* 552–553

Egerton, Sarah Fyge 1670–1723
    poet
    Richard Greene
    Missing Persons 204–205

Egerton, Sarah 1782–1847
    actress
    Joseph Knight
    XVII 159–160; *VI* 577–578

Eleanor, Alienor, or Ænor 1122?–1204
    Queen of France and England
    Thomas Andrew Archer
    XVII 175–178; *VI* 593–596

Eleanor of Castile *d*1290
    wife of Edward I
    William Hunt
    XVII 178–179; *VI* 596–597

Eleanor of Provence *d*1291
    wife of Henry III
    Thomas Andrew Archer
    XVII 179–180; *VI* 597–598

Elizabeth 1437?–1492
    wife of Edward IV
    James Gairdner
    XVII 196–200; *VI* 614–618

Elizabeth 1465–1503
    wife of Henry VII
    James Gairdner
    XVII 200–203; *VI* 618–621

Elizabeth 1533–1603
    Queen of England
    Augustus Jessopp
    XVII 203–231; *VI* 621–649

Elizabeth 1635–1650
    daughter of Charles I
    Gordon Goodwin
    XVII 232–233; *VI* 650–651

Elizabeth 1596–1662
    Queen of Bohemia
    Adolphus William Ward
    XVII 233–240; *VI* 651–658

Elizabeth 1770–1840
    Princess, artist
    Jennett Humphreys
    XVII 240; *VI* 658

Ellerman, Annie Winifred 1894–1983
    Bryher, writer
    Kim Scott Walwyn
    1981–1985 125–127

Elliot, Jane or Jean 1727–1805
    poet
    Thomas Wilson Bayne
    XVII 259–260; *VI* 677–679

Elliott, Charlotte 1789–1871
    hymn writer
    unsigned
    XVII 266; *VI* 684

Elliott, Grace Dalrymple 1758?–1823
    mistress of Prince of Wales
    John Goldworth Alger
    XVII 268–269; *VI* 686–687

Elphinstone, Hester Maria 1762–1857
    friend of Dr Johnson
    Jennett Humphreys
    XVII 321; *VI* 739

Elphinstone, Margaret Mercer 1788–1867
    friend of Princess Charlotte
    Jennett Humphreys
    XVII 325–326; *VI* 743–744

Elsie, Lily 1886–1962
actress
Cecil Beaton
1961–1970 332–334

Elstob, Elizabeth 1683–1756
Anglo–Saxon scholar
Leslie Stephen
XVII 334–335; *VI* 752–753

Emma *d*1052
Ælfgifu, wife of Ethelred III
William Hunt
XVII 360–361; *VI* 778–779

Epine, Francesca Margherita de l' *d*1746
singer
Lydia Miller Middleton
XVII 380–381; *VI* 798–799

Esdaile, Katharine Ada 1881–1950
art historian
Geoffrey Webb
1941–1950 239–240

Ethelburga or Æthelburh *d*676?
saint
William Hunt
XVIII 19; *VI* 883

Etheldreda, 630?–679
saint, Queen of Northumbria, Abbess
of Ely
Edmund Venables
XVIII 19–21; *VI* 883–885

Ethelfleda, Æthelflaed, or Ælfled *d*918?
wife of Æthelred
William Hunt
XVIII 21–22; *VI* 885–886

Evans, Edith Mary 1888–1976
actress
Bryan Forbes
1971–1980 296–297

Ewing, Juliana Horaria 1841–1885
children's writer
Percy Arthur Barnett
XVIII 96; *VI* 960

Fachiri, Adila Adrienne Adalbertina
Maria 1886–1962
violinist
Ivor Newton
1961–1970 342–344

Faithfull, Emily 1835–1895
printer, propagandist for women's
employment
Barry Bloomfield
Missing Persons 220

Fane, Priscilla Anne 1793–1879
linguist, artist
George Clement Boase
XVIII 179; *VI* 1043

Fanshawe, Catherine Maria 1765–1834
poet
William Prideaux Courtney
XVIII 182–183; *VI* 1046–1047

Farjeon, Eleanor 1881–1965
writer
John Bell
1961–1970 346–347

Farmer, Emily 1826–1905
painter
B. S. Long
1901–1911 *II* 6–7

Farren, Ellen 1848–1904
actress
John Parker
1901–1911 *II* 12–14

Farren, Elizabeth 1759?–1829
actress
Joseph Knight
XVIII 230–231; *VI* 1094–1095

Faucit, Helena Saville 1817–1898
actress
Joseph Knight
1901 *II* 202–205; *XXII* 627–630

Fawcett, Millicent 1847–1929
women's suffragist
Ray Strachey
1922–1930 297–299

Felkin, Ellen Thorneycroft 1860–1929
novelist
Edward O'Brien
1922–1930 299–300

Fell, Margaret 1614–1702
Quaker
Augustus Charles Bickley
XVIII 297–298; *VI* 1161–1162

Fenning, Elizabeth 1792–1815
poisoner
Alsager Vian
XVIII 319–320; *VI* 1183–1184

Fenton, Lavinia 1708–1760
actress
Gordon Goodwin
XVIII 324–326; *VI* 1188–1190

Fenwick, Eliza *d*1840
writer
Marilyn L. Brooks
Missing Persons 222

Fenwick, Ethel Gordon 1857–1947
nursing reformer
Alice Stewart Glegg Bryson
1941–1950 246–247

Ferguson, Mary Catherine 1823–1905
biographer
D. J. O'Donoghue
1901–1911 II 18

Fermor, Henrietta Louise *d*1761
letter writer
Gordon Goodwin
XVIII 369; *VI* 1233

Ferrier, Kathleen Mary 1912–1953
singer
Roy Henderson
1951–1960 356–357

Ferrier, Susan Edmondstone 1782–1854
novelist
Leslie Stephen
XVIII 391–392; *VI* 1255–1256

Field, Agnes Mary 1896–1968
film producer
Dilys Powell
1961–1970 357–358

Fielding, Sarah 1710–1768
novelist
Leslie Stephen
XVIII 426; *VI* 1290

Fields, Gracie 1898–1979
music hall artiste, actress
Elizabeth Pollitt
1971–1980 313–315

Fiennes or Fienes, Anne *d*1595
philanthropist
Edmund Venables
XVIII 427–428; *VI* 1291–1292

Fiennes, Celia 1662–1741
traveller, author
David Hey
Missing Persons 222–223

Finch, Anne *d*1720
poet
Mrs A. Murray Smith
XIX 1; *VII* 1

Fisher, Catherine Maria *d*1767
courtesan
Joseph Knight
XIX 53–54; *VII* 53–54

Fisher, Mary *fl*1652–1697
Quaker
Augustus Charles Bickley
XIX 68; *VII* 68

Fitton, Mary *fl*1600
maid of honour to Queen Elizabeth
Sidney Lee
XIX 82–83; *VII* 82–83

Fitzgerald, Elizabeth 1528?–1589
daughter of Earl of Kildare
Sidney Lee
XIX 113; *VII* 113

Fitzgerald, Katherine *d*1604
daughter of Sir John Fitzgerald
William Dunn Macray
XIX 134–135; *VII* 134–135

Fitzgerald, Pamela 1776?–1831
wife of Lord Edward Fitzgerald
John Goldworth Alger
XIX 142–143; *VII* 142–143

Fitzhenry, Mrs *d*1790?
actress
Joseph Knight
XIX 165–166; *VII* 165–166

Fitzherbert, Maria Anne 1756–1837
wife of George IV
Thomas Edward Kebbel
XIX 170–171; *VII* 170–171

Fitzroy, Mary *d*1557
Duchess of Richmond
Gordon Goodwin
XIX 206–207; *VII* 206–207

Fitzwilliam, Fanny Elizabeth 1801–1854
actress
Joseph Knight
XIX 226–227; *VII* 226–227

Fleming, Miss 1796?–1861
Mrs Stanley, actress
Joseph Knight
XIX 271; *VII* 271

Fleming, Margaret 1803–1811
friend of Walter Scott
Leslie Stephen
XIX 281; *VII* 281

Fletcher, Eliza 1770–1858
autobiographer
Gordon Goodwin
XIX 298–299; *VII* 298–299

Flower, Eliza 1803–1846
composer
Lydia Miller Middleton
XIX 340; *VII* 340

Fogerty, Elsie 1865–1945
drama teacher
Muriel H. Wigglesworth
1941–1950 263–264

Follows, Ruth 1718–1809
Quaker
Augustus Charles Bickley
XIX 363; *VII* 363

Foote, Lydia 1844?–1892
actress
Joseph Knight
1901 II 221–222; *XXII* 646–647

Foote, Maria 1797?–1867
actress
Joseph Knight
XIX 369–370; *VII* 369–370

Forbes, Joan Rosita 1890–1967
traveller, writer
Dorothy Middleton
1961–1970 376–377

Fothergill, Jessie 1851–1891
novelist
Bertha Porter
1901 II 233; *XXII* 658

Fox, Caroline 1819–1871
diarist
Richard Garnett
XX 91; *VII* 531

Fox, Elizabeth Vassall 1770–1845
society hostess
James McMullen Rigg
XX 115–117; *VII* 555–557

Fox, Evelyn Emily Marian 1874–1955
mental health worker
Ruth Rees Thomas
1951–1960 372–373

Frampton, Mary 1773–1846
author
Lloyd Charles Sanders
XX 159; *VII* 599

Francis, Anne 1738–1800
poet
James McMullen Rigg
XX 165; *VII* 605

Frankland, Jocosa or Joyce 1531–1587
philanthropist
Alsager Vian
XX 185–186; *VII* 625–626

Franklin, Eleanor Anne 1797?–1825
poet
John Knox Laughton
XX 190–191; *VII* 630–191

Franklin, Jane 1792–1875
traveller
John Knox Laughton
XX 191; *VII* 631

Franklin, Rosalind Elsie 1920–1958
crystallographer
Aaron Klug
Missing Persons 235–236

French, Evangeline Frances 1869–1960
missionary
William James Platt
1951–1960 378

Frere, Mary Eliza Isabella 1845–1911
author
F. H. Brown
1901–1911 II 56–57

Freud, Anna 1895–1982
psychoanalyst
Marie Jahoda
1981–1985 152–153

Frideswide, Fritheswith, or Fredeswitha
*d*735?
saint
William Hunt
XX 275–276; *VII* 715–716

Frith, Mary 1584?–1659
pickpocket, fortune teller, forger
Arthur Henry Bullen
XX 280–281; *VII* 720–721

Fry, Elizabeth 1780–1845
prison reformer
William Garden Blaikie
XX 294–296; *VII* 734–376

Fry, Sara Margery 1874–1958
reformer
Thomas Hodgkin
1951–1960 381–384

Fullerton, Georgiana Charlotte 1812–1855
novelist, philanthropist
Thompson Cooper
XX 325–326; *VII* 765–766

Furse, Katharine 1875–1952
women's military service pioneer
Vera Laughton Mathews
1951–1960 384–385

Fyleman, Rose Amy 1877–1957
children's writer
Iona Opie
1951–1960 386–387

Gabriel, Mary Ann Virginia 1825–1877
composer
Lydia Miller Middleton
XX 344; *VII* 784

Gandhi, Indira Priyadarshani 1917–1984
Indian politician
Mark Tully
1981–1985 156–157

Gardner, Mrs *fl*1763–1782
dramatist, actress
Joseph Knight
XX 429; *VII* 869

Garnett, Constance Clara 1861–1946
translator
Henry Noel Brailsford
1941–1950 288–289

Garrod, Dorothy Anne Elizabeth
1892–1968
archaeologist, pre-historian
Jacquetta Hawkes
Missing Persons 243–244

Gaskell, Elizabeth Cleghorn 1810–1865
novelist
Adolphus William Ward
XXI 49–54; *VII* 928–933

Gatty, Margaret 1809–1873
children's writer
George Clement Boase
XXI 67–69; *VII* 946–948

Gaunt, Elizabeth *d*1685
anabaptist
Mrs A. Murray Smith
XXI 72–73; *VII* 951–952

Geddes, Jenny *fl*1637
dissident
Gordon Goodwin
XXI 102; *VII* 981

Genée, Adeline 1878–1970
ballet dancer
James Monahan
1961–1970 427–428

Gentileschi, Artemisia 1590?–1642
painter
Lionel Henry Cust
XXI 123; *VII* 1002

Gerard, Jane Emily 1849–1905
novelist
Elizabeth Lee
1901–1911 *II* 98–99

Gérin, Winifred Eveleen 1901–1981
biographer
Peter Sutcliffe
1981–1985 159–160

Germain, Elizabeth 1680–1769
friend of Swift
William Prideaux Courtney
XXI 230–231; *VII* 1109–1110

Gethin, Grace 1676–1697
learned lady
Leslie Stephen
XXI 242; *VII* 1121

Gibbs, Mrs *fl*1783–1844
actress
Joseph Knight
XXI 266; *VII* 1145

Gilbert, Ann 1782–1866
poet
Edwin Cannan
XXI 320–321; *VII* 1199–1200

Gilbert, Elizabeth Margaretta Maria
1826–1885
philanthropist
Gordon Goodwin
XXI 324–325; *VII* 1203–1204

Gilbert, Maria Dolores Eliza Rosanna
1818–1861
dancer, adventuress
George Clement Boase
XXI 331–333; *VII* 1210–1212

Gilchrist, Anne 1828–1885
writer
Herbert Harlakenden Gilchrist
XXI 340–341; *VII* 1219–1220

Gillie, Annis Calder 1900–1985
physician
Victor William Michael Drury
1981–1985 162–163

Gillies, Margaret 1803–1887
painter
Robert Edmund Graves
XXI 368–369; *VII* 1247–1248

Girling, Mary Anne 1827–1886
founder of religious sect
George Clement Boase
XXI 396–397; *VII* 1275–1276

Gisborne, Maria 1770–1836
friend of Shelley
Leslie Stephen
XXI 401; *VII* 1280

Glasse, Hannah *fl*1747
writer, habit–maker
Ronald Bayne
XXI 420–421; *VII* 1299–1300

Gleichen, Feodora Georgina Maud
1861–1922
  sculptor
  Tancred Borenius
  1922–1930 341–342

Gleitze, Mercedes 1900–1979
  swimmer
  Doloranda Hannah Pember
  Missing Persons 254

Glover, Jean 1758–1801
  poet
  Thomas Wilson Bayne
  XXII 2; *VIII* 2

Glover, Julia 1779–1850
  actress
  Joseph Knight
  XXII 4–6; *VIII* 4–6

Glyn, Elinor 1864–1943
  novelist
  Helen M. Palmer
  1941–1950 302–303

Glyn, Isabella Dallas 1823–1889
  actress
  Joseph Knight
  XXII 10; *VIII* 10

Godiva or Godgifu *fl*1040–1080
  benefactress
  Alexander Gordon
  XXII 36–38; *VIII* 36–38

Godolphin, Margaret 1652–1678
  friend of John Evelyn
  Leslie Stephen
  XXII 41–42; *VIII* 41–42

Godwin, Catherine Grace 1798–1845
  poet
  Richard Garnett
  XXII 55; *VIII* 55

Godwin, Mary Wollstonecraft 1759–1797
  writer
  Leslie Stephen
  XXII 60–62; *VIII* 60–62

Gonne, Maud Edith 1866–1953
  Irish nationalist
  Margaret Ward
  Missing Persons 257–258

Goodall, Charlotte 1766?–1830
  actress
  Joseph Knight
  XXII 115; *VIII* 115

Goodman, Julia 1812–1906
  painter
  M. Epstein
  1901–1911 II 127

Gordon, Elizabeth 1794–1864
  heiress
  William Garden Blaikie
  XXII 177; *VIII* 177

Gordon, Henrietta *fl*1658
  maid of honour
  James McMullen Rigg
  XXII 203–204; *VIII* 203–204

Gordon, Jane 1749?–1812
  leader of fashion
  Henry Manners Chichester
  XXII 210–211; *VIII* 210–211

Gordon, Lucie or Lucy 1821–1869
  author, translator
  George Clement Boase
  XXII 220–221; *VIII* 220–221

Gore, Catherine Grace Frances
1799–1861
  novelist, dramatist
  George Clement Boase
  XXII 236–238; *VIII* 236–238

Gore-Booth, Constance 1868–1927
  revolutionary
  Margaret MacCurtain
  Missing Persons 262

Gore-Booth, Eva Selina 1870–1926
  suffragist, social worker, poet
  Davina Gifford Lewis
  Missing Persons 262–263

Gosse, Emily 1806–1857
religious writer
Edmund Gosse
XXII 258; *VIII* 258

Goudge, Elizabeth de Beauchamp
1900–1984
author
John Attenborough
1981–1985 167–168

Grace, Mary *d*1786?
painter
Lionel Henry Cust
XXII 307; *VIII* 307

Graddon, Miss 1804–1854?
singer
Lydia Miller Middleton
XXII 309; *VIII* 309

Graham, Clementina Stirling 1782–1877
author
Aeneas James George Mackay
XXII 313; *VIII* 313

Graham, Janet 1723–1805
poet
Gordon Goodwin
XXII 332; *VIII* 332

Grant, Anne 1755–1838
writer
Norman MacColl
XXII 376–378; *VIII* 376–378

Grant, Elizabeth 1745?–1814?
poet
Thomas Wilson Bayne
XXII 385; *VIII* 385

Gray, Kathleen Eileen Moray 1879–1976
designer, architect
Fiona MacCarthy
1971–1980 357–358

Gray, Maria Emma 1787–1876
conchologist
George Simonds Boulger
XXIII 11; *VIII* 454

Green, Alice Sophia Amelia 1847–1929
historian
Janet Penrose Trevelyan
1922–1930 359–361

Green, Eliza S. Craven 1803–1866
poet
Charles William Sutton
XXIII 42; *VIII* 485

Greenaway, Kate 1846–1901
artist
Austin Dobson
1901–1911 II 155–156

Greene, Anne *fl*1650
domestic servant
Alsager Vian
XXIII 62; *VIII* 505

Greenwell, Dora 1821–1882
poet, essayist
William Garden Blaikie
XXIII 82–83; *VIII* 525–526

Gregory, Isabella Augusta 1852–1932
playwright, poet
Lennox Robinson
1931–1940 362–363

Grenfell, Joyce Irene 1910–1979
actress, broadcaster
Virginia Graham
1971–1980 359–361

Grenville, Frances Evelyn 1861–1938
Countess of Warwick
Hector Bolitho
1931–1940 365–366

Grey, Elizabeth 1581–1651
author
Charles Lethbridge Kingsford
XXIII 181–182; *VIII* 624–625

Grey, Maria Georgina 1816–1906
educationist
Elizabeth Lee
1901–1911 II 166–167

Grierson, Constantia 1706?–1733
classical scholar
John Thomas Gilbert
XXIII 220; *VIII* 663

Griffith, Elizabeth 1720?–1793
playwright, novelist
Alsager Vian
XXIII 231; *VIII* 674

Griffiths, Ann 1780–1805
hymn writer
Rees M. Jenkin Jones
XXIII 242; *VIII* 685

Grimston or Grymeston, Elizabeth *d*1603
poet
Alsager Vian
XXIII 256–257; *VIII* 699–700

Grote, Harriet 1792–1878
biographer
George Croom Robertson
XXIII 293–294; *VIII* 736–737

Gundrada de Warenne *d*1085
founder of priory
Kate Norgate
XXIII 338–339; *VIII* 781–782

Gunning, Elizabeth 1734–1790
novelist
William Hunt
XXIII 343–344; *VIII* 786–787

Gunning, Susannah 1740?–1800
novelist
Gordon Goodwin
XXIII 349–350; *VIII* 792–793

Gurney, Anna 1795–1857
Anglo Saxon scholar
George Clement Boase
XXIII 354; *VIII* 797

Gwyn, Eleanor 1650–1687
actress, mistress of Charles II
Joseph Knight
XXIII 401–403; *VIII* 844–846

Gwynne-Vaughan, Helen Charlotte
Isabella 1879–1967
botanist, women's military service
pioneer
Alice Prochaska
1961–1970 467–469

Hack, Maria 1777–1844
children's writer
Gordon Goodwin
XXIII 416; *VIII* 859

Hadow, Grace Eleanor 1875–1940
social work pioneer
Lynda Grier
1931–1940 386

Haldane, Elizabeth Sanderson 1862–1937
political activist
Ella R. Christie
1931–1940 388–389

Halkett, Anne or Anna 1622–1699
royalist, writer
Thomas Finlayson Henderson
XXIV 48–49; *VIII* 932–933

Hall, Agnes C. 1777–1846
writer
James McMullen Rigg
XXIV 53–54; *VIII* 937–938

Hall, Anna Maria 1800–1881
novelist
George Clement Boase
XXIV 54–55; *VIII* 938–939

Hallahan, Margaret Mary 1803–1868
founder of religious order
Thompson Cooper
XXIV 96; *VIII* 980

Hallé, Wilma Maria Francisca 1839–1911
violinist
Henry Davey
1901–1911 *II* 190

Hamilton, Mrs *fl*1715–1772
actress
Joseph Knight
XXIV 132–133; *VIII* 1016–1017

Hamilton, Anne 1766–1846
friend of Queen Caroline
Thomas Finlayson Henderson
XXIV 135; *VIII* 1019

Hamilton, Elizabeth 1641–1708
courtier
James McMullen Rigg
XXIV 146–147; *VIII* 1030–1031

Hamilton, Elizabeth 1758–1816
writer
Thomas Wilson Bayne
XXIV 147–148; *VIII* 1031–1032

Hamilton, Emma 1761?–1815
mistress of Nelson
John Knox Laughton
XXIV 148–154; *VIII* 1032–1038

Hamilton, Janet 1795–1873
poet
Thomas Wilson Bayne
XXIV 190; *VIII* 1074

Hamilton, Mary 1739–1816
novelist
John Goldworth Alger
XXIV 201; *VIII* 1085

Hanbury, Elizabeth 1793–1901
philanthropist
Charlotte Fell-Smith
1901–1911 II 193–194

Hancock, Florence May 1893–1974
trade union leader
Eirene White
1971–1980 376–377

Hanson, Emmeline Jean 1919–1973
biophysicist, zoologist
Hugh Esmor Huxley
1971–1980 377–378

Harari, Manya 1905–1969
publisher, translator
Paul Jacques Victor Rolo
1961–1970 487–488

Harding, Anne Raikes 1780–1858
novelist
Francis Watt
XXIV 335; *VIII* 1219

Hardy, Elizabeth 1794–1854
novelist
Francis Watt
XXIV 353; *VIII* 1237

Hardy, Mary Anne 1825?–1891
novelist, traveller
Elizabeth Lee
1901 II 390; *XXII* 815

Harley, Brilliana 1600?–1643
letter writer
Sidney Lee
XXIV 391–392; *VIII* 1275–1276

Harlowe, Sarah 1765–1852
actress
George Clement Boase
XXIV 409–410; *VIII* 1293–1294

Harraden, Beatrice 1864–1936
novelist
Michael Sadleir
1931–1940 402

Harrison, Jane Ellen 1850–1928
classical scholar
Francis Macdonald Cornford
1922–1930 408–409

Harrison, Mary 1788–1875
painter
Robert Harrison
XXV 37; *IX* 37

Harrison, Mary St Leger 1852–1931
Lucas Malet, novelist
Georgina Battiscombe
1931–1940 405–406

Harrison, Susannah 1752–1784
religious poet
Morgan George Watkins
XXV 40; *IX* 40

Hartley, Elizabeth 1751–1824
actress
Joseph Knight
XXV 69–70; *IX* 69–70

Harvey, Margaret 1768–1858
poet
Francis Watt
XXV 91; *IX* 91

Harwood, Isabella 1840?–1888
novelist, dramatist
Richard Garnett
XXV 104; *IX* 104

Hasell, Elizabeth Julia 1830–1887
writer
Norman Moore
XXV 106; *IX* 106

Haslett, Caroline Harriet 1895–1957
electrical engineer
Walter McLennan Citrine
1951–1960 464–465

Hastings, Anthea Esther 1824–1981
publisher
Victor Morrison
1981–1985 186

Hastings, Elizabeth 1682–1739
philanthropist
John Henry Overton
XXV 114; *IX* 114

Hastings, Flora Elizabeth 1806–1839
Lady of the Bedchamber
Alexander Hastie Millar
XXV 114–115; *IX* 114–115

Hastings, Selina 1707–1791
heiress
John Henry Overton
XXV 133–135; *IX* 133–135

Hatfield, Martha *fl*1652
puritan
Alsager Vian
XXV 154; *IX* 154

Hathaway, Sibyl Mary 1884–1974
dame of Sark
Barbara Stoney
Missing Persons 294

Havergal, Frances Ridley 1836–1879
poet, hymn writer
Ronald Bayne
XXV 180; *IX* 180

Hawker, Mary Elizabeth 1848–1908
Lanoe Falconer, novelist
Elizabeth Lee
1901–1911 II 227–228

Hawkins, Laetitia-Matilda 1759–1835
author
Isobel Grundy
Missing Persons 295–296

Hawkins, Susanna 1787–1868
poet
Thomas Wilson Bayne
XXV 225–226; *IX* 225–226

Hay, Lucy 1599–1660
beauty, wit
Charles Harding Firth
XXV 272–274; *IX* 272–274

Hay, Mary Cecil 1840?–1886
novelist
Gordon Goodwin
XXV 274; *IX* 274

Hayes, Catharine 1690–1726
murderer
Alsager Vian
XXV 288; *IX* 288

Hayes, Catherine 1825–1861
singer
George Clement Boase
XXV 288–289; *IX* 288–289

Hays, Mary 1760–1843
author
Marilyn L. Brooks
Missing Persons 297–298

Haywood, Eliza 1693?–1756
novelist
Sidney Lee
XXV 313–315; *IX* 313–315

Hearn, Mary Anne 1834–1909
Marianne Farningham, hymn writer
and author
J. Cuthbert Hadden
1901–1911 II 233

Heaton, Mary Margaret 1836–1883
writer
William Cosmo Monkhouse
XXV 355; *IX* 355

Hector, Annie French 1825–1902
Mrs Alexander, novelist
Elizabeth Lee
1901–1911 II 235–236

Helena Victoria 1870–1948
granddaughter of Queen Victoria
Hugh Evelyn Wortham
1941–1950 374–375

Hemans, Felicia Dorothea 1793–1835
poet
Charles William Sutton
XXV 382–383; *IX* 382–383

Hemphill, Barbara *d*1858
novelist
William Arthur Jobson Archbold
XXV 387; *IX* 387

Hennell, Mary 1802–1843
author
James Moffat Scott
XXV 424; *IX* 424

Henrietta or Henrietta Anne 1644–1670
daughter of Charles I
Gordon Goodwin
XXV 426–429; *IX* 426–429

Henrietta Maria 1609–1669
wife of Charles I
Samuel Rawson Gardiner
XXV 429–436; *IX* 429–436

Hensey, Florence *fl*1758
spy
Charles Lethbridge Kingsford
XXVI 131–132; *IX* 582–583

Hepworth, Joscelyn Barbara 1903–1975
sculptor
Alan Bowness
1971–1980 398–399

Herbert, Lucy 1669–1744
writer
Thompson Cooper
XXVI 204; *IX* 655

Herbert, Mary 1561–1621
patron of poets
Sidney Lee
XXVI 204–207; *IX* 655–658

Hermes, Gertrude Anna Bertha
1901–1983
engraver, sculptor
Paul Hulton
1981–1985 190–191

Herschel, Caroline Lucretia 1750–1848
astronomer
Agnes Mary Clerke
XXVI 260–263; *IX* 711–714

Hervey, Mary 1700–1768
eulogized by poets
George Fisher Russell Barker
XXVI 289–290; *IX* 740–741

Hesketh, Harriet 1733–1807
friend of Cowper
Gordon Goodwin
XXVI 296; *IX* 747

Hess, Julia Myra 1890–1965
pianist
Harold Ferguson
1961–1970 508–510

Hessel, Phoebe 1713?–1821
soldier
Henry Manners Chichester
XXVI 298; *IX* 749

Honywood, Mary 1527–1620
celebrated for longevity
Edmund Venables
XXVII 249–250; *IX* 1143–1144

Hooten, Elizabeth *d*1672
Quaker minister
Augustus Charles Bickley
XXVII 308; *IX* 1202

Hope, Anne 1809–1887
author
unsigned
XXVII 311; *IX* 1205

Hopkins, Jane Ellice 1836–1904
social reformer
Charlotte Fell-Smith
1901–1911 II 301–302

Hopton, Susanna 1627–1709
writer
John Henry Overton
XXVII 350; *IX* 1244

Horniman, Annie Elizabeth Fredericka
1860–1937
repertory theatre pioneer
John Parker
1931–1940 445–446

Horsbrugh, Florence Gertrude 1889–1969
politician
Katharine Elliott
1961–1970 540–541

Horton, Christiana 1696?–1756?
actress
Joseph Knight
XXVII 389–390; *IX* 1283–1284

Houston, Fanny Lucy 1857–1936
philanthropist, eccentric
Hilary Aidan St George Saunders
1931–1940 453–454

Howard, Henrietta 1681–1767
mistress of George II
James McMullen Rigg
XXVIII 22–23; *X* 22–23

Howard, Louise Ernestine 1880–1969
classicist, civil servant, ecological
pioneer
Sybil Oldfield
Missing Persons 333–334

Howard, Rosalind Frances 1845–1921
women's rights and temperance
reformer
Charles Henry Roberts
1912–1921 274–275

Howitt, Mary 1799–1888
writer
George Clement Boase
XXVIII 122–123; *X* 122–123

Hubback, Eva Marian 1886–1949
social reformer, feminist
Gillian Sutherland
Missing Persons 334–335

Hubbard, Louisa Maria 1836–1906
social reformer
J. E. G. de Montmorency
1901–1911 II 312–313

Hudson, Mary *d*1801
organist, composer
Robert Farquharson Sharp
XXVIII 152; *X* 152

Hughes, Elizabeth Phillipps 1851–1925
teacher, organizer
Godfrey Hugh Lancelot Le May
Missing Persons 35–336

Hughes, Margaret *d*1719
actress, mistress of Prince Rupert
Joseph Knight
XXVIII 185; *X* 185

Humby, Anne *fl*1817–1849
actress
Joseph Knight
XXVIII 207–208; *X* 207–208

Hume, Anna *fl*1644
daughter of David Hume
Thomas Wilson Bayne
XXVIII 213; *X* 213

Hungerford, Margaret Wolfe 1855?–1897
novelist
Elizabeth Lee
1901 III 13; *XXII* 885

Hunt, Agnes Gwendoline 1866–1948
nurse, medical treatment pioneer
Avice E. Sankey
1941–1950 416–417

Hunt, Arabella *d*1705
singer, lutenist
Lydia Miller Middleton
XXVIII 263; *X* 263

Hunter, Anne 1742–1821
poet
George Thomas Bettany
XXVIII 284–285; *X* 284–285

Hunter, Rachel 1754–1813
novelist
Thomas Seccombe
XXVIII 299; *X* 299

Hutchinson, Anne 1590?–1643
preacher
Gordon Goodwin
XXVIII 337–338; *X* 337–338

Hutton, Catherine 1756–1846
writer
George Fisher Russell Barker
XXVIII 351; *X* 351

Hyde, Anne 1637–1671
Duchess of York
Adolphus William Ward
XXVIII 366–369; *X* 366–369

Hyde, Jane *d*1725
celebrated beauty
Adolphus William Ward
XXVIII 394; *X* 394

Ibbetson, Agnes 1757–1823
vegetable physiologist
George Simonds Boulger
XXVIII 409; *X* 409

Inchbald, Elizabeth 1753–1821
novelist, dramatist, actress
Joseph Knight
XXVIII 423–426; *X* 423–426

Ingelow, Jean 1820–1897
poet
Elizabeth Lee
1901 III 31–32; *XXII* 903–904

Inglis, Elsie Maud 1864–1917
physician, surgeon
Edith Palliser
1912–1921 282–283

Inglis, Margaret Maxwell 1774–1843
poet
Thomas Wilson Bayne
XXIX 5–6; *X* 442–443

Inverarity, Elizabeth 1813–1846
singer, actress
James Cuthbert Hadden
XXIX 25; *X* 462

Isabella 1214–1241
wife of Emperor Frederick II
Kate Norgate
XXIX 62–63; *X* 499–500

Isabella of Angoulême *d*1246
wife of King John
William Hunt
XXIX 63–64; *X* 500–501

Isabella of France 1292–1358
wife of Edward II
Thomas Frederick Tout
XXIX 64–67; *X* 501–504

Isabella 1332–1379
daughter of Edward III
William Hunt
XXIX 67–68; *X* 504–505

Isabella of France 1389–1409
wife of Richard II
Thomas Frederick Tout
XXIX 68–71; *X* 505–508

Isaacs, Stella 1894–1971
founder WRVS
Baron Windlesham
1971–1980 445–446

Jackson, Catherine Hannah Charlotte
*d*1891
author
Elizabeth Lee
1901 III 35–36; *XXII* 907–908

James, Eleanor *fl*1715
printer, writer
Charles Welch
XXIX 207–208; *X* 644–645

Jameson, Anna Brownell 1794–1860
author
Richard Garnett
XXIX 230–232; *X* 667–669

Jane or Johanna *d*1445
wife of James I of Scotland
Aeneas James George Mackay
XXIX 240–241; *X* 677–678

Jane Seymour 1509?–1537
wife of Henry VIII
Sidney Lee
XXIX 241–243; *X* 678–680

Jarman, Frances Eleanor 1803–1873
actress
Joseph Knight
XXIX 252–253; *X* 689–690

Jebb, Eglantyne 1876–1928
philanthropist
Ray Strachey
1922–1930 451–452

Jeffery, Dorothy 1685–1777
Dolly Pentreath, fish–seller
George Clement Boase
XXIX 267; *X* 704

Jekyll, Gertrude 1843–1932
garden designer, writer, artist,
craftswoman
Mavis Batey
Missing Persons 349–350

Jenkin, Henrietta Camilla 1807?–1885
novelist
George Thomas Bettany
XXIX 295–296; *X* 732–733

Jevons, Mary Anne 1795–1845
poet
Charles William Sutton
XXIX 374; *X* 811

Jewsbury, Geraldine Endsor 1812–1880
novelist
Charles William Sutton
XXIX 384–385; *X* 821–822

Jewsbury, Maria Jane 1800–1833
author
Charles William Sutton
XXIX 385; *X* 822

Jex-Blake, Sophia Louisa 1840–1912
physician
Katharine Jex-Blake
1912–1921 297–298

Joan, Joanna, Jone, or Jane 1165–1199
Queen of Sicily
Kate Norgate
XXIX 386–388; *X* 823–825

Joan, Joanna, Anna, or Janet *d*1237
daughter of King John
Kate Norgate
XXIX 388; *X* 825

Joan or Joanna 1210–1238
Queen of Scotland
Kate Norgate
XXIX 388–389; *X* 825–826

Joan or Joanna of Acre 1272–1307
daughter of Edward I
Charles Lethbridge Kingsford
XXIX 389–390; *X* 826–827

Joan 1321–1362
Queen of Scotland
James Tait
XXIX 390–392; *X* 827–829

Joan 1328–1385
  wife of the Black Prince
  James Tait
  XXIX 392–393; *X* 829–830

Joan or Joanna of Navarre 1370?–1437
  wife of Henry IV
  Charles Lethbridge Kingsford
  XXIX 393–395; *X* 830–832

Jocelin, Elizabeth 1596–1622
  author
  Edwin Cannan
  XXIX 399; *X* 836

John, Gwendolen Mary 1876–1939
  artist
  Cecily Langdale
  Missing Persons 358–360

Johnson, Amy 1903–1941
  aviator
  Ernest Underwood
  1941–1950 434–435

Johnson, Bertha Jane 1846–1927
  women's educationist
  Janet Howarth
  Missing Persons 360

Johnson, Celia 1908–1982
  actress
  William Douglas–Home
  1981–1985 212–213

Johnson, Pamela Hansford 1912–1981
  novelist, dramatist, critic
  Alan Maclean
  1981–1985 213–214

Johnstone, Christian Isobel 1781–1857
  novelist
  Gordon Goodwin
  XXX 73–74; *X* 961–962

Jones, Agnes Elizabeth 1832–1868
  pioneer of workhouse nursing
  Anne Baker
  Missing Persons 361–362

Jones, Avonia 1839?–1867
  actress
  Joseph Knight
  XXX 90; *X* 978

Jones, Charlotte 1768–1847
  painter
  Catherine Rachel Jones
  XXX 91–92; *X* 979–980

Jones, Mary 1707–1778
  poet
  Richard Greene
  Missing Persons 362

Jordan, Dorothea or Dorothy 1762–1816
  actress
  Joseph Knight
  XXX 192–196; *X* 1080–1084

Jourdain, Emily Margaret 1876–1951
  authority on furniture and
  decoration
  James Lees-Milne
  Missing Persons 365–366

Juliana 1343–1443
  recluse
  William Arthur Jobson Archbold
  XXX 226; *X* 1114

Kauffmann, Angelica 1741–1807
  painter
  Emily Tennyson Bradley
  XXX 241–244; *X* 1129–1132

Kavanagh, Julia 1824–1877
  novelist, biographer
  Thompson Cooper
  XXX 246–247; *X* 1134–1135

Kean, Ellen 1805–1880
  actress
  Joseph Knight
  XXX 265–266; *X* 1153–1154

Keary, Annie 1825–1879
  novelist
  Richard Garnett
  XXX 270–271; *X* 1158–1159

Keeley, Mary Ann 1805?–1899
actress
Joseph Knight
1901 III 56–57; *XXII* 928–929

Kello, Esther or Hester 1571–1624
calligrapher, painter
Thompson Cooper
XXX 346–347; *X* 1234–1235

Kelly, Frances Maria 1790–1882
actress, singer
Charles Kent
XXX 349–350; *X* 1237–1238

Kelly, Isabella *c*1759–1857
poet, novelist
Richard Greene
Missing Persons 371

Kelty, Mary Anne 1789–1873
author
Thomas Seccombe
XXX 360; *X* 1248

Kemble, Adelaide 1814?–1879
singer, author
Lydia Miller Middleton
XXX 363–365; *X* 1251–1253

Kemble, Elizabeth 1763?–1841
actress
Joseph Knight
XXX 367–368; *X* 1255–1256

Kemble, Frances Anne 1809–1893
Fanny Kemble, actress
Joseph Knight
1901 III 57–58; *XXII* 929–930

Kemble, Maria Theresa or Marie Therése
1774–1838
actress
Joseph Knight
XXX 378–379; *X* 1266–1267

Kemble, Priscilla 1756–1845
actress
Joseph Knight
XXX 379–380; *X* 1267–1268

Kempe, Margerie *temp incert*
writer
Charles Lethbridge Kingsford
XXX 394–395; *X* 1282–1283

Kendal, Margaret Shafto 1848–1935
Madge Kendal, actress
St John Ervine
1931–1940 503–504

Kendrick, Emma Eleonora 1788–1871
author, painter
Lionel Henry Cust
XXX 409–410; *X* 1297–1298

Kennedy or Farrell, Mrs *d*1793
actress, singer
Lydia Miller Middleton
XXX 412–413; *X* 1300–1301

Kennedy, Grace 1782–1825
writer
William Alexander Greenhill
XXX 420–421; *X* 1308–1309

Kennedy, Margaret Moore 1896–1967
writer
Richard Bennett
1961–1970 608

Kennet, Edith Agnes Kathleen 1878–1947
Kathleen Scott, sculptor
Geoffrey Dearmer
1941–1950 447–449

Kenney, Annie 1879–1953
suffragette
Hester Burton
1951–1960 572–573

Kenny, Elizabeth 1880–1952
nurse
Abraham Fryberg
1951–1960 575–576

Kent, Victoria Mary Louisa, Duchess of
1786–1861
mother of Queen Victoria
James McMullen Rigg
XXXI 20–21; *XI* 20–21

Kenyon, Kathleen Mary 1906–1978
archaeologist
Peter J. Parr
1971–1980 463–464

Keppel, Alice Frederica 1868–1947
mistress of Edward VII
Theodore Aronson
Missing Persons 374–375

Keroualle, Louise Renée de 1649–1734
mistress of Charles II
Adolphus William Ward
XXXI 59–62; *XI* 59–62

Kettle or Kyteler, Alice *fl*1342
witch
Bever Harry Blacker
XXXI 79; *XI* 79

Kettle, Tilly 1740?–1786
painter
Lionel Henry Cust
XXXI 79–80; *XI* 79–80

Keys, Mary 1540?–1578
sister of Lady Jane Grey
Mandell Creighton
XXXI 87; *XI* 87

Kilham, Hannah 1774–1832
missionary, linguist
Charlotte Fell-Smith
XXXI 103–104; *XI* 103–104

Killigrew, Anne 1660–1685
poet, painter
George Atherton Aitkin
XXXI 106; *XI* 106

Killigrew, Catherine or Katherine
1530?–1583
learned lady
Thomas Finlayson Henderson
XXXI 106; *XI* 106

Kimmins, Grace Thyrza 1870–1954
medical treatment reformer
Brian Kimmins
1951–1960 584–585

Kincaid, Jean 1579–1600
murderer
George Stronach
XXXI 123; *XI* 123

Kingsford, Anna 1846–1888
doctor, writer
William Arthur Jobson Archbold
XXXI 174–175; *XI* 174–175

Kingsley, Mary Henrietta 1862–1900
traveller, writer
Lucy Toulmin Smith
1901 III 67–69; *XXII* 939–941

Kirby, Elizabeth 1823–1873
children's writer
Thomas Seccombe
XXXI 198; *XI* 198

Kirkhoven or Kerckhoven, Catherine
*d*1667
governess to Charles I's daughter
James McMullen Rigg
XXXI 217–219; *XI* 217–219

Klein, Melanie 1882–1960
psychoanalyst
Jean MacGibbon
1951–1960 593–594

Knight, Ellis Cornelia 1757–1837
author
Richard Garnett
XXXI 249–250; *XI* 249–250

Knight, Henrietta *d*1756
poet
James McMullen Rigg
XXXI 252–253; *XI* 252–253

Knight, Mary Anne 1776–1831
painter
Lionel Henry Cust
XXXI 258–259; *XI* 258–259

Knipp or Knep, Mrs *fl*1670
actress
James McMullen Rigg
XXXI 273; *XI* 273

Knowles, Mary 1733–1807
Quaker
Charlotte Fell-Smith
XXXI 302; *XI* 302

Knox, Isa 1831–1903
poet
Thomas Bayne
1901–1911 II 409

Lacy, Harriette Deborah 1807–1874
actress
Thomas Seccombe
XXXI 373; *XI* 373

Laidlaw, Anna Robena 1819–1901
pianist
J. Cuthbert Haddon
1901–1911 II 411

Lamb, Caroline 1785–1828
novelist
George Fisher Russell Barker
XXXI 421–423; *XI* 421–423

Lamburn, Richmal Crompton 1890–1969
author
Mary Cadogan
1961–1970 626–627

Landon, Letitia Elizabeth 1802–1838
poet
Richard Garnett
XXXII 52–54; *XI* 493–495

Landseer, Jessica 1810–1880
painter
William Cosmo Monkhouse
XXXII 68; *XI* 509

Lane, Jane *d*1689
heroine
James McMullen Rigg
XXXII 74–75; *XI* 515–516

Langtry, Emily Charlotte 1853–1929
actress
Theodore Aronson
Missing Persons 388

Lanier, Emilia 1569–1645
poet
Lorna Hutson
Missing Persons 388–389

Latter, Mary 1725–1777
author
Thomas Seccombe
XXXII 184; *XI* 625

Lawrance, Mary *fl*1794–1830
painter
Lionel Henry Cust
XXXII 248; *XI* 689

Lawrence, Arabella Susan 1871–1947
politician
Jane Elizabeth Norton
1941–1950 489

Lawrence, Gertrude 1898–1952
actress
Alan Dent
1951–1960 613–614

Lead or Leade, Jane 1623–1704
mystic
Charlotte Fell-Smith
XXXII 312–313; *XI* 753–754

Leadbeater, Mary 1758–1826
author
Norman Moore
XXXII 313–314; *XI* 754–755

Leapor, Mary 1722–1746
poet
Elizabeth Lee
XXXII 325; *XI* 766

Le Breton, Anna Letitia 1808–1885
author
Albert Nicholson
XXXII 332; *XI* 773

Leclercq, Carlotta 1840?–1893
actress
Joseph Knight
1901 III 86–87; *XXII* 958–959

Lee, Ann 1736–1784
    founder of American Shakers
    James McMullen Rigg
    XXXII 343; *XI* 784

Lee, Harriet 1757–1851
    novelist, dramatist
    Elizabeth Lee
    XXXII 355–356; *XI* 796–397

Lee, Rachel Fanny Antonia 1774?–1829
    heroine of criminal trial
    Richard Garnett
    XXXII 368–369; *XI* 809–810

Lee, Sarah 1791–1856
    artist, author
    Morgan George Watkins
    XXXII 379; *XI* 820

Lee, Sophia 1750–1824
    novelist, dramatist
    Elizabeth Lee
    XXXII 379–380; *XI* 820–821

Lees, Florence Sarah 1840–1922
    district nursing pioneer
    Monica E. Baly
    Missing Persons 394–395

Lehzen, Louise *c*1784–1870
    royal governess
    Harry Griffiths Pitt
    Missing Persons 396–397

Leigh, Vivien 1913–1967
    actress
    Freda Gaye
    1961–1970 645–647

Leitch, Charlotte Cecilia Pitcairn, 'Cecil'
1891–1977
    golfer
    Maureen Susan Millar
    1971–1980 496–497

Lejeune, Caroline Alice 1897–1973
    film critic
    Dilys Powell
    1971–1980 497–498

Lemmens-Sherrington, Helen 1834–1906
    singer
    Henry Davey
    1901–1911 II 452–453

Lennox, Charlotte 1720–1804
    writer
    Gordon Goodwin
    XXXIII 50–51; *XI* 929–930

Le Noir, Elizabeth Anne 1755?–1841
    poet, novelist
    Elizabeth Lee
    XXXIII 52–53; *XI* 931–932

Leverson, Ada Esther 1862–1933
    novelist
    Julie W. Speedie
    Missing Persons 399–400

Leveson-Gower, Harriet Elizabeth
Georgiana 1806–1868
    friend of Queen Victoria
    Lloyd Charles Sanders
    XXXIII 152–153; *XI* 1031–1032

Levy, Amy 1861–1889
    poet, novelist
    Richard Garnett
    XXXIII 162; *XI* 1041

Lewis, Agnes 1843–1926
    ancient manuscript scholar
    Francis Crawford Burkitt
    1922–1930 509–510

Lewis, Joyce or Jocasta *d*1557
    martyr
    William Arthur Jobson Archbold
    XXXIII 190–191; *XI* 1069–1070

Lewis, Maria Theresa 1803–1865
    biographer
    Elizabeth Lee
    XXXIII 191; *XI* 1070

Lewis, Rosa 1867–1952
    hotel owner
    Robin McDouall
    1951–1960 629–630

Lewson, Jane 1700?–1816
eccentric
Thomas Seccombe
XXXIII 202; *XI* 1081

Leyel, Hilda Winifred Ivy 1880–1957
herbalist
Christmas Humphreys
1951–1960 631–632

Lind, Johanna Maria 1820–1887
Jenny Lind, singer
John Alexander Fuller Maitland
XXXIII 273–275; *XI* 1152–1154

Linley, Mary 1758–1787
singer
Lydia Miller Middleton
XXXIII 325–326; *XI* 1204–1205

Linskill, Mary 1840–1891
novelist
Gerald le Grys Norgate
XXXIII 331; *XI* 1210

Linton, Eliza Lynn 1822–1898
writer
Richard Garnett
1901 III 98–100; *XXII* 970–972

Linwood, Mary 1755–1845
composer, needlework artist
William Cosmo Monkhouse
XXXIII 335; *XI* 1214

Lisle, Alice 1614?–1685
murder victim
Sidney Lee
XXXIII 339–340; *XI* 1218–1219

Lister, Anne 1791–1840
traveller, diarist
David Marshall Lang
Missing Persons 404–405

Litchfield, Mrs Harriet 1777–1854
actress
Joseph Knight
XXXIII 358–359; *XI* 1237–1238

Litton, Marie 1847–1884
actress
Joseph Knight
XXXIII 377–378; *XI* 1256–1257

Llewellyn Davies, Margaret Caroline
1861–1944
general secretary of Women's
Co-operative Guild
Mary Stott
Missing Persons 407

Lloyd, Dorothy Jordan 1889–1946
biochemist
Henry Phillips
1941–1950 511–512

Lloyd George, Frances Louise 1888–1972
political secretary
Kenneth O. Morgan
1971–1980 515–516

Lloyd George, Megan 1902–1966
politician
Kenneth O. Morgan
1961–1970 666–668

Lodge, Eleanor Constance 1869–1936
historian
Evelyn Mary Jamison
1931–1940 541

Lofthouse, Mary 1853–1885
water colour painter
Lionel Henry Cust
XXXIV 72; *XII* 72

Long, Amelia 1762–1837
art connoisseur, horticulturist
John Andrew Hamilton
XXXIV 99; *XII* 99

Long, Catharine *d*1867
novelist, writer
Albert Frederick Pollard
XXXIV 99; *XII* 99

Longworth, Maria Theresa 1832–1881
Mrs Yelverton, author
Albert Nicholson
XXXIV 126–127; *XII* 126–127

Lonsdale, Kathleen 1903–1971
  crystallographer
  Hylton Judith Milledge
  1971–1980 517–518

Lopokova, Lydia Vasilievna 1892–1981
  ballerina
  Margot Fonteyn
  1981–1985 248–249

Loraine, Violet Mary 1886–1956
  actress
  William Aubrey Darlington
  1951–1960 652–653

Loudon, Jane 1807–1858
  horticulturist, writer
  George Simonds Boulger
  XXXIV 148–149; *XII* 148–149

Louise Caroline Alberta 1848–1939
  daughter of Queen Victoria
  Dorothy Cantelupe
  1931–1940 544–545

Louise Victoria Alexandra Dagmar
1867–1931
  daughter of Edward VII
  unsigned
  1931–1940 545

Lowe, Eveline Mary 1869–1956
  politician
  Herbert Stanley Morrison
  1951–1960 653–654

Luke, Jemima 1813–1906
  hymn writer
  J. Cuthbert Hadden
  1901–1911 II 489

Lutyens, Agnes Elisabeth 1906–1983
  composer
  James Dalton
  1981–1985 249–250

Lynch, Theodora Elizabeth 1812–1885
  writer
  George Clement Boase
  XXXIV 336–337; *XII* 336–337

Lyon, Agnes 1762–1840
  poet
  James Cuthbert Hadden
  XXXIV 345; *XII* 345

Lytton, Constance Georgina 1869–1923
  suffragette
  Jose Ferial Harris
  Missing Persons 422–423

Macaulay, Catharine 1731–1791
  historian, controversialist
  William Prideaux Courtney
  XXXIV 407–409; *XII* 407–409

Macaulay, Emilie Rose 1881–1958
  author
  Constance Babington Smith
  1951–1960 659–660

McAuley, Catharine 1787–1841
  founder of the Order of Mercy
  Thompson Cooper
  XXXIV 420–421; *XII* 420–421

M'Avoy, Margaret 1800–1820
  blind needlewoman
  Gordon Goodwin
  XXXIV 421; *XII* 421

McCarthy, Emma Maud 1858–1949
  army nurse
  Helen S. Gillespie
  1941–1950 546–547

McCarthy, Lillah 1875–1960
  actress
  John Courtenay Trewin
  1951–1960 666–667

Macdonald, Flora 1722–1790
  Jacobite heroine
  Thomas Finlayson Henderson
  XXXV 33–35; *XII* 477–479

Macfarlane, Mrs *fl*1716–1719
  murderer
  Thomas Finlayson Henderson
  XXXV 74; *XII* 518

Mackarness, Matilda Anne 1826–1881
author
Elizabeth Lee
XXXV 117; *XII* 561

Mackay, Mary 1855–1924
Marie Corelli, novelist
Michael Sadleir
1922–1930 539–542

Mackellar, Mary 1834–1890
poet
James Cuthbert Hadden
XXXV 129; *XII* 573

Mackintosh, Elizabeth 1896–1952
Josephine Tey and Gordon Daviot,
author, dramatist
Gillian Avery
Missing Persons 429–430

Maclean, Ida Smedley 1877–1944
biochemist
Mary R. S. Creese
Missing Persons 433–434

Maclehose, Agnes 1759–1841
'Clarinda'
Thomas Finlayson Henderson
XXXV 207–208; *XII* 651–652

Macleod, Mary 1569–1674
poet
James Ramsay Macdonald
XXXV 214; *XII* 658

McMillan, Margaret 1860–1931
educationist
Albert Mansbridge
1931–1940 587–588

MacMoyer, Florence *d*1713
last keeper of the book of Armagh
Norman Moore
XXXV 233; *XII* 677

Magee, Martha Maria *d*1846
founder of Irish college
Alexander Gordon
XXXV 313; *XII* 757

Maitland, Agnes Catherine 1850–1906
educationist
Elizabeth Lee
1901–1911 *II* 551–552

Makin, Bathsua *fl*1673
learned lady
Gordon Goodwin
XXXV 391; *XII* 835

Malcolm, Sarah 1710?–1733
murderer
Thomas Seccombe
XXXV 414; *XII* 858

Malleson, Elizabeth 1828–1916
educationist, pioneer of rural district
nursing
Owen Stinchcombe
Missing Persons 443–444

Mangnall, Richmal
schoolmistress
Charles William Sutton
XXXVI 34; *XII* 919

Manley, Mary de la Riviere 1663–1724
author
George Atherton Aitkin
XXXVI 35–38; *XII* 920–923

Mann, Cathleen Sabine 1896–1959
painter
Christopher Sykes
1951–1960 685–686

Mannin, Ethel Edith 1900–1984
writer
Harold Frederick Oxbury
1981–1985 263–264

Manning, Anne 1807–1879
writer
Charlotte Fell-Smith
1901 *III* 137–138; *XXII* 1009–1010

Manning, Marie 1821–1849
murderer
George Clement Boase
XXXVI 69; *XII* 954

Manning, Olivia Mary 1908–1980
novelist
Kay Dick
1971–1980 544–545

Manton, Sidnie Milana 1902–1979
zoologist
Geoffrey Fryer
1971–1980 547–548

Mara, Gertrude Elizabeth 1749–1833
singer
James Cuthbert Hadden
XXXVI 118–119; *XII* 1033–1034

Marcet, Jane 1769–1858
children's writer
Elizabeth Lee
XXXVI 122–123; *XII* 1007–1008

Margaret, Saint *d*1093
Queen of Scotland
Aeneas James George Mackay
XXXVI 132–134; *XII* 1017–1019

Margaret 1240–1275
Queen of Scotland
Thomas Frederick Tout
XXXVI 134–136; *XII* 1019–1021

Margaret 1282?–1318
wife of Edward I
William Hunt
XXXVI 136; *XII* 1021

Margaret, the Maid of Norway 1283–1290
Queen of Scotland
William Hunt
1901 III 139–140; *XXII* 1011–1012

Margaret 1425?–1445
daughter of James I of Scotland
James Tait
XXXVI 136–138; *XII* 1021–1023

Margaret of Anjou 1430–1482
wife of Henry VI
Thomas Frederick Tout
XXXVI 138–148; *XII* 1023–1033

Margaret of Denmark 1457?–1486
wife of James III of Scotland
Thomas Finlayson Henderson
XXXVI 148; *XII* 1033

Margaret, Duchess of Burgundy
1446–1503
sister of Edward IV
James Gairdner
XXXVI 148–150; *XII* 1033–1035

Margaret Tudor 1489–1541
Queen of Scotland
James Tait
XXXVI 150–157; *XII* 1035–1042

Marie Louise 1872–1956
granddaughter of Queen Victoria
Kenneth Rose
1951–1960 689–690

Marina 1906–1968
Duchess of Kent
Gerald Kenneth Savery
Hamilton-Edwards
1961–1970 724–726

Markham, Violet Rosa 1872–1959
public servant
Susan Charlotte Buchan
1951–1960 692–693

Marryat, Florence 1838–1899
novelist
Elizabeth Lee
1901 III 141–142; *XXII* 1013–1014

Marsh, Edith Ngaio 1899–1982
novelist, theatre director
Henry Reymond Fitzwalter Keating
1981–1985 265–266

Marsh-Caldwell, Anne 1791–1874
novelist
Elizabeth Lee
XXXVI 219; *XII* 1104

Marshall, Emma 1830–1899
novelist
Elizabeth Lee
1901 III 144; *XXII* 1016

Marshall or Marishall, Jane *fl*1765
novelist, dramatist
Elizabeth Lee
XXXVI 239; *XII* 1124

Martin, Mary Letitia 1815–1850
novelist
Elizabeth Lee
XXXVI 289; *XII* 1174

Martin, Sarah 1791–1843
prison visitor
Charles Harold Evelyn White
XXXVI 296–297; *XII* 1181–1182

Martin, Violet Florence 1862–1915
Martin Ross, novelist
Bertram Coghill Alan Windle
1912–1921 368–369

Martindale, Hilda 1875–1952
civil servant
Evelyn Adelaide Sharp
1951–1960 704–706

Martineau, Harriet 1802–1876
writer
Leslie Stephen
XXXVI 309–314; *XII* 1194–1199

Mary I 1516–1558
Queen of England
Sidney Lee
XXXVI 333–354; *XII* 1218–1239

Mary II 1662–1694
Queen of England
Adolphus William Ward
XXXVI 354–365; *XII* 1239–50

Mary of Modena 1658–1718
wife of James II
Adolphus William Ward
XXXVI 365–373; *XII* 1250–1258

Mary Queen of Scots 1542–1587
daughter of James V of Scotland
Thomas Finlayson Henderson
XXXVI 373–390; *XII* 1258–1275

Mary of Gueldres *d*1463
wife of James II of Scotland
Thomas Finlayson Henderson
XXXVI 390–391; *XII* 1275–1276

Mary of Guise 1515–1560
wife of James V of Scotland
James Tait
XXXVI 391–397; *XII* 1276–1282

Mary of France 1496–1533
daughter of Henry VII
James Gairdner
XXXVI 397–400; *XII* 1282–1285

Mary 1631–1660
daughter of Charles I
Gordon Goodwin
XXXVI 400–404; *XII* 1285–1289

Mary, Princess of Hesse 1723–1772
daughter of George II
James McMullen Rigg
XXXVI 404; *XII* 1289

Mary 1867–1953
Queen-consort of George V
John Gore
1951–1960 706–712

Masham, Abigail *d*1734
esteemed by Swift
George Fisher Russell Barker
XXXVI 410–412; *XII* 1295–1297

Masham, Damaris 1658–1708
writer
Christabel Osborne
XXXVI 412–413; *XII* 1297–1298

Mason, Charlotte Maria Shaw 1842–1923
educational reformer
Barbara Caine
Missing Persons 450–451

Masters, Mary *d*1759?
poet
James Cuthbert Hadden
XXXVII 25; *XIII* 25

Mathews, Elvira Sibyl Marie Laughton
1888–1959
    director of WRNS
    John Wood Palmer
    1951–1960 716–717

Mathews, Lucia Elizabeth or Elizabetta
1797–1856
    singer
    Joseph Knight
    XXXVII 41–43; *XIII* 41–43

Matilda *d*1083
    wife of William the Conqueror
    William Hunt
    XXXVII 49–52; *XIII* 49–52

Matilda, Maud, Mahalde, or Mold
1080–1118
    wife of Henry I
    Kate Norgate
    XXXVII 52–53; *XIII* 52–53

Matilda of Boulogne 1103?–1152
    wife of King Stephen
    Kate Norgate
    XXXVII 53–54; *XIII* 53–54

Matilda, Maud, Mold, Æthelic, or Aaliz
1102–1167
    daughter of Henry I
    Kate Norgate
    XXXVII 54–58; *XIII* 54–58

Matilda, Duchess of Saxony 1156–1189
    daughter of Henry II
    Kate Norgate
    XXXVII 58–59; *XIII* 58–59

Matthews, Jessie Margaret 1907–1981
    actress
    Harold Frederick Oxbury
    1981–1985 272–274

Mattocks, Isabella 1746–1826
    actress
    Joseph Knight
    XXXVII 72–74; *XIII* 72–74

Maud Charlotte Mary Victoria 1869–1938
    daughter of Edward VII
    unsigned
    1931–1940 605–606

Maxwell, Mary Elizabeth 1837–1915
    Miss Braddon, novelist
    Michael Sadleir
    1912–1921 377–378

Mayo, Elizabeth 1793–1865
    education reformer
    Charles Herbert Mayo
    XXXVII 172; *XIII* 172

Mee, Anne 1775?–1851
    miniaturist
    Freeman Marius O'Donoghue
    XXXVII 209; *XIII* 209

Meeke, Mary *d*1816?
    novelist
    Elizabeth Lee
    XXXVII 210; *XIII* 210

Melba, Nellie 1861–1931
    singer
    John Mewburn Levien
    1931–1940 608–610

Mellon, Harriet 1777?–1837
    actress
    Joseph Knight
    XXXVII 223–224; *XIII* 223–224

Mellon, Sarah Jane 1824–1909
    actress
    W. J. Lawrence
    1901–1911 II 602–603

Menken, Adah Isaacs 1835–1868
    actress, writer
    Joseph Knight
    XXXVII 252–253; *XIII* 252–253

Meteyard, Eliza 1816–1879
    author
    Charles William Sutton
    XXXVII 308–309; *XIII* 308–309

Mew, Charlotte Mary 1869–1928
    poet
    Alida Monro
    1922–1930 582

Meynell, Alice Christiana Gertrude
1847–1922
    poet, essayist, journalist
    Frederick Page
    1922–1930 584–586

Milburg, Mildburga, or Mildburh *d*722?
    saint
    William Hunt
    XXXVII 372; *XIII* 372

Mildred or Mildryth *d*700?
    saint
    William Hunt
    XXXVII 376–377; *XIII* 376–377

Miles, Sibella Elizabeth 1800–1882
    poet
    William Prideaux Courtney
    XXXVII 378; *XIII* 378

Millar, Gertie 1879–1952
    actress
    Alan Dent
    1951–1960 738–739

Miller, Anna 1741–1781
    poet
    Elizabeth Lee
    XXXVII 405–406; *XIII* 405–406

Miller, Florence Fenwick 1854–1935
    journalist, lecturer, feminist
    Rosemary T. Van Arsdel
    Missing Persons 464–465

Miller, Lydia Falconer 1811?–1876
    author
    John Andrew Hamilton
    XXXVII 417; *XIII* 417

Milner, Violet Georgina 1872–1958
    Viscountess Milner, editor
    Colin Coote
    1951–1960 741–742

Mitford, Mary Russell 1787–1855
    novelist, dramatist
    Elizabeth Lee
    XXXVIII 84–86; *XIII* 531–533

Mitford, Nancy Freeman- 1904–1973
    novelist, biographer
    James Lees–Milne
    1971–1980 570–572

Modwenna or Moninne *d*518
    saint
    Thomas Olden
    XXXVIII 92–93; *XIII* 539–540

Mohl, Madame Mary 1793–1883
    society hostess
    John Goldworth Alger
    XXXVIII 104–105; *XIII* 551–552

Molesworth, Mary Louisa 1839–1921
    novelist, children's writer
    Gillian Avery
    Missing Persons 472–473

Monck, Mary *d*1715
    poet
    Thompson Cooper
    XXXVIII 162; *XIII* 609

Monckton, Mary 1746–1840
    blue-stocking
    Elizabeth Lee
    XXXVIII 163–164; *XIII* 610–611

Montagu, Elizabeth 1720–1800
    author
    Sidney Lee
    XXXVIII 240–244; *XIII* 687–691

Montagu, Mary Wortley 1689–1762
    writer
    Leslie Stephen
    XXXVIII 259–263; *XIII* 706–710

Montalba, Henrietta Skerrett 1856–1893
    sculptor
    Lionel Henry Cust
    XXXVIII 277–278; *XIII* 724–725

Montfort, Eleanor of 1252–1282
    daughter of Simon de Montfort
    Kate Norgate
    XXXVIII 282–283; *XIII* 729–730

Moore, Ann *fl*1813
fanatic
Thomas Seccombe
XXXVIII 339–340; *XIII* 786–787

Moore, Eleanora *d*1869
Nelly Moore, actress
Joseph Knight
XXXVIII 348; *XIII* 795

More, Hannah 1745–1833
writer
Leslie Stephen
XXXVIII 414–420; *XIII* 861–867

Morgan, Alice Mary 1850–1890
painter
Lionel Henry Cust
XXXIX 11–12; *XIII* 908–909

Morgan, Sydney 1783?–1859
novelist
John Andrew Hamilton
XXXIX 27–29; *XIII* 924–926

Morley, Iris 1910–1953
novelist, ballet writer
Brian Pearce
Missing Persons 477

Morrell, Ottoline Violet Anne
1873–1938
artistic and literary patron
David Cecil
1931–1940 630–631

Morris, Mary 1862–1938
designer, embroideress
Linda Parry
Missing Persons 479

Mortimer, Mrs Favell Lee 1802–1878
author
James McMullen Rigg
XXXIX 125–126; *XIII* 1022–1023

Moser, Mary *d*1819
painter
Freeman Marius O'Donoghue
XXXIX 178–179; *XIII* 1075–1076

Mountain, Rosoman 1768?–1841
singer, actress
Lydia Miller Middleton
XXXIX 208–210; *XIII* 1105–1107

Mountbatten, Edwina Cynthia Annette
1901–1960
Countess Mountbatten of Burma
Alan Campbell–Johnson
1951–1960 751–753

Mozley, Anne 1809–1891
author
Albert Frederick Pollard
XXXIX 249; *XIII* 1146

Mulock, Dinah Maria 1826–1887
Mrs Craik, author
Richard Garnett
XXXIX 280–281; *XIII* 1177–1178

Murphy, Marie Louise 1737–1814
mistress of Louis XV
John Goldworth Alger
XXXIX 341–342; *XIII* 1238–1239

Murray, Amelia Matilda 1795–1884
writer
Gordon Goodwin
XXXIX 347–348; *XIII* 1244–1245

Murray, Elizabeth *d*1697
famous beauty
Alexander Hastie Millar
XXXIX 356–357; *XIII* 1253–1254

Murray, Margaret Alice 1863–1963
Egyptologist
Max Mallowan
1961–1970 777–778

Murry, Kathleen 1888–1923
Katherine Mansfield, writer
Edward O'Brien
1922–1930 629–630

Mutrie, Martha Darley 1824–1885
artist
Robert Edmund Graves
XXXIX 436; *XIII* 1333

Myddleton or Middleton, Jane 1645–1692
 famous beauty
 Thomas Seccombe
 XXXIX 439–440; *XIII* 1336–1337

Naden, Constance Caroline Woodhill
1858–1889
 poet
 unsigned
 XL 18–19; *XIV* 18–19

Nagle, Nano or Honora 1728–1784
 founder of order of nuns
 Pierce Laurence Nolan
 XL 21–22; *XIV* 21–22

Nairne, Carolina 1776–1845
 poet
 Thomas Wilson Bayne
 XL 23–25; *XIV* 23–25

Needham, Elizabeth *d*1731
 procuress
 Thomas Seccombe
 XL 155–156; *XIV* 155–156

Neilson, Julia Emilie 1868–1957
 actress
 Val Henry Gielgud
 1951–1960 766–777

Neilson, Lilian Adelaide 1848–1880
 Elizabeth Ann Brown, actress
 Joseph Knight
 XL 183–184; *XIV* 183–184

Nelson, Frances Herbert 1761–1831
 wife of Horatio Nelson
 John Knox Laughton
 XL 188–189; *XIV* 188–189

Nest or Nesta *fl*1106
 mistress of Henry I
 William Hunt
 XL 228–229; *XIV* 228–229

Nevill, Dorothy Fanny 1826–1913
 hostess, horticulturist, collector
 Wilfred Robert Trotter
 Missing Persons 492

Newall, Bertha Surtees 1877–1932
 Bertha Phillpotts, educationist
 Mary Gwyneth Lloyd Thomas
 1931–1940 649–650

Newbigin, Marion Isabel 1869–1934
 biologist, geographer, editor
 Mary R. S. Creese
 Missing Persons 492–493

Newton, Ann Mary 1832–1866
 painter
 Lionel Henry Cust
 XL 365; *XIV* 365

Nicholson, Margaret 1750?–1828
 housemaid, assailant of George III
 William Hunt
 XLI 22–23; *XIV* 467–468

Nicholson, Rosa Winifred 1893–1981
 painter, writer
 Judith Collins
 Missing Persons 495

Nicol, Mrs *d*1834?
 actress
 unsigned
 XLI 35–36; *XIV* 480–481

Nicol, Emma 1801–1877
 actress
 unsigned
 XLI 36–37; *XIV* 481–482

Nicolson, Adela Florence 1865–1904
 Laurence Hope, poet
 Francis L. Bickley
 1901–1911 *III* 14–15

Nightingale, Florence 1820–1910
 nursing reformer
 Stephen Paget
 1901–1911 *III* 15–19

Nihell, Elizabeth 1723–*post* 1772
 midwife
 Catherine Crawford
 Missing Persons 496

Nisbett, Louisa Cranstoun 1812?–1858
actress
Joseph Knight
XLI 72–74; *XIV* 517–519

Norgate, Kate 1853–1935
historian
Frederick Maurice Powicke and
Percy Millican
1931–1940 653

North, Marianne 1830–1890
painter
Leslie Stephen
XLI 168–169; *XIV* 613–614

Norton, Caroline Elizabeth Sarah
1808–1877
poet
Richard Garnett
XLI 206–208; *XIV* 651–653

Norton, Frances 1640–1731
author
Elizabeth Lee
XLI 212; *XIV* 657

Novello, Clara Anastasia 1818–1908
singer
Henry Davey
1901–1911 III 28–29

Nunn, Marianne 1778–1847
hymn writer
James Cuthbert Hadden
XLI 274; *XIV* 719

O'Brien, Charlotte Grace 1845–1909
author, social reformer
W. B. Owen
1901–1911 III 32

O'Brien, Kate 1897–1974
novelist, playwright, critic
Mary O'Neill
1971–1980 639

O'Carroll, Margaret *d*1451
famous for hospitality
Norman Moore
XLI 350; *XIV* 795

Ogborne, Elizabeth 1763?–1853
historian
Gordon Goodwin
XLII 11; *XIV* 905

Oldfield, Anne 1683–1730
actress
Joseph Knight
XLII 96–100; *XIV* 990–994

O'Leary, Ellen 1831–1889
poet
Michael MacDonagh
XLII 126; *XIV* 1020

Oliphant, Margaret Oliphant 1828–1897
novelist
Richard Garnett
1901 III 230–234; *XXII* 1102–1106

Oliver, Martha Cranmer 1834–1880
Pattie Oliver, actress
George Clement Boase
XLII 148–149; *XIV* 1042–1043

O'Malley, Grace 1530?–1600?
Irish chieftain
Norman Moore
XLII 169–170; *XIV* 1063–1064

O'Meara, Kathleen 1839–1888
novelist, biographer
Thompson Cooper
XLII 172–173; *XIV* 1066–1067

Opie, Amelia 1769–1853
novelist, poet
Elizabeth Lee
XLII 226–230; *XIV* 1120–1124

Orczy, Emma Magdalena Rosalia Marie
Josepha Barbara 1865–1947
Baroness Orczy, novelist
Georgina Battiscombe
1941–1950 644–645

Orger, Mary Ann 1788–1849
actress
Joseph Knight
XLII 253–254; *XIV* 1147–1148

Orme, Eliza 1848–1937
conveyancer, social investigator
Leslie Kathleen Howsam
Missing Persons 505–506

Ormerod, Eleanor Anne 1828–1901
economic entomologist
Robert Wallace
1901–1911 III 53–54

Orr, Alexandra Sutherland 1828–1903
biographer
Elizabeth Lee
1901–1911 III 54–55

Osborne, Ruth 1680–1751
witch
Thomas Seccombe
XLII 293–294; *XIV* 1187–1188

Ostrith or Osthryth *d*697
Queen of Mercia
Edmund Venables
XLII 317–318; *XIV* 1211–1212

Osyth, Osith, or Osgith *fl*7th cent.
saint
William Hunt
XLII 337; *XIV* 1231

Otté, Elise 1818–1903
scholar, historian
Edmund Gosse
1901–1911 III 59–60

Owen, Alice *d*1613
philanthropist
Joseph Hirst Lupton
XLII 398–399; *XIV* 1292–1293

Pagan, Isobel *d*1821
poet
Thomas Wilson Bayne
XLIII 36; *XV* 36

Paget, Mary Rosalind 1855–1948
social reformer, nurse, midwife
Edith Mary Pye
1941–1950 646–647

Paget, Muriel Evelyn Vernon 1876–1938
philanthropist
Grace H. Paget
1931–1940 667

Paget, Violet 1856–1935
Vernon Lee, author
Cecilia M. Ady
1931–1940 668

Pakington, Dorothy *d*1679
writer
William Dunn Macray
XLIII 86–88; *XV* 86–88

Palliser, Fanny Bury 1805–1878
writer
Thompson Cooper
XLIII 114; *XV* 114

Palmer, Alicia Tindal *fl*1810
novelist
Elizabeth Lee
XLIII 119; *XV* 119

Palmer, Charlotte *fl*1780–1797
author, teacher
Elizabeth Lee
XLIII 121; *XV* 121

Palmer, Eleanor 1720?–1818
celebrated beauty
Gerald le Grys Norgate
XLIII 126; *XV* 126

Palmer, Mary 1716–1794
author
Elizabeth Lee
XLIII 145–146; *XV* 145–146

Pankhurst, Christabel Harriette
1880–1958
suffragette
Roger Fulford
1951–1960 789–791

Pankhurst, Emmeline 1858–1928
suffragette
Ray Strachey
1922–1930 652–654

Pankhurst, Estelle Sylvia 1882–1960
  political activist, journalist, artist
  Sylvia Ayling
  Missing Persons 511–512

Pardoe, Julia 1806–1862
  writer
  Elizabeth Lee
  XLIII 201; *XV* 201

Parepa-Rosa, Euphrosyne Parepa de
Boyesku 1836–1874
  singer
  Robin Humphrey Legge
  XLIII 204–205; *XV* 204–5

Parker, Emma *fl*1811
  author
  Elizabeth Lee
  XLIII 233; *XV* 233

Parr, Harriet 1828–1900
  Holme Lee, novelist
  Albert Frederick Pollard
  1901 III 248; *XXII* 1120

Parr, Louisa *d*1903
  novelist
  Elizabeth Lee
  1901–1911 III 73

Parsons, Eliza *d*1811
  novelist, dramatist
  Elizabeth Lee
  XLIII 399; *XV* 399

Parsons, Elizabeth 1749–1807
  'The Cock Lane Ghost'
  Thomas Seccombe
  XLIII 399–400; *XV* 399–400

Parsons, Elizabeth 1812–1873
  hymn writer
  James Cuthbert Hadden
  XLIII 401; *XV* 401

Parsons, Gertrude 1812–1891
  novelist
  George Clement Boase
  XLIII 401–402; *XV* 401–402

Paterson, Emma Anne 1848–1886
  women's trade union organizer
  unsigned
  XLIV 17; *XV* 462

Patey, Janet Monach 1842–1894
  singer
  Robin Humphrey Legge
  XLIV 31; *XV* 476

Paton, Mary Ann 1802–1864
  singer
  Lydia Miller Middleton
  XLIV 36–37; *XV* 481–482

Patti, Carlotta 1835–1889
  singer
  Robin Humphrey Legge
  XLIV 56; *XV* 501

Pattison, Dorothy Wyndlow 1832–1878
  Sister Dora, philanthropist
  George Clement Boase
  XLIV 57–58; *XV* 502–503

Paul, Isabella Howard 1833?–1879
  actress
  Joseph Knight
  XLIV 72; *XV* 517

Pavlova, Anna 1881–1931
  ballerina
  Margot Fonteyn
  Missing Persons 513–514

Peacock, Lucy *fl*1815
  bookseller, author
  Gerald le Grys Norgate
  XLIV 143; *XV* 588

Pearl, Cora 1842–1886
  courtesan
  George Clement Boase
  XLIV 155; *XV* 600

Penrose, Elizabeth 1780–1837
  Mrs Markham, children's writer
  Elizabeth Lee
  XLIV 342–343; *XV* 787–788

Penrose, Emily 1858–1942
 educationist
 Helen Darbishire
 1941–1950 665–666

Penson, Lillian Margery 1896–1963
 historian
 Robert Greaves
 1961–1970 832–834

Perham, Margery Freda 1895–1982
 writer, lecturer
 Frederick Madden
 1981–1985 310–311

Perrers, Alice *d*1400
 mistress of Edward III
 Charles Lethbridge Kingsford
 XLV 12–14; *XV* 898–900

Pery, Angela Olivia 1897–1981
 Red Cross leader
 Anne M. Bryans
 1981–1985 311–312

Peters, Mary 1813–1856
 hymn writer
 William Boswell Lowther
 XLV 77; *XV* 963

Pethick-Lawrence, Emmeline 1867–1954
 suffragette
 Jose Ferial Harris
 Missing Persons 521–522

Pfeiffer, Emily Jane 1827–1890
 poet
 Richard Garnett
 XLV 139–140; *XV* 1025–1026

Philippa of Hainault 1314?–1369
 wife of Edward III
 William Hunt
 XLV 164–167; *XV* 1050–1053

Philippa of Lancaster 1359–1415
 wife of John I of Portugal
 Charles Raymond Beazley
 XLV 167–168; *XV* 1053–1054

Philips, Katherine 1631–1664
 poet
 George Thorn-Drury
 XLV 177–178; *XV* 1063–1064

Phillips, Catherine 1727–1794
 Quaker
 Thomas Seccombe
 XLV 195–196; *XV* 1081–1082

Phillips, Marion 1881–1932
 political party organizer
 Jose Ferial Harris
 Missing Persons 525–526

Phillips, Teresia Constantia 1709–1765
 courtesan
 Thomas Seccombe
 XLV 213–214; *XV* 1099–1100

Pickering, Ellen *d*1843
 novelist
 Elizabeth Lee
 XLV 241; *XV* 1127

Pigot, Elizabeth Bridget 1783–1866
 friend of Byron
 Morgan George Watkins
 XLV 278; *XV* 1164

Pilkington, Laetitia 1712–1750
 adventuress
 Thomas Seccombe
 XLV 295–297; *XV* 1181–1183

Pilkington, Mary 1766–1839
 writer
 Joseph Knight
 XLV 298–299; *XV* 1184–1185

Pinsent, Ellen Frances 1866–1949
 mental health pioneer
 Ruth Rees Thomas
 1941–1950 673

Piozzi, Hester Lynch 1741–1821
 friend of Dr Johnson
 Leslie Stephen
 XLV 323–326; *XV* 1209–1212

Pitt, Ann 1720?–1799
actress
Joseph Knight
XLV 340–342; *XV* 1226–1228

Pix, Mary 1666–1720?
dramatist
Edmund Gosse
XLV 388–390; *XV* 1274–1276

Plath, Sylvia 1932–1963
poet
Anthony Thwaite
Missing Persons 527

Plumptre, Anna or Anne 1760–1818
author
Elizabeth Lee
XLV 435–436; *XV* 1321–1322

Pole, Margaret 1473–1541
governess to Mary Tudor
James Gairdner
XLVI 28–29; *XVI* 28–29

Ponsonby, Emily Charlotte Mary
1817–1877
novelist
Elizabeth Lee
XLVI 79–80; *XVI* 79–80

Poole, Sophia 1804–1891
author
unsigned
XLVI 104; *XVI* 104

Pope, Clara Maria *d*1838
painter
Freeman Marius O'Donoghue
XLVI 130; *XVI* 130

Pope, Elizabeth 1744?–1797
actress
Joseph Knight
XLVI 130–132; *XVI* 130–132

Pope, Jane 1742–1818
actress
Joseph Knight
XLVI 132–134; *XVI* 132–134

Pope, Maria Ann 1775–1803
actress
Joseph Knight
XLVI 134–135; *XVI* 134–135

Porter, Anna Maria 1780–1832
novelist
Elizabeth Lee
XLVI 170; *XVI* 170

Porter, Jane 1776–1850
novelist
Elizabeth Lee
XLVI 182–184; *XVI* 182–184

Porter, Mary *d*1765
actress
Joseph Knight
XLVI 188–190; *XVI* 188–190

Postan, Eileen Edna le Poer 1889–1940
Eileen Power, historian and teacher
Richard Henry Tawney
1931–1940 718–719

Potter, Helen Beatrix 1866–1943
children's writer and illustrator
Margaret Lane
1941–1950 686–687

Powell, Mrs 1761?–1831
actress
James Caxton Dibdin
XLVI 236–237; *XVI* 236–237

Power, Marguerite A. 1815?–1867
author
Elizabeth Lee
XLVI 258; *XVI* 258

Pratt, Anne 1806–1893
botanist
Bernard Barham Woodward
XLVI 284–285; *XVI* 284–285

Pringle, Mia Lilly Kellmer 1920–1983
psychologist
Barbara Tizard
1981–1985 326–327

Pritchard, Hannah 1711–1768
   actress
   Joseph Knight
   XLVI 407–409; *XVI* 407–409

Procter, Adelaide Anne 1825–1864
   poet
   Elizabeth Lee
   XLVI 416; *XVI* 416

Puddicombe, Anne Adalisa 1836–1908
   Allen Raine, novelist
   D. Lleufer Thomas
   1901–1911 III 144–145

Pye, Edith Mary 1876–1965
   midwife, international relief organiser
   Sybil Oldfield
   Missing Persons 538

Pym, Barbara Mary Crampton
1913–1980
   novelist
   Philip Larkin
   1971–1980 695

Radcliffe, Ann 1764–1823
   novelist
   Richard Garnett
   XLVII 120–121; *XVI* 563–564

Radcliffe, Mary Ann *c*1746–*post*1810
   writer
   Isobel Grundy
   Missing Persons 542–543

Radclyffe-Hall, Marguerite Antonia
1880–1943
   Radclyffe Hall, novelist, poet
   Elisabeth Brink
   Missing Persons 544

Raffald, Elizabeth 1733–1781
   cook, author
   Charles William Sutton
   XLVII 159–160; *XVI* 602–603

Rainforth, Elizabeth 1814–1877
   singer
   Robin Humphrey Legge
   XLVII 179; *XVI* 622

Raisin, Catherine Alice 1855–1945
   geologist, educationist
   Mary R. S. Creese
   Missing Persons 544–545

Rambert, Marie 1888–1982
   ballet director
   Ivor Guest
   1981–1985 329–330

Ramsay, Victoria Patricia Helena
Elizabeth 1886–1974
   Princess, granddaughter of
   Queen Victoria
   Kenneth Rose
   1971–1980 700–701

Ranyard, Ellen Henrietta 1810–1879
   writer
   George Clement Boase
   XLVII 296; *XVI* 739

Rathbone, Eleanor Florence 1872–1946
   social reformer
   Mary D. Stocks
   1941–1950 711–713

Rathbone, Hannah Mary 1798–1878
   author
   Adolphus William Ward
   XLVII 308–309; *XVI* 751–752

Raverat, Gwendolen Mary 1885–1957
   artist
   Reynolds Stone
   1951–1960 834–835

Redpath, Anne 1895–1965
   painter
   David Baxandall
   1961–1970 874–875

Read, Catherine *d*1778
   painter
   Freeman Marius O'Donoghue
   XLVII 350; *XVI* 793

Reeve, Clara 1729–1807
   novelist
   Elizabeth Lee
   XLVII 404–405; *XVI* 847–848

Reid, Elisabeth Jesser 1789–1866
anti–slavery activist, educationist
Sybil Oldfield
Missing Persons 550–551

Rich, Mary 1625–1678
writer
Charlotte Fell-Smith
XLVIII 118–119; *XVI* 1004–1005

Rich, Penelope 1562?–1607
adulterer
Sidney Lee
XLVIII 120–123; *XVI* 1006–1009

Richards, Audrey Isabel 1899–1984
social anthropologist
Edmund Leach
1981–1985 336–338

Richardson, Charlotte Caroline
1777–1853
poet
Elizabeth Lee
XLVIII 222–223; *XVI* 1108–1109

Richardson, Dorothy Miller 1873–1957
novelist, journalist, translator
Susanne P. Stark
Missing Persons 554–555

Richardson, Ethel Florence Lindesay
1870–1946
Henry Handel Richardson, novelist
Leonie Judith Kramer
1941–1950 722–723

Riddell, Charlotte Eliza Lawson
1832–1906
F. G. Trafford, novelist
Elizabeth Lee
1901–1911 *III* 193–194

Riddell, Maria Woodley 1772–1808
poet
David Henry Weinglass
Missing Persons 555

Ripley, Dorothy 1767–1831
missionary
Isobel Grundy
Missing Persons 556–557

Rivarol, Louisa Henrietta, Madame de
1749?–1821
translator
John Goldworth Alger
XLVIII 331–332; *XVI* 1217–1218

Roberts, Emma 1794?–1840
author
Stephen Wheeler
XLVIII 377; *XVI* 1263

Roberts, Mary 1788–1864
author
Charlotte Fell-Smith
XLVIII 388–389; *XVI* 1274–1275

Robins, Elizabeth 1862–1952
actress, writer, feminist
Angela V. John
Missing Persons 560–561

Robinson, Anastasia *d*1755
singer
George Atherton Aitkin
XLIX 1–3; *XVII* 1–3

Robinson, Joan Violet 1903–1983
economist
Geoffrey Colin Harcourt
1981–1985 346–347

Robinson, Martha Walker 1822–1888
writer
Elizabeth Lee
XLIX 30; *XVII* 30

Robinson, Mary 1758–1800
Perdita, actress, author, mistress of
George IV
Joseph Knight
XLIX 30–33; *XVII* 30–33

Robson, Flora 1902–1984
actress
Marius Goring
1981–1985 348–349

Roche, Regina Maria 1764?–1845
novelist
David James O'Donoghue
XLIX 71; *XVII* 71

Rogers, Annie Mary Anne Henley
1856–1937
  educationist
  Barbara Elizabeth Gwyer
  1931–1940 745–746

Romer, Emma 1814–1868
  singer
  Lydia Miller Middleton
  XLIX 183–184; *XVII* 183–184

Romer, Isabella Frances *d*1852
  writer
  Elizabeth Lee
  XLIX 184; *XVII* 184

Rossetti, Christina Georgina 1830–1894
  poet
  Richard Garnett
  XLIX 282–284; *XVII* 282–284

Rossetti, Lucy Madox 1843–1894
  painter
  Richard Garnett
  XLIX 289–290; *XVII* 289–290

Rousby, Clara Marion Jessie 1852?–1879
  actress
  Joseph Knight
  XLIX 321–322; *XVII* 321–322

Routh, Martha 1743–1817
  Quaker
  Charlotte Fell-Smith
  XLIX 324; *XVII* 324

Rowan, Frederica Maclean 1814–1882
  author
  Frank Thomas Marzials
  XLIX 336; *XVII* 336

Rowe, Elizabeth 1674–1737
  author
  Sidney Lee
  XLIX 338–339; *XVII* 338–339

Rowlandson, Mary *fl*1682
  colonist
  John Andrew Doyle
  XLIX 357; *XVII* 357

Rowson, Susanna 1762–1824
  novelist, actress
  Elizabeth Lee
  XLIX 367–368; *XVII* 367–368

Royden, Agnes Maud 1876–1956
  preacher
  Percy Maryon-Wilson
  1951–1960 855–856

Ruck, Amy Roberta 1878–1978
  novelist
  Brian Alderson
  1971–1980 740–741

Rundall, Mary Ann *d*1839
  writer
  Elizabeth Lee
  XLIX 403; *XVII* 403

Rundell, Maria Eliza 1745–1828
  writer
  Elizabeth Lee
  XLIX 403; *XVII* 403

Russell, Dorothy Stuart 1895–1983
  pathologist
  John Trevor Hughes
  1981–1985 353

Russell, Lucy *d*1627
  patron of poets
  unsigned
  XLIX 467; *XVII* 467

Russell, Mary Annette 1866–1941
  Elizabeth, Countess Russell, writer
  Gladys Scott Thomson
  1941–1950 748–749

Rutherford, Margaret 1892–1972
  actress
  John Gielgud
  1971–1980 746–747

Ryan, Elizabeth Montague 1892–1979
  tennis champion
  David Gray
  1971–1980 747–748

Rye, Maria Susan 1829–1903
social reformer
W. B. Owen
1901–1911 III 245–246

Ryves, Elizabeth 1750–1797
author
Elizabeth Lee
L 71–72; *XVII* 560–561

Sackville-West, Victoria Mary 1892–1962
writer, gardener
Anne Scott-James
1961–1970 913–915

Saffery, Maria Grace 1772–1858
poet
William Boswell Lowther
L 114; *XVII* 603

St Aubyn, Catherine *d*1836
artist
Freeman Marius O'Donoghue
L 120; *XVII* 609

Sale-Barker, Lucy Elizabeth Drummond
Davies 1841–1892
author
Elizabeth Lee
L 189; *XVII* 678

Salmon, Eliza 1787–1849
singer
Lydia Miller Middleton
L 204–205; *XVII* 693–694

Salt, Barbara 1904–1975
diplomat
Thomas Brimelow
1971–1980 755–756

Sanger, Sophy 1881–1950
internationalist, labour-law reformer
Sybil Oldfield
Missing Persons 583

Sargant, Ethel 1863–1918
botanist
Mary R. S. Creese
Missing Persons 584

Saunders, Edith Rebecca 1865–1945
botanist, educationist
Mary R. S. Creese
Missing Persons 584–585

Saunders, Margaret *fl*1702–1744
actress
Joseph Knight
L 327–328; *XVII* 816–817

Savage, Ethel Mary 1881–1939
Ethel M. Dell, novelist
Michael Sadleir
1931–1940 785–786

Sayers, Dorothy Leigh 1893–1957
writer
John Innes Mackintosh Stewart
1951–1960 864–865

Scharlieb, Mary Ann Dacomb
1845–1930
gynaecological surgeon
Winifred Clara Cullis
1922–1930 749–751

Schimmelpenninck, Mary Anne
1778–1856
author
Elizabeth Lee
L 417–418; *XVII* 906–907

Schreiber, Charlotte Elizabeth 1812–1895
scholar
George Clement Boase
L 440–441; *XVII* 929–930

Schulenburg, Ehrengard Melusina
von der 1667–1743
mistress of George I
Adolphus William Ward
L 441–443; *XVII* 930–932

Scott, Caroline Lucy 1784–1857
novelist
George Clement Boase
LI 14–15; *XVII* 952–953

Scott, Harriet Anne 1819–1894
novelist
George Clement Boase
LI 24; *XVII* 962

Scott, Sarah *d*1795
novelist
William Prideaux Courtney
LI 67; *XVII* 1005

Sedgwick, Amy 1830–1897
actress
Joseph Knight
1901 III 336–337; *XXII* 1208–1209

Sedley, Catharine 1657–1717
mistress of James II
Thomas Seccombe
LI 185–187; *XVII* 1123–1125

Sellon, Priscilla Lydia 1821–1876
founder of order of nuns
William Prideaux Courtney
LI 228–229; *XVII* 1166–1167

Sergeant, Emily Frances Adeline
1851–1904
novelist
Charlotte Fell-Smith
1901–1911 III 291–292

Serres, Olivia 1772–1834
painter, writer
Dalrymple James Belgrave
LI 257–259; *XVII* 1195–1197

Setchel, Sarah 1803–1894
painter
Robert Edmund Graves
LI 259–260; *XVII* 1197–1198

Seward, Anna 1747–1809
author
Elizabeth Lee
LI 280–282; *XVII* 1218–1220

Sewell, Elizabeth Missing 1815–1906
author
Elizabeth Lee
1901–1911 III 293–295

Sewell, Mary 1797–1884
author
Elizabeth Lee
LI 287–288; *XVII* 1225–1226

Sexburga, Seaxburg, or Sexburh *d*673
Queen of West Saxons
William Hunt
LI 291; *XVII* 1229

Sexburga, Saint *d*699?
Queen of Kent
William Hunt
LI 291–292; *XVII* 1229–1230

Seymour, Mrs *fl*1717–1723
actress
Joseph Knight
LI 294–295; *XVII* 1232–1233

Seymour, Catherine 1538?–1568
sister of Lady Jane Grey
Albert Frederick Pollard
LI 296–297; *XVII* 1234–1235

Sharp, Evelyn 1869–1955
writer, women's suffrage campaigner
Janet E. Grenier
Missing Persons 595

Sharp, Evelyn Adelaide 1903–1985
civil servant
James Jones
1981–1985 370–371

Sharpe, Louisa 1798–1843
painter
Freeman Marius O'Donoghue
LI 424–425; *XVII* 1362–1363

Shaw, Hester 1586?–1660
midwife
Ann Christine Hess
Missing Persons 595–596

Shaw, Mary 1814–1876
singer
Edward Irving Carlyle
LI 441–442; *XVII* 1379–1380

Shelley, Mary Wollstonecraft 1797–1851
author
Richard Garnett
LII 29–31; *XVIII* 29–31

Sheppard, Elizabeth Sara 1830–1862
novelist
Elizabeth Lee
LII 58; *XVIII* 58

Sheridan, Caroline Henrietta 1779–1851
novelist
William Fraser Rae
LII 74–75; *XVIII* 74–75

Sheridan, Clare Consuelo 1885–1970
artist, sculptor
Anita Leslie
1961–1970 933–935

Sheridan, Elizabeth Ann 1754–1792
singer
William Fraser Rae
LII 76; *XVIII* 76

Sheridan, Frances 1724–1766
author
William Fraser Rae
LII 77; *XVIII* 77

Sheridan, Helen Selina 1807–1867
song writer
William Fraser Rae
LII 77–78; *XVIII* 77–78

Sherwood, Martha 1775–1851
author
Elizabeth Lee
LII 102–104; *XVIII* 102–104

Shipton, Mother
prophet
Sidney Lee
LII 119–120; *XVIII* 119–120

Shirreff, Emily Anne Eliza 1814–1897
pioneer of women's education
Elizabeth Lee
LII 144–145; *XVIII* 144–145

Shore, Jane *d*1527?
mistress of Edward IV
William Arthur Jobson Archbold
LII 147–148; *XVIII* 147–148

Shore, Louisa Catherine 1824–1895
poet
Lionel Henry Cust
LII 151–152; *XVIII* 151–152

Siddal, Elizabeth Eleanor 1829–1862
painter
Virginia Surtees
Missing Persons 599–600

Siddons, Sarah 1755–1831
actress
Joseph Knight
LII 195–202; *XVIII* 195–202

Sidgwick, Eleanor Mildred 1845–1936
educationist
Blanche E. C. Dugdale
1931–1940 811–812

Simmonds, Martha 1624–1665/7
Quaker
Anne Laurence
Missing Persons 600–601

Simpson, Jane Cross 1811–1886
hymn writer
Thomas Wilson Bayne
LII 273–274; *XVIII* 273–274

Sinclair, Catherine 1800–1864
novelist
Thomas Wilson Bayne
LII 290; *XVIII* 290

Sinclair, Mary Amelia St Clair
1863–1946
author
Susanne P. Stark
Missing Persons 605–606

Sitwell, Edith Louisa 1887–1964
poet, critic
John Lehmann
1961–1970 950–951

Skene, Felicia Mary Frances 1821–1899
novelist
Elizabeth Lee
1901 III 347–348; *XXII* 1219–1220

Slessor, Mary Mitchell 1848–1915
  missionary
  Deborah Jane Birkett
  Missing Persons 609–610

Slingsby, Mary *d*1694
  actress
  Joseph Knight
  LII 377–378; *XVIII* 377–378

Smallwood, Norah Evelyn 1909–1984
  publisher
  John Charlton
  1981–1985 376–377

Smith, Charlotte 1749–1806
  poet, novelist
  Elizabeth Lee
  LIII 27–29; *XVIII* 435–437

Smith, Elizabeth 1776–1806
  oriental scholar
  Alexander Gordon
  LIII 32–33; *XVIII* 440–441

Smith, Elizabeth 1776–1806
  scholar, translator
  Judith Hawley
  Missing Persons 613

Smith, Florence Margaret 1902–1971
  Stevie Smith, poet, novelist
  Kay Dick
  1971–1980 785–786

Smith, Frances 1924–1978
  Bunty Stephens, golfer
  Donald Steel
  1971–1980 786–787

Smith, Lucy Toulmin 1838–1911
  scholar
  Elizabeth Lee
  1901–1911 III 341–342

Smith, Pleasance 1773–1877
  centenarian
  Alexander Gordon
  LIII 100–101; *XVIII* 508–509

Smith, Sarah 1832–1911
  Hesba Stretton, author
  Elizabeth Lee
  1901–1911 III 346–347

Smithson, Harriet Constance 1800–1854
  actress
  Joseph Knight
  LIII 168–171; *XVIII* 576–579

Smyth, Ethel Mary 1858–1944
  composer, author, feminist
  Frank Howes
  1941–1950 804–805

Snell, Hannah 1723–1792
  soldier
  Thomas Seccombe
  LIII 205–206; *XVIII* 613–614

Somerset, Isabella Caroline 1851–1921
  Lady Henry Somerset
  Edward Francis Russell
  1912–1921 501–502

Somerville, Edith Anna Œnone
1858–1949
  writer
  Patrick Coghill
  1941–1950 808–809

Somerville, Mary 1780–1872
  writer on science
  Ellen Mary Clerke
  LIII 254–255; *XVIII* 662–663

Somerville, Mary 1897–1963
  educationist
  Grace Wyndham Goldie
  1961–1970 966–967

Sophia 1630–1714
  princess, mother of George I
  Jeremy Black
  Missing Persons 624–625

Sophia Dorothea 1666–1726
  mother of George II
  Ragnhild Marie Hatton
  Missing Persons 625–626

Sorabji, Cornelia 1866–1954
Indian barrister, social reformer
William A. W. Jarvis
1951–1960 907–909

Southcott, Joanna 1750–1814
religious fanatic
Alexander Gordon
LIII 277–279; *XVIII* 685–687

Southey, Caroline Anne 1786–1854
poet
Richard Garnett
LIII 282–283; *XVIII* 690–691

Soyer, Elizabeth Emma 1813–1842
painter
George Clement Boase
LIII 309–310; *XVIII* 717–718

Spence, Elizabeth Isabella 1768–1832
author
Elizabeth Lee
LIII 334–335; *XVIII* 742–743

Spencer, Dorothy 1617–1684
famous beauty
George Atherton Aitkin
LIII 352–354; *XVIII* 760–762

Spender, Lily 1835–1895
novelist
Edward Irving Carlyle
LIII 380–381; *XVIII* 788–789

Spry, Constance 1886–1960
flower arranger
Julia Cairns
1951–1960 915–916

Stannard, Henrietta Eliza Vaughan
1856–1911
John Strange Winter, novelist
Elizabeth Lee
1901–1911 III 394–395

Stanhope, Hester Lucy 1776–1839
eccentric
Thomas Seccombe
LIV 12–14; *XVIII* 899–901

Stanley, Charlotte 1599–1664
civil war heroine
Albert Frederick Pollard
LIV 48–49; *XVIII* 935–936

Stansfeld, Margaret 1860–1951
physical training pioneer
Katharine Mary Westaway
1951–1960 920

Starke, Mariana 1762?–1838
writer
Charlotte Fell-Smith
LIV 107; *XVIII* 994

Stebbing, Lizzie Susan 1885–1943
philosopher
Margaret Macdonald
1941–1950 828

Steel, Flora Annie 1847–1929
novelist
Eva Mary Bell
1922–1930 809–810

Steele, Anne 1717–1778
hymn writer
James Cuthbert Hadden
LIV 128–129; *XVIII* 1015–1016

Stenton, Doris Mary 1894–1971
historian
Kathleen Major
1971–1980 805–806

Stephens, Catherine 1794–1882
singer, actress
Joseph Knight
LIV 168–170; *XVIII* 1055–1057

Stephens, Jane 1813?–1896
actress
Joseph Knight
LIV 176; *XVIII* 1063

Stephenson, Marjory 1885–1948
biochemist
Muriel Robertson
1941–1950 835–836

Stepney, Catherine *d*1845
novelist
Elizabeth Lee
LIV 190; *XVIII* 1077

Sterling, Antoinette 1843–1904
singer
Henry Davey
1901–1911 III 412–413

Sterry, Charlotte 1870–1966
tennis champion
John George Smyth
1961–1970 982–983

Stewart, Isla 1855–1910
nurse
D'Arcy Power
1901–1911 III 416

Stewart-Mackenzie, Maria Elizabeth
Frederica 1783–1862
friend of Walter Scott
Thomas Finlayson Henderson
LIV 368; *XVIII* 1255

Stewart-Murray, Katharine Marjory
1874–1960
public servant
Mary Danvers Stocks
1951–1960 926–927

Stillman or Spartali, Marie 1843–1927
painter, artist's model
Pamela Gerrish Nunn
Missing Persons 634–635

Stirling, Mary Anne 1815–1895
actress
Joseph Knight
LIV 381–383; *XVIII* 1268–1270

Stocks, Mary Danvers 1891–1975
educationist, broadcaster
Donald Soper
1971–1980 808–809

Stokes, Margaret M'Nair 1832–1900
archaeologist
Caesar Litton Falkiner
1901 III 362–363; *XXII* 1234–1235

Stopes, Marie Charlotte Carmichael
1880–1958
scientist, sex education reformer
James MacGibbon
1951–1960 930–931

Storace, Anna, or Ann Selina 1766–1817
singer, actress
Joseph Knight
LIV 421–423; *XVIII* 1308–1310

Strachey, Rachel Conn 1887–1940
feminist
Jose Ferial Harris
Missing Persons 639–640

Strickland, Agnes 1796–1874
historian
Elizabeth Lee
LV 48–50; *XIX* 48–50

Strong, Eugénie 1860–1943
classical archaeologist, art historian
Jocelyn Mary Catherine Toynbee
1941–1950 848–849

Stuart or Stewart, Frances Teresa
1647–1702
mistress of Charles II
Thomas Seccombe
LV 80–82; *XIX* 80–82

Stuart, Jane *c*1654–1742
natural daughter of James II
Eveline Cruikshanks
Missing Persons 646

Stuart-Wortley, Emmeline Charlotte
Elizabeth 1806–1855
poet, author
Elizabeth Lee
LV 109–110; *XIX* 109–110

Summerskill, Edith Clara 1901–1980
politician
Fred T. Willey
1971–1980 821–822

Sumner, Mary Elizabeth 1828–1921
founder of Mothers' Union
Florence Hill
Missing Persons 651

Sundon, Charlotte Clayton *d*1742
  woman of bedchamber
  George Atherton Aitkin
  LV 170–171; *XIX* 170–171

Sutherland, Lucie Stuart 1903–1980
  historian, administrator
  Anne Whiteman
  1971–1980 827–828

Swanwick, Anna 1813–1899
  author
  Elizabeth Lee
  1901 III 374; *XXII* 1246

Swanwick, Helena Maria Lucy 1864–1939
  suffragist
  Jose Ferial Harris
  Missing Persons 655–656

Swynford, Catherine 1350?–1403
  mistress of John of Gaunt
  Charles Lethbridge Kingsford
  LV 243–244; *XIX* 243–244

Szabo, Violette Reine Elizabeth
1921–1945
  secret agent
  Michael Foot
  Missing Persons 659–660

Taglioni, Marie 1809–1884
  dancer
  Thomas Seccombe
  LV 291–292; *XIX* 291–292

Talbot, Catherine 1721–1770
  author
  Elizabeth Lee
  LV 300–301; *XIX* 300–301

Talbot, Elizabeth 1518–1608
  Bess of Hardwick
  Thomas Seccombe
  LV 309–311; *XIX* 309–311

Talbot, Mary Anne 1778–1808
  drummer boy
  Thomas Seccombe
  LV 325–326; *XIX* 325–326

Tautphoelus, Baroness von 1807–1893
  Jemima Montgomery, novelist
  Richard Garnett
  LV 391–392; *XIX* 391–392

Taylor, Eva Germaine Rimington
1879–1966
  geographer, science historian
  Eila Muriel Joice Campbell
  1961–1970 998–999

Taylor, Harriet Hardy 1807–1858
  philosopher, women's rights activist
  Andrea L. Broomfield
  Missing Persons 663–664

Taylor, Helen 1831–1907
  women's rights advocate
  Elizabeth Lee
  1901–1911 III 483–485

Taylor, Jane 1783–1824
  children's writer
  Thomas Seccombe
  LV 420–422; *XIX* 420–422

Teerlinc, Levina 1510/20?–1576
  painter
  Roy Strong
  Missing Persons 665–666

Tempest, Marie 1864–1942
  actress
  St John Ervine
  1941–1950 867–869

Tennant, Margaret Mary Edith, 'May'
1869–1946
  social work pioneer
  Violet Markham
  1941–1950 873–874

Terry, Alice Ellen 1847–1928
  actress
  Harold Hannyngton Child
  1922–1930 827–830

Teyte, Margaret, 'Maggie' 1888–1976
  singer
  Desmond Shawe-Taylor
  1971–1980 837–838

Thicknesse, Ann 1737–1824
author, musician
Lydia Miller Middleton
LVI 130–131; *XIX* 610–611

Thirkell, Angela Margaret 1890–1961
novelist
Thea Holme
1961–1970 1005–1006

Thomas, Elizabeth 1677–1731
poet
Thomas Seccombe
LVI 178–179; *XIX* 658–659

Thomas, Margaret Haig 1883–1958
Viscountess Rhondda, editor
Anthony Lejeune
1951–1960 968–969

Thompson, Flora Jane 1876–1947
writer
Gillian Lindsay
Missing Persons 668–669

Thompson, Lydia 1836–1908
actress
W. J. Lawrence
1901–1911 III 505–506

Thomson, Katharine 1797–1862
writer
Thomas Seccombe
LVI 265–266; *XIX* 745–746

Thorndike, Agnes Sybil 1882–1976
actress
Sheridan Morley
1971–1980 845–847

Thornton, Alice 1626–1707
autobiographer
Ann L. Hughes
Missing Persons 671–672

Thornycroft, Mary 1814–1895
sculptor
Walter Armstrong
LVI 311–312; *XIX* 791–792

Thurmond, Mrs *fl*1715–1737
actress
Joseph Knight
LVI 350–351; *XIX* 830–831

Thurston, Katherine Cecil 1875–1911
novelist
G. S. Woods
1901–1911 III 524–525

Tighe, Mary 1772–1810
poet
Elizabeth Lee
LVI 388–389; *XIX* 868–869

Tilley, Vesta 1864–1952
male impersonator
Walter James Macqueen Pope
1951–1960 973–974

Titiens, or Tietjens, Teresa Caroline
Johanna 1831–1877
singer
Robin Humphrey Legge
LVI 419; *XIX* 899

Toft or Tofts, Mary 1701?–1763
impostor
Thomas Seccombe
LVI 435–436; *XIX* 915–916

Tofts, Katherine 1680?–1758?
singer
Lydia Miller Middleton
LVI 437–438; *XIX* 917–918

Tollett, Elizabeth 1694–1754
poet
Thompson Cooper
LVI 448; *XIX* 928

Tonna, Charlotte Elizabeth 1790–1846
writer
David James O'Donoghue
LVII 34–35; *XIX* 961–962

Toulmin, Camilla Dufour 1812–1895
writer
Edmund Toulmin Nicolle
LVII 81–82; *XIX* 1008–1010

Trapnel, Anna *fl*1642–1660
prophet
Valerie Drake
Missing Persons 680

Travers, Rebecca 1609–1688
Quaker
Charlotte Fell-Smith
LVII 161–162; *XIX* 1088–1089

Tredway, Letice Mary 1593–1677
abbess
John Goldworth Alger
LVII 168–169; *XIX* 1095–1096

Trench, Melesina 1768–1827
author
Thomas Seccombe
LVII 189–191; *XIX* 1116–1117

Trevelyan, Hilda 1877–1959
actress
John Courtenay Trewin
1951–1960 991–992

Trimmer, Sarah 1741–1810
author
Elizabeth Lee
LVII 231–232; *XIX* 1158–1159

Trollope, Frances 1780–1863
novelist
Richard Garnett
LVII 243–246; *XIX* 1170–1173

Trollope, Theodosia 1825–1865
author
Thomas Seccombe
LVII 248–249; *XIX* 1175–1176

Tucker, Charlotte Maria 1821–1893
children's writer
Elizabeth Lee
LVII 279–280; *XIX* 1206–1207

Tuckwell, Gertrude Mary 1861–1951
philanthropist
Violet Markham
1951–1960 997

Tussaud, Marie 1760–1850
founder of waxwork exhibition
Thomas Seccombe
LVII 378–379; *XIX* 1305–1306

Twining, Louisa 1820–1912
poor-law reformer
Janet E. Grenier
Missing Persons 685

Umphelby, Fanny 1788–1852
author
Robert Avery Ward
LVIII 26; *XX* 26

Underhill, Evelyn 1875–1941
religious writer
Marjorie Vernon
1941–1950 897–898

Unwin, Mary 1724–1796
friend of Cowper
Thomas Seccombe
LVIII 34–35; *XX* 34–35

Ursula *d*238, 283, or 451
saint
Mary Tout
LVIII 53–55; *XX* 53–55

Uttley, Alice Jane 1884–1976
Alison Uttley, author
Brian Alderson
1971–1980 869–870

Vanbrugh, Irene 1872–1949
actress
Samuel Robinson Littlewood
1941–1950 899–901

Vanbrugh, Violet 1867–1942
actress
Samuel Robinson Littlewood
1941–1950 901–902

Vane, Frances Anne 1713–1788
gambler
Thomas Seccombe
LVIII 112–113; *XX* 112–113

Walburga or Walpurga *d*779?
abbess
Mary Bateson
LIX 9; *XX* 466

Waldegrave, Frances Elizabeth Anne
1821–1879
singer
Henry Riversdale Grenfell
LIX 14–15; *XX* 471–472

Waldie, Charlotte Ann 1788–1859
novelist
Elizabeth Lee
LIX 26–27; *XX* 483–484

Walker, Ethel 1861–1951
painter, sculptor
Mary Woodall
1951–1960 1019–1020

Walkinshaw, Clementina 1726?–1802
mistress of Prince Charles Edward
Francis Hindes Groome
LIX 91–93; *XX* 548–550

Wallace, Eglantine *d*1803
author
John Knox Laughton
LIX 97–98; *XX* 554–555

Wallace, Grace *d*1878
author
George Stronach
LIX 98; *XX* 555

Wallis, Miss *fl*1789–1814
actress
Joseph Knight
LIX 139–140; *XX* 596–597

Wallmoden, Amalie Sophie Marianne
1704–1765
mistress of George II
James McMullen Rigg
LIX 149–150; *XX* 606–607

Walter, Lucy 1630?–1658
mistress of Charles II
Thomas Seccombe
LIX 259–260; *XX* 716–717

Ward, Barbara Mary 1814–1981
journalist, broadcaster
Nora Beloff
1981–1985 410–411

Ward, Ida Caroline 1880–1949
phonetician, language scholar
Margaret Mackeson Green
1941–1950 925–926

Ward, Mary 1585–1645
founder of religious order
Edward Irving Carlyle
1901 III 506–508; *XXII* 1378–1380

Ward, Mary Augusta 1851–1920
Mrs Humphry Ward, novelist
Myra Curtis
1912–1921 551–552

Wardlaw, Elizabeth 1677–1727
poet
Thomas Finlayson Henderson
LIX 352; *XX* 809

Waring, Anna Letitia 1823–1910
hymn writer
Alexander Gordon
1901–1911 III 593

Warner, Mary Amelia 1804–1854
actress
Joseph Knight
LIX 397–398; *XX* 854–855

Warner, Sylvia Townsend 1893–1978
novelist, poet
Alexandra Pringle
1971–1980 884–885

Watson, Janet Vida 1923–1985
geologist
Robert M. Shackleton
1981–1985 416–417

Watt, Margaret Rose 1868–1948
Women's Institute pioneer
Frances Farrer
1941–1950 930

Watts, Susanna 1768–1842
  writer
  Isobel Grundy
  Missing Persons 705

Waylett, Harriet 1798–1851
  actress
  Joseph Knight
  LX 83–85; *XX* 994–996

Webb, Mrs *d*1793
  actress
  Joseph Knight
  LX 94–95; *XX* 1005–1006

Webb, Mary Gladys 1881–1927
  novelist, essayist, poet
  Susan Charlotte Buchan
  1922–1930 901–902

Webster, Augusta 1837–1894
  poet
  Elizabeth Lee
  LX 115–116; *XX* 1026–1027

Wellesley, Dorothy Violet 1889–1956
  poet
  Victoria Mary Sackville-West
  1951–1960 1041–1042

Wells, Mary *fl*1781–1812
  actress
  Joseph Knight
  LX 230–231; *XX* 1141–1142

Wenham, Jane *d*1730
  witch
  Thomas Seccombe
  LX 253; *XX* 1164

Wentworth, Henrietta Maria 1657?–1686
  mistress of Duke of Monmouth
  Thomas Seccombe
  LX 257–258; *XX* 1168–1169

Werburga or Werburh *d*700?
  saint
  William Hunt
  LX 294–295; *XX* 1205–1206

Werner, Alice 1859–1935
  Bantu language teacher
  Peter Jeremy Lewinter Frankl
  Missing Persons 707–708

West, Mrs 1790–1876
  actress
  Joseph Knight
  LX 323–324; *XX* 1234–1235

West, Jane 1758–1852
  author
  Elizabeth Lee
  LX 331–332; *XX* 1242–1243

West, Rebecca 1892–1983
  author, reporter, literary critic
  Bernard Levin
  1981–1985 420–422

Weston, Agnes Elizabeth 1840–1918
  sailors' welfare pioneer
  Myra Curtis
  1912–1921 569–571

Weston, Elizabeth Jane 1582–1612
  learned lady, linguist
  Elizabeth Lee
  LX 359–360; *XX* 1270–1271

Wharton, Anne 1632?–1685
  poet
  Thomas Seccombe
  LX 401–402; *XX* 1312–1313

White, Alice Mary Meadows 1839–1884
  composer
  James Cuthbert Hadden
  LXI 31–32; *XXI* 31–32

Whitlock, Elizabeth 1761–1836
  actress
  Joseph Knight
  LXI 140–141; *XXI* 140–141

Whorwood, Jane *fl*1648
  royalist
  Charles Harding Firth
  LXI 170–171; *XXI* 170–171

Wilkinson, Ellen Cicely 1891–1947
trade unionist, politician
Dorothy M. Elliott
1941–1950 955–956

Williams, Anna 1706–1783
poet
William Prideaux Courtney
LXI 378–379; *XXI* 378–379

Williams, Ella Gwendolen Rees
1890?–1979
Jean Rhys, writer
Diana Athill
1971–1980 903–905

Williams, Helen Maria 1762–1827
author
John Knox Laughton
LXI 404–405; *XXI* 404–405

Williams, Ivy 1877–1966
barrister
Hazel Fox
1961–1970 1081–1082

Williams, Jane 1806–1885
historian, writer
Daniel Lleufer Thomas
LXI 411–412; *XXI* 411–412

Wilson, Mrs *d*1786
actress
Joseph Knight
LXII 73–74; *XXI* 544–545

Wilson, Caroline 1787–1846
author
Elizabeth Lee
LXII 85–86; *XXI* 556–557

Wilson, Mrs Cornwall Baron, Margaret
1797–1846
author
Elizabeth Lee
LXII 87; *XXI* 558

Wilson, Harriette 1789–1846
woman of fashion
Thomas Seccombe
LXII 95–96; *XXI* 566–567

Wilson, Margaret 1667–1685
martyr
Thomas Seccombe
LXII 118–119; *XXI* 589–590

Winefride or Gwenfrewi
saint
Mary Bateson
LXII 179; *XXI* 650

Winkworth, Catherine 1827–1878
author
Elizabeth Lee
LXII 194–196; *XXI* 665–666

Wiskemann, Elizabeth Meta 1899–1971
historian, journalist
James Joll
1971–1980 918–919

Woffington, Margaret 1714?–1760
actress
Joseph Knight
LXII 281–284; *XXI* 752–755

Wood, Ellen 1814–1887
novelist
Thomas Seccombe
LXII 355–357; *XXI* 826–828

Wood, Mary Anne Everett 1818–1895
historian
Adolphus William Ward
LXII 369–370; *XXI* 840–841

Wood, Matilda Alice Victoria 1870–1922
Marie Lloyd, music hall comedian
Harold Hannyngton Child
1922–1930 921–922

Woodham, Mrs 1743–1803
singer, actress
Joseph Knight
LXII 398; *XXI* 869

Woodroffe, Anne 1766–1830
author
Elizabeth Lee
LXII 407; *XXI* 878

Woolf, Adeline Virginia 1882–1941
novelist, critic
David Cecil
1941–1950 975–976

Woolley or Wolley, Hannah *fl*1670
writer
Bertha Porter
LXII 431–432; *XXI* 902–903

Worboise, Emma Jane 1825–1887
author
Elizabeth Lee
LXII 440–441; *XXI* 911–912

Wordsworth, Dorothy 1771–1855
writer
Alan G. Hill
Missing Persons 731–732

Wordsworth, Elizabeth 1840–1932
educationist
Evelyn Mary Jamison
1931–1940 921–922

Wright, Helena Rosa 1887–1981
physician
Josephine Barnes
1981–1985 431–432

Wright, Mehetabel Wesley 1697–1750
poet
Richard Greene
Missing Persons

Wright, Patience 1725–1786
wax modeller
Freeman Marius O'Donoghue
LXIII 121–122; *XXI* 1036–1037

Wroth, Mary *fl*1621
author
Sidney Lee
LXIII 161–162; *XXI* 1076–1077

Wyndham, Mary 1861–1931
Mary Moore, actress and
theatre manager
William Aubrey Darlington
1931–1940 924–925

Wynn, Charlotte Williams 1807–1869
diarist
William Prideaux Courtney
LXIII 256; *XXI* 1171

Wynyard, Diana 1906–1964
actress
William Aubrey Darlington
1961–1970 1118–1119

Yates, Elizabeth 1799–1860
actress
Joseph Knight
LXIII 290–292; *XXI* 1205–1207

Yates, Frances Amelia 1899–1981
historian
Joseph Burney Trapp
1981–1985 433–434

Yates, Mary Ann 1728–1787
actress
Joseph Knight
LXIII 298–301; *XXI* 1213–1216

Yearsley, Ann 1756–1806
poet
Elizabeth Lee
LXIII 310–311; *XXI* 1225–1226

Yonge, Charlotte Mary 1823–1901
novelist and children's writer
Edith Sichel
1901–1911 *III* 717–719

Younger, Elizabeth 1699?–1762
actress
Joseph Knight
LXIII 403–404; *XXI* 1318–1319

Younghusband, Eileen Louise 1902–1981
social work pioneer
Lucy Faithfull
1981–1985 434–435

Part 2

WOMEN CONTRIBUTORS

Women contributors 1885-1985 and *Missing Persons*

This section consists of two parts. The first is an alphabetical list of contributors, arranged by volume. The second is arranged alphabetically by contributor across all the volumes. Here, under the contributor's name, is the list of subjects on which she wrote, arranged alphabetically regardless of volume, followed by the volume reference. Where references are to the 1885–1901 volumes, two references are given, the first to the 66-volume set, the second to the 22-volume reissue.

Women contributors, arranged by *DNB* volume:

Volumes I–LXIII, 1885–1900, and 1901 supplement

Mary Bateson
Rose Marian Bradley
Frances Bushby
Agnes Mary Clerke
Ellen Mary Clerke
Edith Coleridge
Alice Margaret Cooke
Cornelia Augusta Hewett Crosse
Anne Gilchrist
Jennett Humphreys
Alice Mary Humphry
Elizabeth Ingall
Catherine Rachel Jones
Elizabeth Lee
Margaret MacArthur
Agnes Macdonell
Alice Macdonell
Mrs S. L. May
Lydia Miller Middleton
Rosa Harriet Newmarch
Kate Norgate
Eliza Orme
Christabel Osborne
Bertha Porter
Eleanor Grace Powell
Emma Louise Radford
Anne Isabella Ritchie
Julia Anne Elizabeth Roundell
Ghetal Burdon-Sanderson
Lucy Maude Manson Scott
Eva Blantyre Simpson
Mrs A. Murray Smith, formerly Emily
  Tennyson Bradley
Charlotte Fell-Smith
Lucy Toulmin Smith
Caroline Emelia Stephen
Julia Prinsep Stephen
Charlotte Carmichael Stopes
Beatrix Marion Sturt
Emma Catharine Sutton
Elizabeth Marion Todd
Mary Tout
Louisa Charlotte Tyndall
Margaret Maria Verney
Ellen Williams
Sarah Wilson

1901-1911

Elizabeth S. Haldane
Edith S. Hooper
Elizabeth Lee
Annie Matheson
Miss S. Morrison
Edith Sichel
Charlotte Fell-Smith
Mrs A. B. White

1912-1921

Helen Bosanquet
Myra Curtis
Ellinor Flora Bosworth Grogan
Nina Louisa Hills
Katharine Jex-Blake
Fanny Cecilia Johnson
Hilda Johnstone
May Morris
Edith Palliser
Rachael Emily Poole
Margaret Thyra Barbara Stephen

1922-1930

Cecilia Mary Ady
Eva Mary Bell
Janet Marjorie Close
Mary Coate
Winifred Clara Cullis
Eveline Charlotte Godley
Elizabeth Sanderson Haldane
Dorothea Hosie
Alida Monro
Jane Thompson Stoddart
Ray Strachey
Margaret Ruth Toynbee
Janet Penrose Trevelyan
Susan Charlotte Buchan

1931-1940

Cecilia Mary Ady
Hilda Andrews
Agnes Arber
Georgina Battiscombe
Doris Blacker
Ellen Sophia Bosanquet
Dorothy Jeffreys Cantelupe

Ella Robertson Christie
Gladys Laura Clapperton
Blanche Elizabeth Campbell Dugdale
Dorothy Mary Emmet
Viola Gerard Garvin
Eveline Charlotte Godley
Lynda Grier
Barbara Elizabeth Gwyer
Mary Agnes Hamilton
Agnes Yelland Hay
Pamela Hinkson
Clara Joyce Elizmar Hollins
Elspeth Josceline Huxley
Evelyn Mary Jamison
Amice Lee
Sylvia Lynd
Agnes Mure Mackenzie
Lucy Masterman
Violet Georgina Milner
Louise Morgan
Grace Hartley Paget
Olive Purser
Mary Gwyneth Lloyd Thomas
Gladys Scott Thomson
Jocelyn Mary Catherine Toynbee
Margaret Ruth Toynbee
Maisie Ward
Marion Evelyn Wood

1941-1950

Mosa Isabel Anderson
Constance Babington Smith
Georgina Battiscombe
Margaret Bellasis
Gertrud Bing
Elsie Edith Bowerman
Alice Stewart Glegg Bryson
Hope Danby
Helen Darbishire
Sybil Frances Dawson Eccles
Dorothy Mary Elliott
Dorothy Everett
Frances Margaret Farrer
Dorothy Galton
Helen Shiels Gillespie
Margaret Mackeson Green
Lynda Grier
Mary Agnes Hamilton
Jacquetta Hawkes
Mary Thalassa Alford Cruso Hencken

Leonie Judith Kramer
Margaret Lane
Margaret Macdonald
Violet Rosa Markham
Hilda Martindale
Diana Morgan
Jane Elizabeth Norton
Annette Jocelyn Otway-Ruthven
Helen Maud Palmer
Myfanwy Piper
Edith Mary Pye
Muriel Robertson
Lennox Robinson
Monica Salmond
Avice Edith Sankey
Gladys Scott Thomson
Mary Danvers Stocks
Ruth Rees Thomas
Jocelyn Mary Catherine Toynbee
Marjorie Vernon
Cicely Veronica Wedgwood
Muriel Helen Wigglesworth
Mary Woodall

1951-1960

Constance Babington Smith
Ida Phyllis Barclay-Smith
Margaret Rosa Bellasis
Ruth Elizabeth Mary Bowden
Dorothea Elizabeth Brunner
Hester Burton
Ruth Florence Butler
Julia Cairns
Harriette Chick
Margaret Isabel Cole
Winifred Kathleen Davin
Molina Fullman
Freda Gaye
Grace Wyndham Goldie
Isabella Gordon
Mary Agnes Hamilton
Mary Isobel Henderson
Margaret Cameron Hogarth
Sylvia Jewkes
Jean MacGibbon
Violet Rosa Markham
Vera Laughton Mathews
Mary Munro
Iona Opie
Helen Maud Palmer

Elizabeth Kennard Whittington
  Rothenstein
Dorothy Stuart Russell
Victoria Mary Sackville-West
Ruth Lydia Saw
Evelyn Adelaide Sharp
Isobel Agnes Smith
Mary Danvers Stocks
Ruth Rees Thomas
Susan Charlotte Buchan
Mary Walton
Katharine Mary Westaway
Elizabeth Meta Wiskemann
Mary Woodall

1961-1970

Gillian Elise Avery
Anne Olivier Bell
Kathleen Mary Bliss
Mary Cadogan
Eila Muriel Joice Campbell
Marian Laura Campbell
Mary Lucy Cartwright
Margaret Isabel Cole
Pamela Joy Coote
Janet Dunbar
Katherine Elliott
Hazel Mary Fox
Christina Agnes Lilian Foyle
Enriqueta Eva Frankfort
Helen Louise Gardner
Alice Garnett
Freda Gaye
Mary Cecilia Glasgow
Grace Wyndham Goldie
Margaret Mary Gowing
Joyce Irene Grenfell
Betty Kathleen Hance
Dorothy Frances Hollingsworth
Thea Holme
Joan Mervyn Hussey
Anita Leslie
Sarah Frances McCabe
Kathleen Major
Dorothy Middleton
Elizabeth Monroe
Christine Stephanie Nicholls
Kathleen Mary Norman
Lillian Mary Pickford
Helen Kemp Porter

Elizabeth Dilys Powell
Alice Marjorie Sheila Prochaska
Patricia Marie Pugh
Jean Robertson
Anne Eleanor Scott-James
Marion Ursula Howard Spring
Eleanor Dale Putnam Symons
Kathleen Mary Tillotson
Stella Archer Walker
Eirene Lloyd White
Anne Yates

1971-1980

Madge Gertrude Adam
Diana Athill
Vera May Atkins
Constance Babington Smith
Joyce Margaret Bellamy
Lettice Cooper
Freda Kunzlen Corbet
Beatrice Yvonne Cormeau
Ina Mary Cumpston
Brenda Davies
Kay Dick
Frances Annesley Donaldson
Dorothy Drake
Judy Egerton
Patty Beatrice Fisher
Margot Fonteyn
Christina Agnes Lilian Foyle
Victoria Glendinning
Virginia Graham
Jacquetta Hawkes
Evelyn Mansfield King
Jennie Lee
Daphne Mair Mitchell Lennie
Anita Leslie
Elizabeth Pakenham Longford
Fiona MacCarthy
Diana Mary McVeagh
Hilary Barrow Magnus
Kathleen Major
Catherine Makepeace Thackeray
  Martineau
Maureen Susan Millar
Hylton Judith Milledge
Elizabeth Monroe
Doris Langley Moore
Christine Stephanie Nicholls
Mary O'Neill

Louise Orr
Claire Dorothea Taylor Palley
Constance Anne Parker
Elizabeth Pollitt
Elizabeth Dilys Powell
Alexandra Jane Reina Pringle
Betty Radice
Margaret Richardson
Mary Soames
Kathryn Margaret Stansfield
Kathleen Elizabeth Stevens
Wendy Trewin
Sheila Mosley Walker
Helen Mary Warnock
Pamela Mabel Waterworth
Eirene Lloyd White
Elizabeth Anne Osborn Whiteman
Anthea Williams
Amabel Williams-Ellis

1981-1985

Sara Trerice Adams
Gillian Elise Avery
Josephine Barnes
Nora Beloff
Sophie Bowness
Anne Margaret Bryans
Angela Joan Cunningham
Katherine Elliot
Lucy Faithfull
Margot Fonteyn
Margaret Mary Gowing
Beryl Grey
Jenifer Margaret Hart
Sheila Hodges
Marie Jahoda
Dorothy Mary Kosinski
Rachael Low
Diana Mary McVeagh
Christine Stephanie Nicholls
Marjorie Nicholson
Frances Catherine Partridge
Miriam Louisa Rothschild
Sarah Caroline Jane Street
Barbara Patricia Tizard
Joan Ursula Penton Vaughan Williams
Kim Scott Walwyn
Mary Teresa Josephine Webber
Elizabeth Anne Osborn Whiteman

Missing Persons

Patricia Helen Allderidge
Gillian Elise Avery
Sylvia Ayling
Anne Pimlott Baker
Monica Eileen Baly
Jane Barbour
Elaine Barr
Mavis Lilian Batey
Margaret Rachel Beetham
Alison Sarah Bendall
Deborah Jane Birkett
Maureen Doris Borland
Elisabeth Brink
Marilyn Lily Brooks
Andrea Lynn Broomfield
Barbara Caine
Maryann Feola Castelucci
Judith Frances Champ
Margaret Anne Clennett
Judith Mary Vaughan Collins
Joan Mary Bermingham Counihan
Catherine Joan Crawford
Mary Rose Stewart Creese
Eveline Cruickshanks
Helen Mary Davies
Madeleine Elizabeth Vinicombe Davis
Margaret Ellen Eisenstein DeLacy
Valerie Christine Drake
Ruth Dudley Edwards
Marianne Elliott
Mary Phyllis English
Naomi Irene Evetts
Jean Dorothy Young Farrugia
Christine Yvonne Ferdinand
Joyce Pease Fitch
Sheila Margaret Fletcher
Sibylla Jane Pickering Flower
Margot Fonteyn
Janet Ing Freeman
Kathryn Fuller
Margaret Templeton Gibson
Philippa Jane Glanville
Janet Anne Gough
Penelope Mary Gouk
Jane Elizabeth Grenier
Isobel Mary Grundy
Bridget Charlotte Hadaway
Joan Hasler
Ragnhild Marie Hatton

Jacquetta Hawkes
Judith Victoria Hawley
Joan Catherine Henderson
Ann Christine Hess
Bridget Irene Hill
Florence Mary Hill
Rosemary Hill
Rosemary Elizabeth Horrox
Brenda Lilian Hough
Janet Hilary Howarth
Leslie Kathleen Howsam
Anne Mary Hudson
Ann Laura Hughes
Lorna Margaret Hutson
Joanna Mary Innes
Angela Vaughan John
Harriet Clare Jordan
Averill Alison Kelly
Cecily Alice Langdale
Elizabeth Anne Laurence
Deborah Margaret Lavin
Davina Gifford Lewis
Gillian Phyllis Lindsay
Valerie Lloyd
Susan Jennifer Loach
Elizabeth Pakenham Longford
Rachel Low
Fiona MacCarthy
Anita McConnell
Margaret Bernadette MacCurtain
Frances Margaret Stewart McDonald
Elizabeth Letitia Malcolm
Mavis Evelyn Mate
Helen Miller
Margaret Frances Mulvuhill
Ann Katharine Newmark
Pamela Gerrish Nunn
Sheila Mary O'Connell
Margaret Rosemary O'Day
Hilary Seton Offler
Ann Sybil Oldfield
Elaine Margaret Paintin
Katharine Ferriday Pantzer
Susan Mary Parkes
Linda Lou Alberta Parry
Frances Catherine Partridge
Valerie Louise Pearl
Margaret Hansen Pelling
Dorlanda Hannah Pember
Sandra Joan Raphael
Eleanor Alexandra Reid

Adrienne Elaine Reynolds
Vivian Gladys Salmon
Carolyn Poling Schriber
Alison Eva Mary Shell
Valentine Mary Kennerley Sillery
Barbara Mary Dimond Smith
Julia Jane Smith
Julia Winifred Speedie
Ann Hazel Spokes Symonds
Liz Stanley
Susanne Petra Stark
Barbara Mary Stoney
Charlotte Mary Stott
Elizabeth Bridget Stuart
Susan Agnes Stussy
Virginia Surtees
Gillian Ray Sutherland
Nicola Mary Sutherland
Irene Joan Thirsk
Elizabeth Mary Vallance
Rosemary Thorstenson Van Arsdel
Helen Margaret Wallis
Grace Margaret Ward
Jocelin Slingsby Winthrop-Young
Meta Zimmeck

MADGE GERTRUDE ADAM
Plaskett, Harry Hemley *1971–1980*

SARA TRERICE ADAMS
Adams, Mary Grace Agnes *1981–1985*

CECILIA MARY ADY
Armstrong, Edward *1922–1930*
Paget, Violet *1931–1940*
Toynbee, Paget Jackson *1931–1940*

PATRICIA HELEN ALLDERIDGE
Dadd, Richard *Missing Persons*

MOSA ISABEL ANDERSON
Noel-Buxton, Noel Edward *1941–1950*

HILDA ANDREWS
Terry, Richard Runciman *1931–1940*

AGNES ARBER
Scott, Dukinfield Henry *1931–1940*

DIANA ATHILL
Williams, Ella Gwendolen Rees *1971–1980*

VERA MAY ATKINS
De Baissac, Marc Claude de Boucherville
  1971–1980
Heslop, Richard Henry *1971–1980*

GILLIAN ELISE AVERY
Browne, Frances *Missing Persons*
Burnett, Frances Eliza Hodgson
  Missing Persons
Lofting, Hugh John *Missing Persons*
Mackintosh, Elizabeth *Missing Persons*
Molesworth, Mary Louisa *Missing Persons*
Opie, Peter Mason *1981–1985*
Ransome, Arthur Michell *1961–1970*

SYLVIA AYLING
Pankhurst, Estelle Sylvia *Missing Persons*

CONSTANCE BABINGTON SMITH
Fielden, Edward Hedley *1971–1980*
Macaulay, Emilie Rose *1951–1960*
Warburton, Adrian *1941–1950*

ANNE PIMLOTT BAKER
Burgess, Guy Francis de Moncy
  Missing Persons

Cannon, Thomas *Missing Persons*
Fitzsimmons, Robert *Missing Persons*
Jones, Agnes Elizabeth *Missing Persons*
Kimber, William *Missing Persons*
Maskelyne, John Nevil *Missing Persons*
Merrick, Joseph Carey *Missing Persons*
Preston, Thomas *Missing Persons*
Prince, Henry James *Missing Persons*
Thomas, Hugh Owen *Missing Persons*
Tosti, Francesco Paolo *Missing Persons*

MONICA EILEEN BALY
Lees, Florence Sarah *Missing Persons*

JANE BARBOUR
Sumner, George Heywood Maunoir
  Missing Persons

IDA PHYLLIS BARCLAY–SMITH
Kinnear, Norman Boyd *1951–1960*

ALICE JOSEPHINE MARY TAYLOR BARNES
Wright, Helena Rosa *1981–1985*

ELAINE BARR
Wickes, George *Missing Persons*

MARY BATESON
Leofric of Bourne *XXXIII, XI*
Liulf or Ligulf *XXXIII, XI*
Livinus, Saint *XXXIII, XI*
Lucius *XXXIV, XII*
Lugid or Molua, Saint *XXXIV, XII*
Maglorius, Saint *XXXV, XII*
Maildulf or Mailduf *XXXV, XII*
Marleberge, Thomas de *XXXVI, XII*
Mellitus *XXXVII, XIII*
Mirk, John *XXXVIII, XIII*
Misyn, Richard *XXXVIII, XIII*
Modestus, Saint *XXXVIII, XIII*
Moinenno, Saint *XXXVIII, XIII*
Monan, Saint *XXXVIII, XIII*
Mo-nennius *XXXVIII, XIII*
More, William *XXXVIII, XIII*
Mortain, Robert of *XXXIX, XIII*
Morton, Robert *XXXIX, XIII*
Narford, Nerford, or Nereford, Robert
  XL, XIV
Necton or Nechodun, Humphrey *XL, XIV*
Neot, Saint *XL, XIV*

MAVIS LILIAN BATEY

GEORGINA BATTISCOMBE
Anderson, Stella *1931–1940*
Caine, Thomas Henry Hall *1931–1940*
Ford, Ford Madox *1931–1940*
Harrison, Mary St Leger *1931–1940*
McNeile, Herman Cyril *1931–1940*
Orczy, Emma Magdalena Rosalia Marie
  Josepha Barbara *1941–1950*

ANNE OLIVIER BELL
Bell, Vanessa *1961–1970*

EVA MARY BELL
Steel, Flora Annie *1922–1930*

JOYCE MARGARET BELLAMY
Barnes, Alfred John *1971–1980*
Postgate, Raymond William *1971–1980*

MARGARET ROSA BELLASIS
Arlen, Michael *1951–1960*
Dashwood, Edmée Elizabeth Monica
  1941–1950
Farnol, John Jeffery *1951–1960*
Hannay, James Owen *1941–1950*
Hichens, Robert Smyth *1941–1950*
Mercer, Cecil William *1951–1960*
Oppenheim, Edward Phillips *1941–1950*

NORA BELOFF
Ward, Barbara Mary *1981–1985*

MARGARET RACHEL BEETHAM
Beeton, Isabella Mary *Missing Persons*

ALISON SARAH BENDALL
Langdon, Thomas *Missing Persons*

GERTRUD BING
Saxl, Friedrich *1941–1950*

DEBORAH JANE BIRKETT
Slessor, Mary Mitchell *Missing Persons*

DORIS BLACKER
Peel, William Robert Wellesley *1931–1940*

KATHLEEN MARY BLISS
Oldham, Joseph Houldsworth *1961–1970*

MAUREEN DORIS BORLAND
Ross, Robert Baldwin *Missing Persons*

ELLEN SOPHIA BOSANQUET
Bosanquet, Robert Carr *1931–1940*

HELEN BOSANQUET
Hill, Octavia

RUTH ELIZABETH MARY BOWDEN
Cullis, Winifred Clara *1951–1960*

ELSIE EDITH BOWERMAN
Dove, Jane Frances *1941–1950*

SOPHIE and Alan BOWNESS
Nicholson, Benjamin Lauder *1981–1985*

ROSE MARIAN BRADLEY
Gale, Dunstan *XX, VII*
Gisborne, John *XXI, VII*

ELISABETH BRINK
Radclyffe-Hall, Marguerite Antonia
  Missing Persons

MARILYN LILY BROOKS
Fenwick, Eliza *Missing Persons*
Hays, Mary *Missing Persons*

ANDREA LYNN BROOMFIELD
Taylor, Harriet Hardy *Missing Persons*

ANNE MARGARET BRYANS
Pery, Angela Olivia *1981–1985*

DOROTHEA ELIZABETH BRUNNER
Denman, Gertrude Mary *1951–1960*

ALICE STEWART GLEGG BRYSON
Fenwick, Ethel Gordon *1941–1950*

SUSAN CHARLOTTE BUCHAN
Markham, Violet Rosa *1951–1960*
Webb, Mary Gladys *1922–1930*

HESTER BURTON
Kenney, Annie *1951–1960*

FRANCES BUSHBY
North, Dudley *XLI, XIV*
North, Roger *XLI, XIV*
North, Roger *XLI, XIV*
North, Thomas *XLI, XIV*

RUTH FLORENCE BUTLER
Burrows, Christine Mary Elizabeth
1951–1960

MARY CADOGAN
Lamburn, Richmal Crompton– *1961–1970*

BARBARA CAINE
Mason, Charlotte Maria Shaw *Missing
Persons*

JULIA CAIRNS
Spry, Constance *1951–1960*

EILA MURIEL JOICE CAMPBELL
Taylor, Eva Germaine Rimington
1961–1970

MARIAN LAURA CAMPBELL
Lindsay, John Seymour *1961–1970*

DOROTHY JEFFREYS CANTELUPE
Princess Louise Caroline Alberta
1931–1940

MARY LUCY CARTWRIGHT
Collingwood, Edward Foyle *1961–1970*
Titchmarsh, Edward Charles *1961–1970*

MARYANN FEOLA CASTELUCCI
Bishop, George *Missing Persons*

JUDITH FRANCES CHAMP
Talbot, George *Missing Persons*

HARRIETTE CHICK
Martin, Charles James *1951–1960*

ELLA ROBERTSON CHRISTIE
Haldane, Elizabeth Sanderson *1931–1940*

GLADYS LAURA CLAPPERTON
Yapp, Arthur Keysall *1931–1940*

MARGARET ANNE CLENNETT
Smith, John *Missing Persons*

AGNES MARY CLERKE
Adams, John Couch *1901 I, XXII*
Adrian, Robert *I, I*
Airy, George Biddell *1901 I, XXII*

Anderson, Alexander *I, I*
Anderson, George *I, I*
Anderson, George *I, I*
Anderson, Robert *I, I*
Andrews, Henry *I, I*
Atwood, George *II, I*
Aubert, Alexander *II, I*
Aylesbury, Thomas *II, I*
Babbage, Charles *II, I*
Baily, Francis *II, I*
Ball or Balle, William *III, I*
Barlow, Peter *III, I*
Beaufoy, Mark *IV, II*
Bernard, Edward *IV, II*
Bevis or Bevans, John *IV, II*
Bird, John *V, II*
Birmingham, John *V, II*
Bishop, George *V, II*
Black, Joseph *V, II*
Blair, Robert *V, II*
Bliss, Nathaniel *V, II*
Boyle, Robert *VI, II*
Bradley, James *VI, II*
Breen, James *VI, II*
Brinkley, John *VI, II*
Brisbane, Thomas Makdougall- *VI, II*
Broun, John Allan *VI, II*
Bruhl, John Maurice *VII, III*
Burton, Charles Edward *VIII, III*
Caldecott, John *VIII, III*
Carrington, Richard Christopher *IX, III*
Cary, William *IX, III*
Catton, Thomas *IX, III*
Challis, James *IX, III*
Charnock, Thomas *X, IV*
Chary, Chintamanny Ragoonatha *X, IV*
Chester, Robert *X, IV*
Chillingworth, John *X, IV*
Chillingworth, John *X, IV*
Cockayne, William *XI, IV*
Coddington, Henry *XI, IV*
Coggeshall, Henry *XI, IV*
Collingwood, Roger *XI, IV*
Collins, John *XI, IV*
Cooke, Thomas *XII, IV*
Cooper, Edward Joshua *XII, IV*
Costard, George *XII, IV*
Cotes, Roger *XII, IV*
Cunningham, Timothy *XIII, V*
Dalton, John *XIII, V*
Dawes, William Rutter *XIV, V*

Dick, Thomas *XV, V*
Digges, Leonard *XV, V*
Dollond, George *XV, V*
Dollond, John *XV, V*
Dollond, Peter *XV, V*
Drew, John *XVI, VI*
Dunlop, James *XVI, VI*
Dunthorne, Richard *XVI, VI*
Fallows, Fearon *XVIII, VI*
Ferguson, James *XVIII, VI*
Fisher, George *XIX, VII*
Flamsteed, John *XIX, VII*
Goodricke, John *XXII, VIII*
Grant, James William *XXII, VIII*
Grant, Robert *1901 II, XXII*
Gregory, David *XXIII, VIII*
Gregory, James *XXIII, VIII*
Groombridge, Stephen *XXIII, VIII*
Grubb, Thomas *XXIII, VIII*
Hall, Chester Moor *XXIV, VIII*
Halley, Edmund or Edmond *XXIV, VIII*
Halton, Immanuel *XXIV, VIII*
Harriot, Thomas *XXIV, VIII*
Henderson, Thomas *XXV, IX*
Herschel, Caroline Lucretia *XXVI, IX*
Herschel, John Frederick William *XXVI, IX*
Herschel, William *XXVI, IX*
Hind, John Russell *1901 II, XXII*
Hooke, Robert *XXVII, IX*
Hornsby, Thomas *XXVII, IX*
Horrocks, Jeremiah *XXVII, IX*
Irvine, William *XXIX, X*
Jacob, William Stephen *XXIX, X*
Johnson, Manuel John *XXX, X*
Kirwan, Richard *XXXI, XI*
Lamont, Johann von *XXXII, XI*
Landen, John *XXXII, XI*
Lassell, William *XXXII, XI*
Lawson, Henry *XXXII, XI*
Lax, William *XXXII, XI*
Leadbetter, Charles *XXXII, XI*
Lloyd, William Forster *XXXIII, XI*
Long, Roger *XXXIV, XII*
Lubbock, John William *XXXIV, XII*
Luby, Thomas *XXXIV, XII*
Lynn, George *XXXIV, XII*
Lynn, Thomas *XXXIV, XII*
Machin, John *XXXV, XII*
Maclear, Thomas *XXXV, XII*
Maddy, Watkin *XXXV, XII*

Main, Robert *XXXV, XII*
Main, Thomas John *XXXV, XII*
Mann, William *XXXVI, XII*
Maskelyne, Nevil *XXXVI, XII*
Mason, Charles *XXXVI, XII*
Melvill, Thomas *XXXVII, XIII*
Michell, John *XXXVII, XIII*
Miller, William Allen *XXXVII, XIII*
Mitchell, James *XXXVII, XIII*
Moivre, Abraham de *XXXVIII, XIII*
Molyneux, Samuel *XXXVIII, XIII*
Moore, Jonas *XXXVIII, XIII*
Murray or Moray, Robert *XXXIX, XIII*
Narrien, John *XL, XIV*
Neile, William *XL, XIV*
Newall, Robert Stirling *XL, XIV*
Nichol, John Pringle *XL, XIV*
Parker, George *XLIII, XV*
Parsons, William *XLIII, XV*
Pearson, William *XLIV, XV*
Pell, John *XLIV, XV*
Perry, Stephen Joseph *XLV, XV*
Phelps, Thomas *XLV, XV*
Pigott, Edward *XLV, XV*
Pigott, Nathaniel *XLV, XV*
Pond, John *XLVI, XVI*
Pope, Walter *XLVI, XVI*
Pound, James *XLVI, XVI*
Pritchard, Charles *XLVI, XVI*
Ramsden, Jesse *XLVII, XVI*
Reeve, Henry *XLVII, XVI*
Reeve, Henry *XLVII, XVI*
Sheepshanks, Richard *LII, XVIII*
Short, James *LII, XVIII*
Smith, Henry John Stephen *LIII, XVIII*
Smyth, Charles Piazzi *1901 III, XXII*
South, James *LIII, XVIII*
Stone, Edward James *LIV, XVIII*
Symons, George James *1901 III, XXII*
Taylor, Thomas Glanville *LV, XIX*
Troughton, Edward *LVII, XIX*
Ussher, Henry *LVIII, XX*
Vince, Samuel *LVIII, XX*
Wallis, John *LIX, XX*
Whipple, George Mathews *LXI, XXI*
Wing, Vincent *LXII, XXI*

ELLEN MARY CLERKE
Adelaide *I, I*
Albertazzi, Emma *I, I*
Forrester, Joseph James *XX, VII*

Proctor, Richard Anthony *XLVI, XVI*
Somerville, Mary *LIII, XVIII*
Somerville, William *LIII, XVIII*

JANET MARJORIE CLOSE
Palmer, George Herbert *1922–1930*

MARY COATE
Baring-Gould, Sabine *1922–1930*

MARGARET ISABEL COLE
Horrabin, James Francis *1961–1970*
Middleton, James Smith *1961–1970*
Pease, Edward Reynolds *1951–1960*

EDITH COLERIDGE
Coleridge, Herbert *XI, IV*

JUDITH MARY VAUGHAN COLLINS
Nicholson, Rosa Winifred *Missing Persons*

ALICE MARGARET COOKE
Nicholas of Meaux *XL, XIV*
Nigel *XLI, XIV*
Norman, John *XLI, XIV*
O'Heney, Matthew *XLII, XIV*
Olaf Godfreyson *XLII, XIV*
Olaf Sitricson *XLII, XIV*
Olaf *XLII, XIV*
Peche, Richard *XLIV, XV*
Pecock, Reginald *XLIV, XV*
Penketh, Thomas *XLIV, XV*
Peter *XLV, XV*
Philip of Poitiers *XLV, XV*
Ralph *XLVII, XVI*
Ralph *XLVII, XVI*
Reginald *XLVII, XVI*
Reginald *XLVII, XVI*
Richard *XLVIII, XVI*
Robert *XLVIII, XVI*
Rochfort, Simon *XLIX, XVII*
Sansetun, Benedict of *L, XVII*
Sawtrey, William *L, XVII*
Serlo *LI, XVII*
Simon of Faversham *LII, XVIII*
Stephen *LIV, XVIII*
Thomas *LVI, XIX*
Thrucytel *LVI, XIX*
Thurkill, Thorkill, or Turgesius *LVI, XIX*
Thurkill or Thorkill *LVI, XIX*
Tilney, John *LVI, XIX*

Vinsauf, Geoffrey de *LVIII, XX*
Wakefield, Peter of *LVIII, XX*
Werferth, Werefrid, or Hereferth *LX, XX*
Wiglaf *LXI, XXI*
Wihtgar *LXI, XXI*
Wihtred *LXI, XXI*
Willehad or Wilhead *LXI, XXI*
Willibald *LXII, XXI*
Withman *LXII, XXI*
Wodehouse or Woodhouse, Robert de
   LXII, XXI
Wulfwig or Wulfwy *LXIII, XXI*

LETTICE COOPER
Bentley, Phyllis Eleanor *1971–1980*

PAMELA JOY COOTE
Turrill, William Bertram *1961–1970*

FREDA KUNZLEN CORBET
Hayward, Isaac James *1971–1980*

BEATRICE YVONNE CORMEAU
Starr, George Reginald *1971–1980*

**JOAN MARY BERMINGHAM
COUNIHAN**
Armitage, Ella Sophia *Missing Persons*

CATHERINE JOAN CRAWFORD
Nihell, Elizabeth *Missing Persons*

MARY ROSE STEWART CREESE
Maclean, Ida Smedley *Missing Persons*
Newbigin, Marion Isabel *Missing Persons*
Raisin, Catherine Alice *Missing Persons*
Sargant, Ethel *Missing Persons*
Saunders, Edith Rebecca *Missing Persons*

**CORNELIA AUGUSTA HEWETT
CROSSE**
Knox, Alexander Andrew *XXXI, XI*

EVELINE CRUICKSHANKS
Stuart, Jane *Missing Persons*

WINIFRED CLARA CULLIS
Scharlieb, Mary Ann Dacomb *1922–1930*

INA MARY CUMPSTON
Bustamante, William Alexander *1971–1980*

ANGELA JOAN CUNNINGHAM
Demant, Vigo Auguste *1981–1985*

MYRA CURTIS
Broughton, Rhoda *1912–1921*
Gorst, John Eldon *1912–1921*
Ward, Mary Augusta *1912–1921*
Weston, Agnes Elizabeth *1912–1921*

HOPE DANBY
Backhouse, Edmund Trelawny *1941–1950*

HELEN DARBISHIRE
Penrose, Emily *1941–1950*
Selincourt, Ernest de *1941–1950*

BRENDA DAVIES
Reed, Carol *1971–1980*

HELEN MARY DAVIES
Cadbury, John *Missing Persons*

WINIFRED KATHLEEN DAVIN
Cary, Arthur Joyce Lunel *1951–1960*

MADELEINE ELIZABETH
VINICOMBE DAVIS
Winnicott, Donald Woods *Missing Persons*

MARGARET ELLEN EISENSTEIN
DELACY
Alanson, Edward *Missing Persons*

KAY DICK
Manning, Olivia Mary *1971–1980*
Smith, Florence Margaret *1971–1980*

FRANCES ANNESLEY DONALDSON
Wodehouse, Pelham Grenville *1971–1980*

DOROTHY DRAKE
Methven, Malcolm John *1971–1980*

VALERIE CHRISTINE DRAKE
Trapnel, Anna *Missing Persons*

BLANCHE ELIZABETH CAMPBELL
DUGDALE
Sidgwick, Eleanor Mildred *1931–1940*

JANET DUNBAR
Knight, Harold *1961–1970*

SYBIL FRANCES DAWSON ECCLES
Dawson, Bertrand Edward *1941–1950*

RUTH DUDLEY EDWARDS
Connolly, James *Missing Persons*
Pearse, Patrick Henry *Missing Persons*

JUDY EGERTON
Monnington, Walter Thomas *1971–1980*

DOROTHY MARY ELLIOTT
Wilkinson, Ellen Cicely *1941–1950*

KATHERINE ELLIOTT
Davidson, Frances Joan *1981–1985*
Horsbrugh, Florence Gertrude *1961–1970*

MARIANNE ELLIOTT
Simms, Robert *Missing Persons*
Simms, William *Missing Persons*

DOROTHY MARY EMMET
Stocks, John Leofric *1931–1940*

MARY PHYLLIS ENGLISH
Cooke, Mordecai Cubitt *Missing Persons*

DOROTHY EVERETT
Chambers, Raymond Wilson *1941–1950*

NAOMI IRENE EVETTS
Steers, Thomas *Missing Persons*

LUCY FAITHFULL
Younghusband, Eileen Louise *1981–1985*

FRANCES MARGARET FARRER
Watt, Margaret Rose *1941–1950*

JEAN DOROTHY YOUNG
FARRUGIA
Witherings, Thomas *Missing Persons*

CHRISTINE YVONNE FERDINAND
Herringman, Henry *Missing Persons*

PATTY BEATRICE FISHER
Mottram, Vernon Henry *1971–1980*

JOYCE PEASE FITCH
Fitch, Thomas *Missing Persons*

SHEILA MARGARET FLETCHER
Bryant, Sophie *Missing Persons*

SIBYLLA JANE PICKERING
FLOWER
Auldjo, John *Missing Persons*

MARGOT FONTEYN
Blair, David *1971–1980*
Lopokova, Lydia Vasilievna *1981–1985*
Pavlova, Anna *Missing Persons*

HAZEL MARY FOX
Williams, Ivy *1961–1970*

CHRISTINA AGNES LILIAN FOYLE
Mackenzie, Edward Montague Compton
1971–1980
Foyle, William Alfred *1961–1970*

ENRIQUETA EVA FRANKFORT
Bing, Gertrud *1961–1970*

JANET ING FREEMAN
Harris, John *Missing Persons*

KATHRYN FULLER
Boyle, Constance Antonina *Missing
Persons*

MOLINA FULLMAN
Jowitt, William Allen *1951–1960*

DOROTHY GALTON
Pares, Bernard *1941–1950*

HELEN LOUISE GARDNER
Simpson, Percy *1961–1970*

ALICE GARNETT
Fleure, Herbert John *1961–1970*

FREDA GAYE
Leigh, Vivien *1961–1970*
Parker, John *1951–1960*

VIOLA GERARD GARVIN
Wolfe, Humbert *1931–1940*

MARGARET TEMPLETON GIBSON
Achard of St Victor *Missing Persons*
Andrew of St Victor *Missing Persons*

ANNE GILCHRIST
Betham, Mary Matilda *IV, II*
Blake, William *V, II*

HELEN SHIELS GILLESPIE
McCarthy, Emma Maud *1941–1950*

PHILIPPA JANE GLANVILLE
De Lamerie, Paul Jacques *Missing Persons*

MARY CECILIA GLASGOW
Wilson, James Steuart *1961–1970*

VICTORIA GLENDINNING
Bowen, Elizabeth Dorothea Cole
1971–1980

EVELINE CHARLOTTE GODLEY
Godley, Alfred Dennis *1922–1930*
Godley, John Arthur *1931–1940*

GRACE WYNDHAM GOLDIE
Armstrong, William *1951–1960*
Somerville, Mary *1961–1970*

ISABELLA GORDON
Calman, William Thomas *1951–1960*

JANET ANNE GOUGH
Buss, Frances Mary *Missing Persons*

PENELOPE MARY GOUK
Mercator, Nicolaus *Missing Persons*

MARGARET MARY GOWING
Darwin, Charles Galton *1961–1970*
Hinton, Christopher *1981–1985*

VIRGINIA GRAHAM
Grenfell, Joyce Irene *1971–1980*

MARGARET MACKESON GREEN
Ward, Ida Caroline *1941–1950*

JOYCE IRENE GRENFELL
Potter, Stephen Meredith *1961–1970*

JANE ELIZABETH GRENIER
Black, Clementina Maria *Missing Persons*
Courtney, Kathleen D'Olier *Missing Persons*
Sharp, Evelyn *Missing Persons*
Twining, Louisa *Missing Persons*

BERYL GREY
Dolin, Anton *1981–1985*

LYNDA GRIER
Hadow, Grace Eleanor *1931–1940*
Sadler, Michael Ernest *1941–1950*

ELLINOR FLORA BOSWORTH GROGAN
Bourchier, James David *1912–1921*

ISOBEL MARY GRUNDY
Collier, Jane *Missing Persons*
Hawkins, Laetitia-Matilda *Missing Persons*
Heyrick, Elizabeth *Missing Persons*
Radcliffe, Mary Ann *Missing Persons*
Ripley, Dorothy *Missing Persons*
Watts, Susanna *Missing Persons*

BARBARA ELIZABETH GWYER
Rogers, Annie Mary Anne Henley *1931–1940*

BRIDGET CHARLOTTE HADAWAY
Hammerton, John Alexander *Missing Persons*

ELIZABETH SANDERSON HALDANE
Bain, Alexander *1901–1911 I*
Haldane, Richard Burton *1922–1930*
Ritchie, David George *1901–1911 III*
Stirling, James Hutchison *1901–1911 III*

MARY AGNES HAMILTON
Bondfield, Margaret Grace *1951–1960*
Henderson, Arthur *1931–1940*
Lansbury, George *1931–1940*
Smillie, Robert *1931–1940*
Webb, Sidney James *1941–1950*

JENIFER MARGARET HART
Corbett Ashby, Margery Irene *1981–1985*

JOAN HASLER
Morice, James *Missing Persons*

RAGNHILD MARIE HATTON
Sophia Dorothea *Missing Persons*

JACQUETTA HAWKES
Garrod, Dorothy Anne Elizabeth *Missing Persons*
Turner, Walter James Redfern *1941–1950*

BETTY KATHLEEN HANCE
Round, Henry Joseph *1961–1970*

JUDITH VICTORIA HAWLEY
Smith, Elizabeth *Missing Persons*

JACQUETTA HAWKES
Wheeler, Robert Eric Mortimer *1971–1980*

AGNES YELLAND DALRYMPLE-HAY
Hay, Harley Hugh Dalrymple- *1931–1940*

MARY THALASSA ALFORD CRUSO HENCKEN
Randall-MacIver, David *1941--1950*

JOAN CATHERINE HENDERSON
Godolphin, Francis *Missing Persons*

MARY ISOBEL HENDERSON
Murray, George Gilbert Aimé *1951–1960*

ANN CHRISTINE HESS
Shaw, Hester *Missing Persons*

BRIDGET IRENE HILL
Blaugdone, Barbara *Missing Persons*
Drake, Judith *Missing Persons*

FLORENCE MARY HILL
Sumner, Mary Elizabeth *Missing Persons*

ROSEMARY HILL
Dresser, Christopher *Missing Persons*

NINA LOUISA HILLS
Robson, William Snowdon *1912–1921*

PAMELA HINKSON
Harrel, David *1931–1940*

SHEILA HODGES
Cronin, Archibald Joseph *1981–1985*

MARGARET CAMERON HOGARTH
Campbell, James Macnabb *1951–1960*

DOROTHY FRANCES
HOLLINGSWORTH
Wright, Norman Charles *1961–1970*

CLARA JOYCE ELIZMAR HOLLINS
McCormick, William Symington
1931–1940

THEA HOLME
Thirkell, Angela Margaret *1961–1970*

EDITH S. HOOPER
Butler, Josephine Elizabeth *1901–1911 I*
Huntington, George *1901–1911 II*
Podmore, Frank *1901–1911 III*
Prynne, George Rundle *1901–1911 III*
Skipsey, Joseph *1901–1911 III*

ROSEMARY ELIZABETH HORROX
Brampton, Edward *Missing Persons*

DOROTHEA HOSIE
Jordan, John Newell *1922–1930*

BRENDA LILIAN HOUGH
Crockford, John *Missing Persons*

JANET HILARY HOWARTH
Johnson, Bertha Jane *Missing Persons*

LESLIE KATHLEEN HOWSAM
Orme, Eliza *Missing Persons*

ANNE MARY HUDSON
Swinderby, William *Missing Persons*

ANN LAURA HUGHES
Thornton, Alice *Missing Persons*

JENNETT HUMPHREYS
Acton, Eliza *I, I*
Acton, Henry *I, I*

Amelia *I, I*
Amner, Richard *I, I*
Armstrong, Thomas *II, I*
Ashdowne, William *II, I*
Aspland, Robert *II, I*
Aspland, Robert Brook *II, I*
Augusta, Sophia *II, I*
Bakewell, Robert *III, I*
Bakewell, Robert *III, I*
Bales, Peter *III, I*
Balfour, Clara Lucas *III, I*
Barber, Mary *III, I*
Belsham, Thomas *IV, II*
Benger, Elizabeth Ogilvy *IV, II*
Bennet, Thomas *IV, II*
Bennet, Agnes Maria *IV, II*
Berkeley, Eliza *IV, II*
Bicknell, Elhanan *V, II*
Biffin or Beffin, Sarah *V, II*
Billingsley, Martin *V, II*
Bland, John *V, II*
Blount, Martha *V, II*
Bonhote, Elizabeth *V, II*
Booth, Benjamin *V, II*
Booth, Peniston *V, II*
Boothroyd, Benjamin *V, II*
Boucher, John *VI, II*
Boucher, John *VI, II*
Bouchier, Barton *VI, II*
Bovey or Boevey, Catharina *VI, II*
Bowen, James *VI, II*
Bowen, John *VI, II*
Bowtell, John *VI, II*
Boyd, Mark *VI, II*
Boys, William *VI, II*
Brackenbury, Joseph *VI, II*
Bradshaw, James *VI, II*
Bradstreet, Anne *VI, II*
Brewer, George *VI, II*
Bright, Mynors *VI, II*
Brock, William John *VI, II*
Brook, Charles *VI, II*
Brooke, Elizabeth *VI, II*
Brooke, Frances *VI, II*
Brougham, Henry *VI, II*
Browne, Lyde *VII, III*
Bryan, Margaret *VII, III*
Bulkeley, Sophia *VII, III*
Bullokar, John *VII, III*
Bullokar, William *VII, III*
Burges, Mary Anne *VII, III*

Burnet, Elizabeth *VII, III*
Burney, Sarah Harriet *VII, III*
Burrell, Sophia *VII, III*
Bury, Elizabeth *VIII, III*
Byrne, Anne Frances *VIII, III*
Byrne, Letitia *VIII, III*
Campbell, Archibald *VIII, III*
Campbell, Harriette *VIII, III*
Candler, Ann *VIII, III*
Caraccioli, Charles *IX, III*
Carey, George Saville *IX, III*
Carleton, Mary *IX, III*
Carlile or Carlisle, Anne *IX, III*
Carmichael, James *IX, III*
Carrick, John Donald *IX, III*
Cartwright, Frances Dorothy *IX, III*
Carwardine, Penelope *IX, III*
Catley, Ann *IX, III*
Cawthorn, James *IX, III*
Chaigneau, William *IX, III*
Chamberlain, Robert *X, IV*
Chandler, Johanna *X, IV*
Chandler, Mary *X, IV*
Chapman, John *X, IV*
Chapone, Hester *X, IV*
Cheyne, Jane *X, IV*
Cholmondeley, Mary *X, IV*
Chudleigh, Mary *X, IV*
Clement or Clements, Margaret *XI, IV*
Clerke, Gilbert *XI, IV*
Cobbold, Elizabeth *XI, IV*
Cokayne, Thomas *XI, IV*
Cokayne, Thomas *XI, IV*
Dick, Anne *XV, V*
Dickson, Elizabeth *XV, V*
Digby, Lettice *XV, V*
Dod, Henry *XV, V*
Dorset, Catherine Ann *XV, V*
Du Bois, Dorothea *XVI, VI*
Duncombe, Susanna *XVI, VI*
Elizabeth *XVII, VI*
Elphinstone, Hester Maria *XVII, VI*
Elphinstone, Margaret Mercer *XVII, VI*
Entick, John *XVII, VI*
Estlin, John Prior *XVIII, VI*

ALICE MARY HUMPHRY
Humphry, William Gilson *XXVIII, X*

JOAN MERVYN HUSSEY
Baynes, Norman Hepburn *1961–1970*

LORNA MARGARET HUTSON
Lanier, Emilia *Missing Persons*

ELSPETH JOSCELINE HUXLEY
Cholmondeley, Hugh *1931–1940*

ELIZABETH INGALL
Bathurst, Henry *III, I*
Beard, John Relly *IV, II*

JOANNA MARY INNES
Byng, John *Missing Persons*

MARIE JAHODA
Freud, Anna *1981–1985*

EVELYN MARY JAMISON
Lodge, Eleanor Constance *1931–1940*
Wordsworth, Elizabeth *1931–1940*

SYLVIA JEWKES
Clay, Henry *1951–1960*

KATHARINE JEX-BLAKE
Jex-Blake, Sophia Louisa *1912–1921*

ANGELA VAUGHAN JOHN
Robins, Elizabeth *Missing Persons*

FANNY CECELIA JOHNSON
Anderson, Elizabeth *1912–1921*

HILDA JOHNSTONE
Edwards, Matilda Barbara Betham-
  1912–1921

CATHERINE RACHEL JONES
Jones, Charlotte *XXX, X*

HARRIET CLARE JORDAN
Mawson, Thomas Hayton *Missing Persons*

AVERILL ALISON KELLY
Coade, Eleanor *Missing Persons*

EVELYN MANSFIELD KING
Silkin, Lewis *1971–1980*

DOROTHY MARY KOSINSKI
Cooper, Arthur William Douglas
  1981–1985

LEONIE JUDITH KRAMER
Richardson, Ethel Florence Lindesay
1941–1950

MARGARET LANE
Potter, Helen Beatrix *1941–1950*

CECILY ALICE LANGDALE
John, Gwendolen Mary *Missing Persons*

ELIZABETH ANNE LAURENCE
Bachilor, John *Missing Persons*
Hobson, Paul *Missing Persons*
Simmonds, Martha *Missing Persons*

DEBORAH MARGARET LAVIN
Macmillan, William Miller *Missing
Persons*

AMICE LEE
Macdonell, Philip James *1931–1940*

ELIZABETH LEE
Banks, Isabella *1901 I, XXII*
Bayly, Ada Ellen *1901–1911 I*
Beale, Dorothea *1901–1911 I*
Bloomfield, Georgiana *1901–1911 I*
Bray, Caroline *1901–1911 I*
Busk, Rachel Harriette *1901–1911 I*
Byrne, Julia Clara *1901 I, XXII*
Carey, Rosa Nouchette *1901–1911 I*
Charles, Elizabeth *1901 I, XXII*
Clough, Anne Jemima *1901 II, XXII*
Corner, Julia *1901 II, XXII*
Cornwell, James *1901–1911 I*
Craven, Pauline Marie Armande Aglae
1901 II, XXII
Currie, Mary Montgomerie *1901–1911 I*
De la Ramée, Marie Louise *1901–1911 I*
De Vere, Aubrey Thomas *1901–1911 I*
De Vere, Stephen Edward *1901–1911 I*
Gerard, Jane Emily *1901–1911 II*
Grey, Maria Georgina *1901–1911 II*
Hardy, Mary Anne *1901 II, XXII*
Hawker, Mary Elizabeth *1901–1911 II*
Hector, Annie French *1901–1911 II*
Hoey, Frances Sarah *1901–1911 II*
Hungerford, Margaret Wolfe *1901 III,
XXII*
Ingelow, Jean *1901 III, XXII*
Jackson, Catherine Hannah Charlotte

1901 III, XXII
Leapor, Mary *XXXII, XI*
Lee, Harriet *XXXII, XI*
Lee, Sophia *XXXII, XI*
Lee-Hamilton, Eugene Jacob *1901–1911 II*
Le Noir, Elizabeth Anne *XXXIII, XI*
Lewis, Maria Theresa *XXXIII, XI*
Mackarness, Matilda Anne *XXXV, XII*
Maitland, Agnes Catherine *1901–1911 II*
Marcet, Jane *XXXVI, XII*
Marryat, Florence *1901 III, XXII*
Marsh-Caldwell, Anne *XXXVI, XII*
Marshall, Emma *1901 III, XXII*
Marshall or Marishall, Jane *XXXVI, XII*
Martin, Mary Letitia *XXXVI, XII*
Meeke, Mary *XXXVII, XIII*
Merivale, Herman Charles *1901–1911 II*
Miller, Anna *XXXVII, XIII*
Mitford, Mary Russell *XXXVIII, XIII*
Monckton, Mary *XXXVIII, XIII*
Murray, David Christie *1901–1911 II*
Norton, Frances *XLI, XIV*
Ogle, George *XLII, XIV*
Opie, Amelia *XLII, XIV*
Orr, Alexandra Sutherland *1901–1911 III*
Palmer, Alicia Tindal *XLIII, XV*
Palmer, Charlotte *XLIII, XV*
Palmer, Mary *XLIII, XV*
Pardoe, Julia *XLIII, XV*
Parker, Emma *XLIII, XV*
Parr, Louisa *1901–1911 III*
Parsons, Eliza *XLIII, XV*
Penrose, Elizabeth *XLIV, XV*
Pickering, Ellen *XLV, XV*
Plumptre, Anna or Anne *XLV, XV*
Ponsonby, Emily Charlotte Mary *XLVI,
XVI*
Porter, Anna Maria *XLVI, XVI*
Porter, Jane *XLVI, XVI*
Power, Marguerite A. *XLVI, XVI*
Procter, Adelaide Anne *XLVI, XVI*
Reeve, Clara *XLVII, XVI*
Richardson, Charlotte Caroline *XLVIII,
XVI*
Riddell, Charlotte Eliza *1901–1911 III*
Robinson, Martha Walker *XLIX, XVII*
Romer, Isabella Frances *XLIX, XVII*
Rowson, Susanna *XLIX, XVII*
Rundall, Mary Ann *XLIX, XVII*
Rundell, Maria Eliza *XLIX, XVII*
Ryves, Elizabeth *L, XVII*

Sale-Barker, Lucy Elizabeth Drummond
Davies *L, XVII*
Schimmelpenninck, Mary Anne *L, XVII*
Seward, Anna *LI, XVII*
Sewell, Elizabeth Missing *1901–1911 III*
Sewell, Mary *LI, XVII*
Shaw, Thomas Budge *LI, XVII*
Sheppard, Elizabeth Sara *LII, XVIII*
Sherwood, Mary Martha *LII, XVIII*
Shirreff, Emily Anne Eliza *LII, XVIII*
Skene, Felicia Mary Frances *1901 III,
XXII*
Smith, Charlotte *LIII, XVIII*
Smith, Lucy Toulmin *1901–1911 III*
Smith, Sarah *1901–1911 III*
Spence, Elizabeth Isabella *LIII, XVIII*
Stannard, Henrietta Eliza Vaughan
1901–1911 III
Stepney, Catherine *LIV, XVIII*
Strickland, Agnes *LV, XIX*
Stuart-Wortley, Emmeline Charlotte
Elizabeth *LV, XIX*
Sturgis, Julian Russell *1901–1911 III*
Swanwick, Anna *1901 III, XXII*
Talbot, Catherine *LV, XIX*
Taylor, Helen *1901–1911 III*
Tighe, Mary *LVI, XIX*
Trimmer, Sarah *LVII, XIX*
Tucker, Charlotte Maria *LVII, XIX*
Veley, Margaret *LVIII, XX*
Waldie, Charlotte Ann *LVIII, XX*
Webster, Augusta *LX, XX*
West, Jane *LX, XX*
Weston, Elizabeth Jane *LX, XX*
Wilson, Caroline *LXII, XXI*
Wilson, Mrs Cornwell Baron *LXII, XXI*
Winkworth, Catherine *LXII, XXI*
Woodroffe, Anne *LXII, XXI*
Worboise, Emma Jane *LXII, XXI*
Yearsley, Ann *LXIII, XXI*

JENNIE LEE
Levy, Benn Wolfe *1971–1980*

DAPHNE MAIR MITCHELL LENNIE
Brittain, Vera Mary *1971–1980*
Browne, John Francis Archibald
1971–1980

ANITA LESLIE
Leslie, John Randolph *1971–1980*
Sheridan, Clare Consuelo *1961–1970*

DAVINA GIFFORD LEWIS
Gore-Booth, Eva Selina *Missing Persons*

GILLIAN PHYLLIS LINDSAY
Thompson, Flora Jane *Missing Persons*

VALERIE LLOYD
Fenton, Roger *Missing Persons*

SUSAN JENNIFER LOACH
Cawarden, Thomas *Missing Persons*
Throckmorton, George *Missing Persons*

ELIZABETH PAKENHAM
LONGFORD
Arbuthnot, Harriet *Missing Persons*
Brown, John *Missing Persons*
Conroy, John Ponsonby *Missing Persons*
Stockmar, Christian Friedrich *Missing
Persons*
Woodham-Smith, Cecil Blanche
1971–1980

RACHAEL LOW
Jennings, Frank Humphrey Sinkler
Missing Persons
Rotha, Paul *1981–1985*

SYLVIA LYND
Hinkson, Katharine *1931–1940*

MARGARET MACARTHUR
Beaton or Bethune, David *IV, II*
Beaton or Bethune, James *IV, II*
Beaton or Bethune, James *IV, II*
Callow, John *VIII, III*

SARAH FRANCES MCCABE
Henriques, Basil Lucas Quixano
1961–1970
Silverman, Samuel Sydney *1961–1970*

FIONA MACCARTHY
Gimson, Ernest William *Missing Persons*
Gray, Kathleen Eileen Moray *1971–1980*

ANITA MCCONNELL
Bate, Robert Brettell *Missing Persons*
Six, James *Missing Persons*

MARGARET BERNADETTE
MACCURTAIN
Gore-Booth, Constance *Missing Persons*

Goldwin or Golding, John *XXII, VIII*
Goodgroome, John *XXII, VIII*
Goodson, Richard *XXII, VIII*
Gordon, John *XXII, VIII*
Graddon, Miss *XXII, VIII*
Greatorex, Ralph *XXIII, VIII*
Greatorex, Thomas *XXIII, VIII*
Greaves, Thomas *XXIII, VIII*
Green, James *XXIII, VIII*
Green, Samuel *XXIII, VIII*
Greeting, Thomas *XXIII, VIII*
Gregory, William *XXIII, VIII*
Griffin, Thomas *XXIII, VIII*
Guest, George *XXIII, VIII*
Gunn, Barnabas *XXIII, VIII*
Gunn, John *XXIII, VIII*
Gutteridge, William *XXIII, VIII*
Haigh, Thomas *XXIII, VIII*
Haite, John James *XXIV, VIII*
Hall, Henry *XXIV, VIII*
Hall, Henry *XXIV, VIII*
Hamilton, James Alexander *XXIV, VIII*
Harper, Thomas *XXIV, VIII*
Harris, Joseph *XXV, IX*
Harris, Joseph Macdonald *XXV, IX*
Harris, Renatus or Réné *XXV, IX*
Harrison, Samuel *XXV, IX*
Hart, Charles *XXV, IX*
Hart, Joseph Binns *XXV, IX*
Hart, Philip *XXV, IX*
Harvey, Edmund George *XXV, IX*
Hasse, Christian Frederick *XXV, IX*
Hawkins, James *XXV, IX*
Hayden, George *XXV, IX*
Heather or Heyther, William *XXV, IX*
Henstridge, Daniel *XXVI, IX*
Heseltine, James *XXVI, IX*
Hindle, John *XXVI, IX*
Hine, William *XXVII, IX*
Hingston, John *XXVII, IX*
Hodges, Edward *XXVII, IX*
Holborne, Anthony *XXVII, IX*
Holmes, Alfred *XXVII, IX*
Holmes, Edward *XXVII, IX*
Holmes, George *XXVII, IX*
Holmes, John *XXVII, IX*
Hook, James *XXVII, IX*
Hooper, Edmund *XXVII, IX*
Horn, Charles Edward *XXVII, IX*
Howard, Samuel *XXVIII, X*
Humphries, John *XXVIII, X*

Hunt, Arabella *XXVIII, X*
Husk, William Henry *XXVIII, X*
Hutcheson, Francis *XXVIII, X*
Incledon, Charles *XXVIII, X*
Ive, Simon *XXIX, X*
Jackson, Arthur Herbert *XXIX, X*
Jackson, John *XXIX, X*
Jackson, William *XXIX, X*
Jacob, Benjamin *XXIX, X*
Janiewicz, Felix *XXIX, X*
Jarvis, Samuel *XXIX, X*
Jay, John George Henry *XXIX, X*
Jeffreys, George *XXIX, X*
Jewett, Randolph or Randal *XXIX, X*
Johnson, Edward *XXX, X*
Johnson, Robert *XXX, X*
Johnstone, John Henry *XXX, X*
Jones, John *XXX, X*
Julien or Jullien, Louis Antoine *XXX, X*
Kearns, William Henry *XXX, X*
Keeble, John *XXX, X*
Keith, Robert William *XXX, X*
Keller, Gottfried or Godfrey *XXX, X*
Kellner, Ernest Augustus *XXX, X*
Kelly, Michael *XXX, X*
Kelway, Joseph *XXX, X*
Kelway, Thomas *XXX, X*
Kemble, Adelaide *XXX, X*
Kemp, Joseph *XXX, X*
Kennedy, or Farrell, Mrs *XXX, X*
Lenton, John *XXXIII, XI*
Leveridge, Richard *XXXIII, XI*
Light, Edward *XXXIII, XI*
Lingard, Frederick *XXXIII, XI*
Linley, Francis *XXXIII, XI*
Linley, George *XXXIII, XI*
Linley, Mary *XXXIII, XI*
Linley, William *XXXIII, XI*
Loder, George *XXXIV, XII*
Loder, John David *XXXIV, XII*
Loosemore, Henry *XXXIV, XII*
Loosemore, John *XXXIV, XII*
Lowe, Thomas *XXXIV, XII*
Lumley, Benjamin *XXXIV, XII*
Marsh, Alphonso *XXXVI, XII*
Marsh, Alphonso *XXXVI, XII*
Martin, Jonathan *XXXVI, XII*
Maynard, John *XXXVII, XIII*
Mazzinghi, Joseph *XXXVII, XIII*
Mitchell, John *XXXVIII, XIII*
Moorehead, John *XXXVIII, XIII*

MAUREEN SUSAN MILLAR
Leitch, Charlotte Cecilia Pitcairn *1971–1980*

HYLTON JUDITH MILLEDGE
Lonsdale, Kathleen *1971–1980*

HELEN MILLER
Garrard, William *Missing Persons*
Stumpe, William *Missing Persons*

VIOLET GEORGINA MILNER
Maxse, Leopold James *1931–1940*

ALIDA MONRO
Mew, Charlotte Mary *1922–1930*

ELIZABETH MONROE
Bullard, Reader William *1971–1980*
Kirkbride, Alec Seath *1971–1980*
Loraine, Percy Lyham *1961–1970*
MacMichael, Harold Alfred *1961–1970*

DORIS LANGLEY MOORE
Laver, James *1971–1980*

LOUISE MORGAN
Ellerman, John Reeves *1931–1940*

MARY DIANA MORGAN
Braithwaite, Florence Lilian *1941–1950*

MAY MORRIS
De Morgan, William Frend *1912–1921*
Webb, Philip Speakman *1912–1921*

MISS S. MORRISON
Moore, Arthur William *1901–1911 II*

MARGARET FRANCES MULVUHILL
Despard, Charlotte *Missing Persons*

MARY MUNRO
Lenox-Conyngham, Gerald Ponsonby
1951–1960

ROSA HARRIET NEWMARCH
Elvey, George Job *1901 II, XXII*
Pierson, Henry Hugo *XLV, XV*
Quarles, Charles *XLVII, XVI*
Smith, John *LIII, XVIII*
Smith, John Christopher *LIII, XVIII*
Smith, John Stafford *LIII, XVIII*
Travers, John *LVII, XIX*

ANN KATHARINE NEWMARK
Messel, Rudolph *Missing Persons*
Muspratt, Max *Missing Persons*
Phillips, Peregrine *Missing Persons*
Shanks, James *Missing Persons*

CHRISTINE STEPHANIE NICHOLLS
Boot, Henry Albert Howard *1981–1985*
Clayton, Philip Thomas Byard *1971–1980*
Martin, William Keble *1961–1970*
Nelson, George Horatio *1961–1970*
Tovey, John Cronyn *1971–1980*

MARJORIE NICHOLSON
Citrine, Walter McLennan *1981–1985*

KATE NORGATE
Geoffrey *XXI, VII*
Grim, Edward *XXIII, VIII*
Gundrada de Warenne *XXIII, VIII*

Guthlac, Saint *XXIII, VIII*
Guthrum or Guthorm *XXIII, VIII*
Henry II *XXVI, IX*
Henry of Scotland *XXVI, IX*
Henry *XXVI, IX*
Henry, Saint *XXVI, IX*
Herbert of Bosham *XXVI, IX*
Hubert, Walter *XXIX, X*
Isabella *XXIX, X*
Joan, Joanna, Jone, or Jane *XXIX, X*
Joan, Joanna, Anna, or Janet *XXIX, X*
Joan or Joanna *XXIX, X*
Langton, Simon *XXXII, XI*
Langton, Stephen *XXXII, XI*
Longchamp, William of *XXXIV, XII*
Matilda, Maud, Mahalde, Mold *XXXVII, XIII*
Matilda of Boulogne *XXXVII, XIII*
Matilda, Maud, Mold, Æthelic, Aaliz *XXXVII, XIII*
Matilda *XXXVII, XIII*
Montfort, Almeric of *XXXVIII, XIII*
Montfort, Eleanor of *XXXVIII, XIII*
Montfort, Guy of *XXXVIII, XIII*
Montfort, Henry of *XXXVIII, XIII*
Montfort, Simon of *XXXVIII, XIII*
Montfort, Simon of *XXXVIII, XIII*
Richard of Ilchester *XLVIII, XVI*
Ridel, Geoffrey *XLVIII, XVI*
Robert *XLVIII, XVI*
Roger *XLIX, XVII*
Samson *L, XVII*
Stephen *LIV, XVIII*
Thomas à Becket *LVI, XIX*
Tracy, William de *LVII, XIX*
Wace *LVIII, XX*
William II *LXI, XXI*
William *LXI, XXI*
William *LXI, XXI*
William of Malmesbury *LXI, XXI*
William of Ypres *LXI, XXI*
William of Newburgh *LXI, XXI*

KATHLEEN MARY NORMAN
Jarvis, John Layton *1961–1970*

JANE ELIZABETH NORTON
Lawrence, Arabella Susan *1941–1950*

PAMELA GERRISH NUNN
Stillman, Marie *Missing Persons*

SHEILA MARY O'CONNELL
Larkin, William *Missing Persons*

MARGARET ROSEMARY O'DAY
Thoroughgood, John *Missing Persons*

HILARY SETON OFFLER
William of Ste Barbe *Missing Persons*

ANN SYBIL OLDFIELD
Howard, Louise Ernestine *Missing Persons*
Pye, Edith Mary *Missing Persons*
Reid, Elisabeth Jesser *Missing Persons*
Sanger, Sophy *Missing Persons*

MARY O'NEILL
O'Brien, Kate *1971–1980*

IONA OPIE
Fyleman, Rose Amy *1951–1960*

ELIZA ORME
Hunter, William Alexander *1901 III, XXII*
Plimsoll, Samuel *1901 III, XXII*
Potter, Thomas Bayley *1901 III, XXII*

LOUISE ORR
Toynbee, Arnold Joseph *1971–1980*

CHRISTABEL OSBORNE
Masham, Damaris *XXXVI, XII*
Miller, James *XXXVII, XIII*
Mortimer, Thomas *XXXIX, XIII*
Musgrave, Christopher *XXXIX, XIII*

ANNETTE JOCELYN OTWAY-
RUTHVEN
Phillips, Walter Alison *1941–1950*

GRACE HARTLEY PAGET
Paget, Muriel Evelyn Vernon *1931–1940*

ELAINE MARGARET PAINTIN
Barnard, Frederick Augusta *Missing Persons*

CLAIRE DOROTHEA TAYLOR
PALLEY
Beadle, Thomas Hugh William *1971–1980*
Tredgold, Robert Clarkson *1971–1980*

EDITH PALLISER
Inglis, Elsie Maud *1912–1921*

HELEN MAUD PALMER
Bevan, Aneurin *1951–1960*
Blogg, Henry George *1951–1960*
Boothman, John Nelson *1951–1960*
Dampier, William Cecil *1951–1960*
George VI *1951–1960*
Glyn, Elinor *1941–1950*
Hardinge, Alexander Henry Louis
1951–1960
Hirst, Hugo *1941–1950*
Hopwood, Francis John Stephens
1941–1950
Livingstone, Richard Winn *1951–1960*
Stanley, Arthur
Tagore, Rabindranath *1941–1950*
Turing, Alan Mathison *1951–1960*
Wood, Howard Kingsley *1941–1950*

KATHARINE FERRIDAY PANTZER
Berthelet, Thomas *Missing Persons*

CONSTANCE ANNE PARKER
Shepard, Ernest Howard *1971–1980*

SUSAN MARY PARKES
Keenan, Patrick Joseph *Missing Persons*

FRANCES CATHERINE PARTRIDGE
Carrington, Dora de Houghton *Missing Persons*

LINDA LOU ALBERTA PARRY
Morris, Mary *Missing Persons*

FRANCIS CATHERINE PARTRIDGE
Garnett, David *1981–1985*

VALERIE LOUISE PEARL
Thomson, Maurice *Missing Persons*
Whitaker, Lawrence *Missing Persons*

MARGARET HANSEN PELLING
Baker, Robert *Missing Persons*
Lewis, Timothy Richards *Missing Persons*
Pemell, Robert *Missing Persons*

DORLANDA HANNAH PEMBER
Gleitze, Mercedes *Missing Persons*

LILLIAN MARY PICKFORD
Verney, Ernest Basil *1961–1970*

MARY MYFANWY PIPER
Nash, Paul *1941–1950*

ELIZABETH POLLITT
Fields, Gracie *1971–1980*

RACHAEL EMILY POOLE
Riviere, Briton *1912–1921*

BERTHA PORTER
Fothergill, Jessie *1901 II, XXII*
Goldicutt, John *XXII, VIII*
Goodwin, Francis *XXII, VIII*
Gough, Alexander Dick *XXII, VIII*
Graham, James Gillespie *XXII, VIII*
Griffith, William Pettit *XXIII, VIII*
Gwilt, George *XXIII, VIII*
Gwynn, Gwyn, or Gwynne, John *XXIII, VIII*
Halfpenny, Joseph *XXIV, VIII*
Halfpenny, William *XXIV, VIII*
Hamilton, Thomas *XXIV, VIII*
Hanmer, John *XXIV, VIII*
Hanmer, Jonathan *XXIV, VIII*
Hardcastle, Thomas *XXIV, VIII*
Hardwick, Philip *XXIV, VIII*
Hardwick, Thomas *XXIV, VIII*
Hardy, Nathaniel *XXIV, VIII*
Hawksmoor, Nicholas *XXV, IX*
Henderson, John *XXV, IX*
Holland, Henry *XXVII, IX*
Hosking, William *XXVII, IX*
Ivory, Thomas *XXIX, X*
Ivory, Thomas *XXIX, X*
James, John *XXIX, X*
Johnston, David *XXX, X*
Keith, George Skene *XXX, X*
Kennedy, John *XXX, X*
King, Robert *XXXI, XI*
Kingsnorth, Richard *XXXI, XI*
Lacy, William *XXXI, XI*
Langley, Batty *XXXII, XI*
Laurence, Roger *XXXII, XI*
Lawrence or Laurence, Edward *XXXII, XI*
Lawrence, George *XXXII, XI*
Lee, Francis *XXXII, XI*
Lee, Samuel *XXXII, XI*
Leoni, Giacomo *XXXIII, XI*

Leverton, Thomas *XXXIII, XI*
Lingard or Lyngard, Richard *XXXIII, XI*
Long, Thomas *XXXIV, XII*
Love, Nicholas *XXXIV, XII*
Lushington, Thomas *XXXIV, XII*
Lye, Lee, or Leigh, Thomas *XXXIV, XII*
Mandevil, Robert *XXXVI, XII*
Mapletoft, John *XXXVI, XII*
Marshall, Thomas *XXXVI, XII*
Mason, Charles *XXXVI, XII*
Mason, Francis *XXXVI, XII*
Mason, John *XXXVI, XII*
Mason, Thomas *XXXVI, XII*
Master, William *XXXVII, XIII*
Mayer, John *XXXVII, XIII*
Mayne, Zachary *XXXVII, XIII*
Melbancke, Brian *XXXVII, XIII*
Meriton or Meryton, George *XXXVII, XIII*
Meriton or Merriton, George *XXXVII, XIII*
Meriton, John *XXXVII, XIII*
Merriot, Thomas *XXXVII, XIII*
Miege, Guy *XXXVII, XIII*
Mill, John *XXXVII, XIII*
Miller, John *XXXVII, XIII*
Milward, Richard *XXXVIII, XIII*
Mitchell or Mitchel, James *XXXVIII, XIII*
Mitchell, Robert *XXXVIII, XIII*
Mocket, Moket, or Moquet, Richard *XXXVIII, XIII*
Molloy, Charles *XXXVIII, XIII*
Monson, John *XXXVIII, XIII*
Montagu, Edward *XXXVIII, XIII*
Montagu, Edward *XXXVIII, XIII*
Monteage, Stephen *XXXVIII, XIII*
Moore, Richard *XXXVIII, XIII*
Morris, Robert *XXXIX, XIII*
Morton, Richard *XXXIX, XIII*
Munday, Henry *XXXIX, XIII*
Murphy, James Cavanah *XXXIX, XIII*
Mylne or Myln, John *XL, XIV*
Mylne, John *XL, XIV*
Mylne, Robert *XL, XIV*
Mylne, Robert *XL, XIV*
Mylne, William Chadwell *XL, XIV*
Needler, Benjamin *XL, XIV*
Newman, John *XL, XIV*
Newstead, Christopher *XL, XIV*
Nicholson, John *XLI, XIV*
Nicholson, Peter *XLI, XIV*

Nicolls, Ferdinando *XLI, XIV*
Nobbes, Robert *XLI, XIV*
Norris, William *XLI, XIV*
Norton, Robert *XLI, XIV*
Norton, Samuel *XLI, XIV*
Norton, Thomas *XLI, XIV*
Oakley, Edward *XLI, XIV*
Oasland or Osland, Henry *XLI, XIV*
O'Neill, Hugh *XLII, XIV*
Owen, Jacob *XLII, XIV*
Owen, Richard *XLII, XIV*
Pakington, John *XLIII, XV*
Pakington, John *XLIII, XV*
Palmer, John *XLIII, XV*
Palmer, Thomas *XLIII, XV*
Parry, William *XLIII, XV*
Parsons, Benjamin *XLIII, XV*
Parsons, Edward *XLIII, XV*
Parsons, James *XLIII, XV*
Parsons, Philip *XLIII, XV*
Parsons, Richard *XLIII, XV*
Parsons, Robert *XLIII, XV*
Pasor, Matthias *XLIII, XV*
Pattrick or Patrick, George *XLIV, XV*
Paulden, Thomas *XLIV, XV*
Peckwell, Henry *XLIV, XV*
Penn, John *XLIV, XV*
Pennie, John Fitzgerald *XLIV, XV*
Peyton, John *XLV, XV*
Sharrock, Robert *LI, XVII*
Skinner, Stephen *LII, XVIII*
Smith, Henry *LIII, XVIII*
Stapley, Anthony *LIV, XVIII*
Temple, James *LVI, XIX*
Temple, Peter *LVI, XIX*
Thomas, William *LVI, XIX*
Thorpe, Francis *LVI, XIX*
Towerson, Gabriel *LVII, XIX*
Trapp, John *LVII, XIX*
Truman, Joseph *LVII, XIX*
Valentine, Benjamin *LVIII, XX*
Vassall, John *LVIII, XX*
Vassall, Samuel *LVIII, XX*
Vaughan, Thomas *LVIII, XX*
Vulliamy, Benjamin Lewis *LVIII, XX*
Vulliamy, Lewis *LVIII, XX*
Wagstaffe, John *LVIII, XX*
Wallop, Richard *LIX, XX*
Wallop, Robert *LIX, XX*
Waring, Robert *LIX, XX*
Warmestry, Gervase *LIX, XX*

Warmestry, Thomas *LIX, XX*
Webster, John *LX, XX*
Weston, Richard *LX, XX*
Wharton, Thomas *LX, XX*
White, Jeremiah *LXI, XXI*
White, Thomas *LXI, XXI*
Whitehall, Robert *LXI, XXI*
Whitlock, John *LXI, XXI*
Williams, Edward *LXII, XXI*
Willis, Thomas *LXII, XXI*
Willis, Timothy *LXII, XXI*
Wingate, Edmund *LXII, XXI*
Wogan, Thomas *LXII, XXI*
Wolrich or Wolryche, Thomas *LXII, XXI*
Wood, William *LXII, XXI*
Woodbridge, Benjamin *LXII, XXI*
Woodward, Hezekiah or Ezekias *LXII, XXI*
Woolley or Wolley, Hannah *LXII, XXI*
Wright, Laurence *LXIII, XXI*
Wyndham, Hugh *LXIII, XXI*

HELEN KEMP PORTER
Blackman, Vernon Herbert *1961–1970*
Gregory, Frederick Gugenheim *1961–1970*
Richards, Francis John *1961–1970*

ELEANOR GRACE POWELL
Neale, William *XL, XIV*
Newton, Adam *XL, XIV*
Norwych, George *XLI, XIV*
Raleigh, William de *XLVII, XVI*

ELIZABETH DILYS POWELL
Balcon, Michael Elias *1971–1980*
Chaplin, Charles Spencer *1971–1980*
Field, Agnes Mary *1961–1970*
Lejeune, Caroline Alice *1971–1980*
Mackworth-Young, Gerard *1961–1970*

ALEXANDRA JANE REINA PRINGLE
Warner, Sylvia Townsend *1971–1980*

ALICE MARJORIE SHEILA PROCHASKA
Crowdy, Rachel Eleanor *1961–1970*
Gwynne-Vaughan, Helen Charlotte Isabella *1961–1970*

PATRICIA MARIE PUGH
Jones, Arthur Creech *1961–1970*

OLIVE PURSER
Purser, Louis Claud *1931–1940*

EDITH MARY PYE
Paget, Mary Rosalind *1941–1950*

EMMA LOUISE RADFORD
Larkham, Thomas *XXXII, XI*
Newsam, Bartholomew *XL, XIV*
Quare, Daniel *XLVII, XVI*
Radford, John *XLVII, XVI*
Russell, Francis *XLIX, XVII*
Spode, Josiah *LIII, XVIII*
Tompion, Thomas *LVII, XIX*
Tremayne, Edmund *LVII, XIX*
Vivian, Hussey Crespigny *LVIII, XX*
Wrey, Bourchier *LXIII, XXI*

BETTY RADICE
Rieu, Emile Victor *1971–1980*

SANDRA JOAN RAPHAEL
Cox, Richard *Missing Persons*
Furber, Robert *Missing Persons*
Gray, Christopher *Missing Persons*
Gurle, Leonard *Missing Persons*
Looker, Roger *Missing Persons*
Robinson, William *Missing Persons*
Rose, John *Missing Persons*
Sutton, Martin Hope *Missing Persons*

ELEANOR ALEXANDRA REID
Evelyn, John *Missing Persons*
Evelyn, John *Missing Persons*
Holland, John *Missing Persons*

ADRIENNE ELAINE REYNOLDS
Atkinson, Edward Leicester *Missing Persons*

MARGARET RICHARDSON
Maufe, Edward Brantwood *1971–1980*

ANNE ISABELLA RITCHIE
Browning, Elizabeth Barrett *VII, III*

JEAN ROBERTSON
Wilson, Frank Percy *1961–1970*

MURIEL ROBERTSON
Stephenson, Marjory *1941–1950*

ESME STUART LENNOX ROBINSON
Fay, William George *1941–1950*

ELIZABETH KENNARD
WHITTINGTON ROTHENSTEIN
Spencer, Stanley *1951–1960*

MIRIAM LOUISA ROTHSCHILD
Foster, John Galway *1981–1985*

JULIA ANNE ELIZABETH
ROUNDELL
Browne, Anthony *VII, III*

DOROTHY STUART RUSSELL
Turnbull, Hubert Maitland *1951–1960*

VICTORIA MARY SACKVILLE-WEST
Wellesley, Dorothy Violet *1951–1960*

MONICA SALMOND
Grenfell, Edward Charles *1941–1950*

VIVIAN GLADYS SALMON
Lodwick, Francis *Missing Persons*

GHETAL BURDON-SANDERSON
Herschell, Ridley Haim *XXVI, IX*

AVICE EDITH SANKEY
Hunt, Agnes Gwendoline *1941–1950*

RUTH LYDIA SAW
Joad, Cyril Edwin Mitchinson *1951–1960*

CAROLYN POLING SCHRIBER
Arnulf *Missing Persons*

LUCY MAUDE MANSON SCOTT
Monck, Christopher *XXXVIII, XIII*
Montagu, James *XXXVIII, XIII*
Mushet, William *XXXIX, XIII*

ANNE ELEANOR SCOTT–JAMES
Sackville-West, Victoria Mary *1961–1970*

GLADYS SCOTT-THOMSON
Russell, Mary Annette *1941–1950*

EVELYN ADELAIDE SHARP
Douglas, William Scott *1951–1960*
Martindale, Hilda *1951–1960*

ALISON EVA MARY SHELL
Barker, Jane *Missing Persons*
Lane, William *Missing Persons*

**VALENTINE MARY KENNERLEY
SILLERY**
Fry, Thomas *Missing Persons*

EVA BLANTYRE SIMPSON
Simpson, James Young *LII, XVIII*

EDITH SICHEL
Ainger, Alfred *1901–1911 I*
Coleridge, Mary Elizabeth *1901–1911 I*
Yonge, Charlotte Mary *1901–1911 III*

**MRS A. MURRAY SMITH, formerly
EMILY TENNYSON BRADLEY**
Fairborne, Palmes *XVIII, VI*
Feckenham, John de *XVIII, VI*
Felix, John *XVIII, VI*
Fermor, Farmer, or Fermour, William
  XVIII, VI
Ferne, Henry *XVIII, VI*
Finch, Anne *XIX, VII*
Finch, Heneage *XIX, VII*
Finch, Heneage *XIX, VII*
Finingham, Robert de *XIX, VII*
Fisher, Jasper *XIX, VII*
Fisher, Payne *XIX, VII*
Flete, John *XIX, VII*
Gage, John *XX, VII*
Galeon, William *XX, VII*
Gardiner, Thomas *XX, VII*
Gaunt, Elizabeth *XXI, VII*
Gerard, John *XXI, VII*
Gerard, Garret, or Garrard, Thomas *XXI,
  VII*
Gifford, George *XXI, VII*
Gilby, Anthony *XXI, VII*
Godwin, Thomas *XXII, VIII*
Goffe or Gough, Thomas *XXII, VIII*
Goldwell, James *XXII, VIII*
Gondibour or Goudibour, Thomas *XXII,
  VIII*
Goodman, Christopher *XXII, VIII*
Gourdon, William *XXII, VIII*

Gove, Richard *XXII, VIII*
Gower, Thomas *XXII, VIII*
Grayle or Graile, John *XXIII, VIII*
Green, Bartholomew or Bartlet *XXIII,
  VIII*
Gregory, David *XXIII, VIII*
Grey, Henry *XXIII, VIII*
Grey, Lord John *XXIII, VIII*
Grey, Thomas *XXIII, VIII*
Guest, Gheast, or Geste, Edmund *XXIII,
  VIII*
Guthrie, David *XXIII, VIII*
Hall, James *XXIV, VIII*
Hallam, John *XXIV, VIII*
Harding, Thomas *XXIV, VIII*
Harington, John *XXIV, VIII*
Harington, John *XXIV, VIII*
Harris, Robert *XXV, IX*
Horne, Robert *XXVII, IX*
Horne, Thomas *XXVII, IX*
Howard, Thomas *XXVIII, X*
Hyde, Alexander *XXVIII, X*
Hyde, Thomas *XXVIII, X*
Ingmethorpe, Thomas *XXIX, X*
Jackson, Thomas *XXIX, X*
Jacombe, Thomas *XXIX, X*
James, William *XXIX, X*
Jermin or German, Michael *XXIX, X*
Jerningham, Henry *XXIX, X*
Joscelyn or Jesselin, John *XXX, X*
Kauffmann, Angelica *XXX, X*
Kingston, Anthony *XXXI, XI*
Kirton, Edmund *XXXI, XI*
Knightley, Richard *XXXI, XI*
Knipe, Thomas *XXXI, XI*
Knolles, Thomas *XXXI, XI*
Knyvet or Knevet, Edmund *XXXI, XI*
Kynaston or Kinaston, Francis *XXXI, XI*
Lamphire, John *XXXII, XI*
Langton, Thomas *XXXII, XI*
Laurence, Thomas *XXXII, XI*
Lawrence *XXXII, XI*
Laxton, William *XXXII, XI*
Leigh, Ferdinand *XXXII, XI*
Levinz, Levens or Levinge, Robert
  XXXIII, XI
Lewis, William *XXXIII, XI*
Lily or Lilly, Peter *XXXIII, XI*
Litlington, Nicholas *XXXIII, XI*
Lloyd, George *XXXIII, XI*
Lockey, Thomas *XXXIV, XII*

Love, Richard *XXXIV, XII*
Lynde, Humphrey *XXXIV, XII*
Millyng, Thomas *XXXVII, XIII*
Monck or Monk, Nicholas *XXXVIII, XIII*
Monson, Thomas *XXXVIII, XIII*
Montaigne or Mountain, George
 XXXVIII, XIII
More or Moore, George *XXXVIII, XIII*

BARBARA MARY DIMOND SMITH
Nettlefold, Joseph Henry *Missing Persons*

ISOBEL AGNES SMITH
McKenzie, Alexander *1951–1960*

JULIA JANE SMITH
Traherne, Thomas *Missing Persons*

CHARLOTTE FELL–SMITH
Barton, John *1901–1911 I*
Bellows, John *1901–1911 I*
Blackburn, Helen *1901–1911 I*
Blackwell, Elizabeth *1901–1911 I*
Boucherett, Emilia Jessie *1901–1911 I*
Brown, Hugh Stowell *1901 I, XXII*
Burns, Dawson *1901–1911 I*
Hanbury, Elizabeth *1901–1911 II*
Hopkins, Jane Ellice *1901–1911 II*
Horniman, Frederick John *1901–1911 II*
Jenkins, Ebenezer Evans *1901–1911 II*
Kendall, John *XXX, X*
Kilham, Hannah *XXXI, XI*
Knibb, William *1901 III, XXII*
Knowles, Mary *XXXI, XI*
Latey, Gilbert *XXXII, XI*
Lawson, Thomas *XXXII, XI*
Lead or Leade, Jane *XXXII, XI*
Leatham, William Henry *XXXII, XI*
Leddra, William *XXXII, XI*
Letchworth, Thomas *XXXIII, XI*
Lord, Thomas *1901–1911 II*
Macgowan, John *XXXV, XII*
Mallory or Mallorie, Thomas *XXXV, XII*
Manning, Anne *1901 III, XXII*
Manton, Thomas *XXXVI, XII*
Marshall, Charles *XXXVI, XII*
Marshall, Walter *XXXVI, XII*
Martin, John *XXXVI, XII*
Martin, Josiah *XXXVI, XII*
Mason, Martin *XXXVI, XII*
Mather, William *XXXVII, XIII*

Maton, Robert *XXXVII, XIII*
Matthews or Mathews, Lemuel *XXXVII,
 XIII*
Maude, Thomas *XXXVII, XIII*
Maxwell, James *XXXVII, XIII*
Maynard, John *XXXVII, XIII*
Mead, William *XXXVII, XIII*
Meidel, Christopher *XXXVII, XIII*
Middleton, Joshua *XXXVII, XIII*
Milward, John *XXXVIII, XIII*
Möens, William John Charles *1901–1911
 II*
More, Robert *XXXVIII, XIII*
Morehead, William *XXXIX, XIII*
Morgan, Hector Davies *XXXIX, XIII*
Mucklow, William *XXXIX, XIII*
Murray, Lindley *XXXIX, XIII*
Naish, William *XL, XIV*
Neale, Samuel *XL, XIV*
Newcomen, Matthew *XL, XIV*
Newlin, Thomas *XL, XIV*
Newton, Benjamin *XL, XIV*
Newton, William *XL, XIV*
Nicholas, Henry, or Niclaes, Henrick *XL,
 XIV*
Nicholas, Thomas *XL, XIV*
Nicholls, Degory *XL, XIV*
Nicholls, John *XL, XIV*
Nickolls, John *XLI, XIV*
Norton, Humphrey *XLI, XIV*
Norton, John *XLI, XIV*
Nutt, Joseph *XLI, XIV*
Nyndge, Alexander *XLI, XIV*
Ogborne, David *XLII, XIV*
Oldisworth, Giles *XLII, XIV*
Ollyffe, John *XLII, XIV*
Osborn, Elias *XLII, XIV*
O'Sullivan, Mortimer *XLII, XIV*
Ouseley, Gideon *XLII, XIV*
Overton, Constantine *XLII, XIV*
Owen, Griffith *XLII, XIV*
Owen, John *XLII, XIV*
Oxley, Joseph *XLIII, XV*
Pakeman, Thomas *XLIII, XV*
Pardoe, William *XLIII, XV*
Park or Parkes, James *XLIII, XV*
Parker, Alexander *XLIII, XV*
Parkhurst, Nathaniel *XLIII, XV*
Parkinson, Sydney *XLIII, XV*
Parnell, James *XLIII, XV*
Parry, Joshua *XLIII, XV*

Parry, Richard *XLIII, XV*
Paske, Thomas *XLIII, XV*
Patient or Patience, Thomas *XLIV, XV*
Pearson, Anthony *XLIV, XV*
Pease, Edward *XLIV, XV*
Pease, Joseph Whitwell *1901–1911 III*
Penington or Pennington, Isaac *XLIV, XV*
Penington or Pennington, Isaac *XLIV, XV*
Penn, Granville *XLIV, XV*
Penn, James *XLIV, XV*
Penn, John *XLIV, XV*
Penn, Richard *XLIV, XV*
Penn, Thomas *XLIV, XV*
Pennyman, John *XLIV, XV*
Perrot, John *XLV, XV*
Philipps, Jenkin Thomas *XLV, XV*
Philp, Robert Kemp *XLV, XV*
Phipps, Joseph *XLV, XV*
Pickworth, Henry *XLV, XV*
Pike, John Deodatus Gregory *XLV, XV*
Pinke, William *XLV, XV*
Pittis, Thomas *XLV, XV*
Plume, Thomas *1901 III, XXII*
Pollard, William *XLVI, XVI*
Pomfret, Samuel *XLVI, XVI*
Pory, John *XLVI, XVI*
Post, Jacob *XLVI, XVI*
Price, William *XLVI, XVI*
Price, William *XLVI, XVI*
Pridden, John *XLVI, XVI*
Priestman, John *XLVI, XVI*
Pullen, Pullein, or Pulleyne, Samuel
    XLVII, XVI
Pullen or Pullein, Samuel *XLVII, XVI*
Pullen, Tobias *XLVII, XVI*
Purver, Anthony *XLVII, XVI*
Randall, John *XLVII, XVI*
Ranew, Nathanael *XLVII, XVI*
Ransome, Robert *XLVII, XVI*
Ratcliffe or Ratliffe, Thomas *XLVII, XVI*
Read or Reade, Thomas *XLVII, XVI*
Reede, John de, Baron Reede *XLVII, XVI*
Reeve, Edmund *XLVII, XVI*
Resbury, Nathaniel *XLVIII, XVI*
Reyner, Edward *XLVIII, XVI*
Reynolds or Rainolde, Richard *XLVIII,
    XVI*
Reynolds, Richard *XLVIII, XVI*
Rhodes, Ebenezer *XLVIII, XVI*
Rich, Mary *XLVIII, XVI*
Rich, Richard *XLVIII, XVI*

Rich, Robert *XLVIII, XVI*
Richards, Thomas *XLVIII, XVI*
Richards, William *XLVIII, XVI*
Richardson, George *XLVIII, XVI*
Richardson, John *XLVIII, XVI*
Richardson, John *XLVIII, XVI*
Richardson, Thomas *XLVIII, XVI*
Rickman, Thomas *XLVIII, XVI*
Rigg or Rigge, Ambrose *XLVIII, XVI*
Roach, Richard *XLVIII, XVI*
Roberts, Francis *XLVIII, XVI*
Roberts, John *XLVIII, XVI*
Roberts, Joseph *XLVIII, XVI*
Roberts, Mary *XLVIII, XVI*
Robertson, James *XLVIII, XVI*
Robertson, Joseph *XLVIII, XVI*
Robinson, Hastings *XLIX, XVII*
Robinson, Ralph *XLIX, XVII*
Roebuck, Thomas *XLIX, XVII*
Rogers, Daniel *XLIX, XVII*
Rogers, Nathaniel *XLIX, XVII*
Rogers, Nehemiah *XLIX, XVII*
Rolle or Rolls, Samuel *XLIX, XVII*
Rosewell, Samuel *XLIX, XVII*
Rothe, Robert *XLIX, XVII*
Rous, John *XLIX, XVII*
Rous, John *XLIX, XVII*
Rouse or Russe, John *XLIX, XVII*
Routh, Martha *XLIX, XVII*
Row, Thomas *XLIX, XVII*
Rowlands, Henry *XLIX, XVII*
Rowlands or Verstegen, Richard *XLIX,
    XVII*
Rowntree, Joseph *XLIX, XVII*
Rudd, Sayer *XLIX, XVII*
Russel, William *XLIX, XVII*
Russell, John *XLIX, XVII*
Rutter, John *L, XVII*
Rutter, Joseph *L, XVII*
Ryan, Edward *L, XVII*
Ryland, John Collett *L, XVII*
Sadler, Anthony *L, XVII*
Salthouse, Thomas *L, XVII*
Samble, Richard *L, XVII*
Sams, Joseph *L, XVII*
Sandford or Sanford, John *L, XVII*
Scott, John *LI, XVII*
Seagrave, Robert *LI, XVII*
Secker, William *LI, XVII*
Seed, Jeremiah *LI, XVII*
Sergeant, Lewis *1901–1911 III*

Sewel, William *LI, XVII*
Sharp, Isaac *1901 III, XXII*
Shaw, John *LI, XVII*
Shaw, John *LI, XVII*
Shewen, William *LII, XVIII*
Shillitoe, Thomas *LII, XVIII*
Shute, Josias or Josiah *LII, XVIII*
Simpson or Sympson, William *LII, XVIII*
Slade, Matthew *LII, XVIII*
Smith, Humphrey *LIII, XVIII*
Smith, Stephen *LIII, XVIII*
Smith, William *LIII, XVIII*
Stalham, John *LIII, XVIII*
Starke, Mariana *LIV, XVIII*
Sterry, Peter *LIV, XVIII*
Stockton, Owen *LIV, XVIII*
Story, Thomas *LIV, XVIII*
Sturge, Joseph *LV, XIX*
Swinden, Henry *LV, XIX*
Tallents, Francis *LV, XIX*
Tattersall, William de Chair *LV, XIX*
Taylor, John *LV, XIX*
Taylor, John *LV, XIX*
Taylor, Thomas *LV, XIX*
Taylor, Thomas *LV, XIX*
Terry or Tirreye, John *LVI, XIX*
Theyer, John *LVI, XIX*
Timberlake, Henry *LVI, XIX*
Tipping, William *LVI, XIX*
Tomkins, John *LVII, XIX*
Tozer, Henry *LVII, XIX*
Travers, Rebecca *LVII, XIX*
Travers, Walter *LVII, XIX*
Tregelles, Edwin Octavius *LVII, XIX*
Tuke, Henry *LVII, XIX*
Turford, Hugh *LVII, XIX*
Turner, Daniel *LVII, XIX*
Turner, William *LVII, XIX*
Vincent, Nathaniel *LVIII, XX*
Vitell or Vitells, Christopher *LVIII, XX*
Vokins, Joan *LVIII, XX*
Wadsworth, James *LVIII, XX*
Wadsworth, James *LVIII, XX*
Walker, George Washington *LIX, XX*
Walker, John *LIX, XX*
Watkins, Morgan *LIX, XX*
Watts, Gilbert *LX, XX*
Watts, William *LX, XX*
Wells, Samuel *LX, XX*
Western, Charles Callis *LX, XX*
Whateley, William *LX, XX*

Wheeler, David *LX, XX*
White, John *LXI, XXI*
White, William *LXI, XXI*
Whitehead, George *LXI, XXI*
Whitehead, John *LXI, XXI*
Whitfeld or Whitfield, Henry *LXI, XXI*
Whiting, John *LXI, XXI*
Wild or Wylde, Robert *LXI, XXI*
Wilkinson, Henry *LXI, XXI*
Wilkinson, Henry *LXI, XXI*
Wilson, Thomas *LXII, XXI*
Wolrich, Woolrich, or Wooldridge,
   Humphrey *LXII, XXI*
Woodall, William *1901–1911 III*
Woolman, John *LXII, XXI*
Wyeth, Joseph *LXIII, XXI*
Yeardley, John *LXIII, XXI*

LUCY TOULMIN SMITH
Glanville, Bartholomew de *XXI, VII*
Kingsley, Maria Henrietta *1901 III, XXII*
Kynewulf, Cynewulf, or Cynwulf *XXXI,
   XI*
Nicholson, Brinsley *XLI, XIV*
Smith, Joshua Toulmin *LIII, XVIII*

MARY SOAMES
Churchill, Clementine Ogilvy Spencer-
   1971–1980

JULIA WINIFRED SPEEDIE
Leverson, Ada Esther *Missing Persons*

MARION URSULA HOWARD
SPRING
Spring, Robert Howard *1961–1970*

KATHRYN MARGARET
STANSFIELD
Sharp, Thomas Wilfred *1971–1980*

CAROLINE EMELIA STEPHEN
Aikenhead, Mary *I, I*

JULIA PRINSEP STEPHEN
Cameron, Julia Margaret *VIII, III*

MARGARET THYRA BARBARA
STEPHEN
Davies, Sarah Emily *1912–1921*

KATHLEEN ELIZABETH STEVENS
Curtis Brown, Spencer *1971–1980*

MARY DANVERS STOCKS
Rathbone, Eleanor Florence *1941–1950*
Simon, Oliver Joseph *1951–1960*
Stewart-Murray, Katharine Marjory
   1951–1960

JANE THOMPSON STODDART
Nicoll, William Robertson *1922–1930*

CHARLOTTE CARMICHAEL STOPES
Stopes, Leonard *LIV, XVIII*
Stopes, Richard *LIV, XVIII*

RAY STRACHEY
Aldrich-Blake, Louisa Brandreth
   1922–1930
Fawcett, Millicent *1922–1930*
Jebb, Eglantyne *1922–1930*
Pankhurst, Emmeline *1922–1930*

SARAH CAROLINE JANE STREET
Boulting, John *1981–1985*

BEATRIX MARION STURT
Sturt, Charles *LV, XIX*
Muirhead, George *1901 III, XXII*
Muirhead, James Patrick *1901 III, XXII*

EMMA CATHARINE SUTTON
Fisher, Joseph *XIX, VII*
Fleming, George *XIX, VII*

LIZ STANLEY
Davison, Emily Wilding *Missing Persons*

SUSANNE PETRA STARK
Richardson, Dorothy Miller *Missing
   Persons*
Sinclair, Mary Amelia St Clair *Missing
   Persons*

BARBARA MARY STONEY
Hathaway, Sibyl Mary *Missing Persons*

CHARLOTTE MARY STOTT
Llewelyn Davies, Margaret Caroline
   Missing Persons

ELIZABETH BRIDGET STUART
Talbot, John *Missing Persons*

SUSAN AGNES STUSSY
Sparke, Michael *Missing Persons*

VIRGINIA SURTEES
Siddal, Elizabeth Eleanor *Missing Persons*

GILLIAN RAY SUTHERLAND
Hubback, Eva Marian *Missing Persons*

NICOLA MARY SUTHERLAND
Herle, William *Missing Persons*

ANN HAZEL SPOKES SYMONDS
Herschel, William Kames *Missing Persons*

ELEANOR DALE PUTNAM SYMONS
Franklin, Charles Samuel *1961–1970*

IRENE JOAN THIRSK
Stratford, John *Missing Persons*
Webb, Benedict *Missing Persons*

MARY GWYNETH LLOYD THOMAS
Newall, Bertha Surtees *1931–1940*

RUTH REES THOMAS
Fox, Evelyn Emily Marian *1951–1960*
Pinsent, Ellen Frances *1941–1950*

GLADYS SCOTT THOMSON
Russell, Herbrand Arthur *1931–1940*

KATHLEEN MARY TILLOTSON
Darbishire, Helen *1961–1970*

BARBARA PATRICIA TIZARD
Pringle, Mia Lilli Kellmer *1981–1985*

ELIZABETH MARION TODD
Todd, James Henthorn *LVI, XIX*
Todd, Robert Bentley *LVI, XIX*

MARY TOUT
Richard de Wyche *XLVIII, XVI*
Ursula *LVIII, XX*
Wakering, John *LIX, XX*
Walerand, Robert *LIX, XX*
Wallingford, William *LIX, XX*

Waltham, John de *LIX, XX*
Wesham or Weseham, Roger de *LX, XX*
William of Sainte-Mere-Eglise *LXI, XXI*
Willibrord or Wilbrord, Saint *LXII, XXI*
Windsor, William de *LXII, XXI*
Wulfhere *LXIII, XXI*

JOCELYN MARY CATHERINE TOYNBEE
Gardner, Percy *1931–1940*
Strong, Eugénie *1941–1950*

MARGARET RUTH TOYNBEE
Bell, Alexander Graham *1922–1930*
Finberg, Alexander Joseph *1931–1940*
Wain, Louis William *1931–1940*

JANET PENROSE TREVELYAN
Green, Alice Sophia Amelia *1922–1930*

WENDY TREWIN
Albery, Bronson James *1971–1980*

LOUISA CHARLOTTE TYNDALL
Tyndall, John *LVII, XIX*

ELIZABETH MARY VALLANCE
Braddock, Elizabeth Margaret *Missing Persons*

ROSEMARY THORSTENSON VAN ARSDEL
Miller, Florence Fenwick *Missing Persons*

JOAN URSULA PENTON VAUGHAN WILLIAMS
Holst, Imogen Clare *1981–1985*

MARGARET MARIA VERNEY
Verney, Edmund *LVIII, XX*
Verney, Edmund *LVIII, XX*
Verney, Francis *LVIII, XX*
Verney, Harry *LVIII, XX*
Verney, Ralph *LVIII, XX*
Verney, Ralph *LVIII, XX*

MARJORIE VERNON
Underhill, Evelyn *1941–1950*

SHEILA MOSLEY WALKER
Baden–Powell, Olave St Clair *1971–1980*

STELLA ARCHER WALKER
Edwards, Lionel Dalhousie Robertson *1961–1970*

HELEN MARGARET WALLIS
Rotz, Jean *Missing Persons*

MARY WALTON
Balfour, Arthur *1951–1960*

KIM SCOTT WALWYN
Ellerman, Annie Winifred *1981–1985*

GRACE MARGARET WARD
Gonne, Maud Edith *Missing Persons*

MAISIE WARD
Chesterton, Gilbert Keith *1931–1940*

HELEN MARY WARNOCK
Anderson, Kitty *1971–1980*

PAMELA MABEL WATERWORTH
Garrod, Lawrence Paul *1971–1980*

MARY TERESA JOSEPHINE WEBBER
Ker, Neil Ripley *1981–1985*

CICELY VERONICA WEDGWOOD
Wedgwood, Josiah Clement *1941–1950*

KATHARINE MARY WESTAWAY
Stansfeld, Margaret *1951–1960*

MRS A. B. WHITE
Dibbs, George Richard *1901–1911 I*
Hall, John *1901–1911 II*
Huddart, James *1901–1911 II*
M'Kenzie, John *1901–1911 II*
Seddon, Richard John *1901–1911 III*
Stafford, Edward William *1901–1911 III*
Syme, David *1901–1911 III*
Whitmore, George Stoddart *1901–1911 III*

EIRENE LLOYD WHITE
Brittain, Vera Mary *1961–1970*
Hancock, Florence May *1971–1980*

ELIZABETH ANNE OSBORN WHITEMAN
Aldridge, John Arthur Malcolm *1981–1985*

Clark, George Norman *1971–1980*
Sutherland, Lucy Stuart *1971–1980*

MURIEL HELEN WIGGLESWORTH
Fogerty, Elsie *1941–1950*

ANTHEA WILLIAMS
Elmhirst, Leonard Knight *1971–1980*

ELLEN WILLIAMS
Williams, Rowland *LXI, XXI*

AMABEL WILLIAMS-ELLIS
Hughes, Richard Arthur Warren
1971–1980

SARAH WILSON
Salvin, Anthony *L, XVII*
Tate, George *LV, XIX*
Tate, Thomas *LV, XIX*

JOCELIN SLINGSBY WINTHROP-
YOUNG
Slingsby, William Cecil *Missing Persons*

ELIZABETH META WISKEMANN
Voigt, Frederick Augustus *1951–1960*

MARION EVELYN WOOD
Ashton, Thomas Gair *1931–1940*

MARY WOODALL
Walker, Ethel *1951–1960*
Whitley, William Thomas *1941–1950*

ANNE YATES
Luthuli, Albert John *1961–1970*

META ZIMMECK
Anderson, Adelaide Mary *Missing Persons*

Part 3

MALE CONTRIBUTORS

Male contributors with contributions on women

OSMUND AIRY
Burnet, Margaret *VII*; *III*
Campbell, Anna Mackenzie *VIII*; *III*

GEORGE ATHERTON AITKIN
Killigrew, Anne *XXXI*; *XI*
Manley, Mary de la Riviere *XXXVI*; *XII*
Robinson, Anastasia *XLIX*; *XVII*
Spencer, Dorothy *LIII*; *XVIII*
Sundon, Charlotte Clayton *LV*; *XIX*

BRIAN ALDERSON
Attwell, Mabel Lucie *1961–1970*
Challans, Eileen Mary *1981–1985*
Ruck, Amy Roberta *1971–1980*
Uttley, Alice Jane *1971–1980*

JOHN GOLDWORTH ALGER
Dawes or Daw, Sophia *XIV*; *V*
Elliott, Grace Dalrymple *XVII*; *VI*
Fitzgerald, Pamela *XIX*; *VII*
Hamilton, Mary *XXIV*; *VIII*
Hollond, Ellen Julia *XXVII*; *IX*
Mohl, Madame Mary *XXXVIII*; *XIII*
Murphy, Marie Louise *XXXIX*; *XIII*
Rivarol, Louisa Henrietta *XLVIII*; *XVI*
Tredway, Letice Mary *LVII*; *XIX*

J. P. ANDERSON
Burdett-Coutts, Angela Georgina
   1901–1911 I

WILLIAM ARTHUR JOBSON
ARCHBOLD
Hemphill, Barbara *XXV*; *IX*
Juliana *XXX*; *X*
Kingsford, Anna *XXXI*; *XI*
Lewis, Joyce *XXXIII*; *XI*
Shore, Jane *LII*; *XVIII*

THOMAS ANDREW ARCHER
Bathilda *III*; *I*
Cannera *VIII*; *III*
Cecilia *IX*; *III*
Clifford, Margaret *XI*; *IV*
Clifford, Rosamond *XI*; *IV*
Eleanor *XVII*; *VI*
Eleanor of Provence *XVII*; *VI*

WALTER ARMSTRONG
Thornycroft, Mary *LVI*; *XIX*

THEODORE ARONSON
Keppel, Alice Frederica *Missing Persons*
Langtry, Emily Charlotte *Missing Persons*

GEORGE COMPTON ARCHIBALD
ARTHUR
Alexandra *1922–1930*

JOHN ASHTON
Caroline Amelia Elizabeth *IX*; *III*

JOHN BLACK ATKINS
Butler, Elizabeth Southerden *1931–1940*

JOHN ATTENBOROUGH
Goudge, Elizabeth de Beauchamp
   1981–1985

WILLIAM EDWARD ARMYTAGE
AXON
Ball, Hannah *III*; *I*
Bowes, Mary Eleanor *VI*; *II*
Brettargh, Katharine *VI*; *II*
Brunton, Mary *VII*; *III*

GEORGE FISHER RUSSELL BARKER
Brownrigg, Elizabeth, *VII*; *III*
Carter, Elizabeth *IX*; *III*
Clifford, Anne *XI*; *IV*
Clive, Caroline *XI*; *IV*
Hervey, Mary *XXVI*; *IX*
Hutton, Catherine *XXVIII*; *X*
Lamb, Caroline *XXXI*; *XI*
Masham, Abigail *XXXVI*; *XII*

PERCY ARTHUR BARNETT
Ewing, Juliana Horaria *XVIII*; *VI*

JOHN BARRETT
Dod, Charlotte *Missing Persons*

RONALD BAYNE
Booth, Catherine *1901 I*; *XXII*
Glasse, Hannah *XXI*; *VII*
Havergal, Frances Ridley *XXV*; *IX*

DAVID BAXANDALL
Redpath, Anne *1961–1970*

THOMAS WILSON BAYNE
Elliot, Jane or Jean *XVII*; *VI*
Glover, Jean *XXII*; *VIII*
Grant, Elizabeth *XXII*; *VIII*
Hamilton, Elizabeth *XXIV*; *VIII*
Hamilton, Janet *XXIV*; *VIII*
Hawkins, Susanna *XXV*; *IX*
Hume, Anna *XXVIII*; *X*
Inglis, Margaret Maxwell *XXIX*; *X*
Knox, Isa *1901–1911 II*
Nairne, Carolina *XL*; *XIV*
Pagan, Isobel *XLIII*; *XV*
Simpson, Jane Cross *LII*; *XVIII*
Sinclair, Catherine *LII*; *XVIII*

CECIL BEATON
Elsie, Lily *1961–1970*

CHARLES RAYMOND BEAZLEY
Philippa of Lancaster *XLV*; *XV*

DALRYMPLE JAMES BELGRAVE
Serres, Olivia *LI*; *XVII*

JOHN BELL
Farjeon, Eleanor *1961–1970*

RICHARD BENNETT
Kennedy, Margaret Moore *1961–1970*

GEORGE VERE BENSON
Bankes, Mary *III*; *I*

GEORGE THOMAS BETTANY
Blackburne, Anna *V*; *II*
Hunter, Anne *XXVIII*; *X*
Jenkin, Henrietta Camilla *XXIX*; *X*

AUGUSTUS CHARLES BICKLEY
Camm, Anne *VIII*; *III*
Fell, Margaret *XVIII*; *VI*
Fisher, Mary *XIX*; *VII*
Follows, Ruth *XIX*; *VII*
Hooten, Elizabeth *XXVII*; *IX*

FRANCIS L. BICKLEY
Nicolson, Adela Florence *1901–1911 III*

ALAN GORDON BISHOP
Holtby, Winifred *Missing Persons*

BEVER HARRY BLACKER
Kettle or Kyteler, Alice *XXXI*; *XI*

WILLIAM GARDEN BLAIKIE
Campbell, Willielma *VIII*; *III*
Davidson, Harriet Miller *XIV*; *V*
Fry, Elizabeth *XX*; *VII*
Gordon, Elizabeth *XXII*; *VIII*
Greenwell, Dora *XXIII*; *VIII*

JEREMY BLACK
Sophia *Missing Persons*

HERBERT EDWARD DOUGLAS BLAKISTON
Verney, Margaret Maria *1922–1930*

BARRY BLOOMFIELD
Faithfull, Emily *Missing Persons*

GEORGE CLEMENT BOASE
Broderip, Frances Freeling *VI*; *II*
Bunsen, Frances *VII*; *III*
Bury, Charlotte Susan Maria *VIII*; *III*
Buxton, Bertha H. *VIII*; *III*
Carne, Elizabeth Catherine Thomas *IX*; *III*
Charlesworth, Maria Louisa *X*; *IV*
Chatelain, Clara de *X*; *IV*
Chatterton, Henrietta Georgiana Marcia Lascelles *X*; *IV*
Chisholm, Caroline *X*; *IV*
Costello, Louisa Stuart *XII*; *IV*
Crampton, Victoire *XIII*; *V*
Davies, Lucy Clementina *XIV*; *V*
Eden, Emily *XVI*; *VI*
Fane, Priscilla Anne *XVIII*; *VI*
Gatty, Margaret *XXI*; *VII*
Gilbert, Maria Dolores Eliza Rosanna *XXI*; *VII*
Girling, Mary Anne *XXI*; *VII*
Gordon, Lucie or Lucy *XXII*; *VIII*
Gore, Catherine Grace Frances *XXII*; *VIII*
Gurney, Anna *XXIII*; *VIII*
Hall, Anna Maria *XXIV*; *VIII*
Harlowe, Sarah *XXIV*; *VIII*
Hayes, Catherine *XXV*; *IX*
Howitt, Mary *XXVIII*; *X*
Jeffery, Dorothy *XXIX*; *X*
Lynch, Theodora Elizabeth *XXXIV*; *XII*
Manning, Marie *XXXVI*; *XII*

Oliver, Martha Cranmer *XLII*; *XIV*
Parsons, Gertrude *XLIII*; *XV*
Pattison, Dorothy Wyndlow *XLIV*; *XV*
Pearl, Cora *XLIV*; *XV*
Ranyard, Ellen Henrietta *XLVII*; *XVI*
Schreiber, Charlotte Elizabeth *L*; *XVII*
Scott, Caroline Lucy *LI*; *XVII*
Scott, Harriet Anne *LI*; *XVII*
Soyer, Elizabeth Emma *LIII*; *XVIII*

HECTOR BOLITHO
Grenville, Frances Evelyn *1931–1940*

TANCRED BORENIUS
Gleichen, Feodora Georgina Maud
1922–1930

GEORGE SIMONDS BOULGER
Gray, Maria Emma *XXIII*; *VIII*
Ibbetson, Agnes *XXVIII*; *X*
Loudon, Jane *XXXIV*; *XII*

ALAN BOWNESS
Hepworth, Joscelyn Barbara *1971–1980*

HENRY NOEL BRAILSFORD
Garnett, Constance Clara *1941–1950*

THOMAS BRIMELOW
Salt, Barbara *1971–1980*

ROBERT HENRY BRODIE
Bland, Elizabeth *V*; *II*

ARTHUR AIKIN BRODRIBB
Aikin, Lucy *I*; *I*
Barbauld, Anna Letitia *III*; *I*

F. H. BROWN
Frere, Mary Eliza Isabella *1901–1911 II*

IVOR BROWN
Ashwell, Lena Margaret *1951–1960*

RICHARD CHARLES BROWNE
Arundell, Blanche *II*; *I*

HUGO BRUNNER
Ashford, Margaret Mary Julia *1971–1980*

ARTHUR HENRY BULLEN
Cooper, Elizabeth *XII*; *IV*
Frith, Mary *XX*; *VII*

FRANCIS CRAWFORD BURKITT
Lewis, Agnes *1922–1930*

PATRICK CADELL
Besant, Annie *1931–1940*

ALAN CAMPBELL-JOHNSON
Mountbatten, Edwina Cynthia Annette
1951–1960

EDWIN CANNAN
Gilbert, Ann *XXI*; *VII*
Jocelin, Elizabeth *XXIX*; *X*

BERNARD CAPP
Cary, Mary *Missing Persons*

EDWARD IRVING CARLYLE
Alexander, Cecil Frances *1901 I*; *XXII*
Shaw, Mary *LI*; *XVII*
Spender, Lily *LIII*; *XVIII*
Vaux, Anne *LVIII*; *XX*
Wakefield, Priscilla *LVIII*; *XX*
Ward, Mary *1901 III*; *XXII*

DAVID CECIL
Asquith, Cynthia Mary Evelyn *1951-1960*
Woolf, Adeline Virginia *1941–1950*

JOHN CHARLTON
Smallwood, Norah Evelyn *1981–1985*

HENRY MANNERS CHICHESTER
Gordon, Jane *XXII*; *VIII*
Hessel, Phoebe *XXVI*; *IX*

HAROLD HANNYNGTON CHILD
Terry, Alice Ellen *1922–1930*
Wood, Matilda Alice Victoria *1922–1930*

RICHARD COPLEY CHRISTIE
Volusene, Florence *LVIII*; *XX*

WALTER MCLENNAN CITRINE
Haslett, Caroline Harriet *1951–1960*

PATRICK COGHILL
Somerville, Edith Anna Œnone *1941–1950*

EDWARD DUTTON COOK
Abington, Frances *I*; *I*
Addison, Laura *I*; *I*
Anspach, Elizabeth, Margravine of *II*; *I*

THOMPSON COOPER
Baker, Anne Elizabeth *III*; *I*
Ball, Frances *III*; *I*
Bannerman, Anne *III*; *I*
Bertie, Catharine *IV*; *II*
Brand, Barbarina *VI*; *II*
Burton, Catharine *VIII*; *III*
Cellier, Elizabeth *IX*; *III*
Clitherow, Margaret *XI*; *IV*
Collignon, Catherine *XI*; *IV*
Collyer, Mary *XI*; *IV*
Conway, Anne *XII*; *IV*
Corbaux, Marie Françoise Catherine
  Doetter *XII*; *IV*
Cornwallis, Jane *XII*; *IV*
Davys, Mary *XIV*; *V*
Drane, Augusta Theodosia *1901 II*; *XXII*
Fullerton, Georgiana Charlotte *XX*; *VII*
Hallahan, Margaret Mary *XXIV*; *VIII*
Herbert, Lucy *XXVI*; *IX*
Kavanagh, Julia *XXX*; *X*
Kello, Esther or Hester *XXX*; *X*
McAuley, Catharine *XXXIV*; *XII*
Monck, Mary *XXXVIII*; *XIII*
O'Meara, Kathleen *XLII*; *XIV*
Palliser, Fanny Bury *XLIII*; *XV*
Tollett, Elizabeth *LVI*; *XIX*

COLIN COOTE
Milner, Violet Georgina *1951–1960*

FREDERICK CORDER
Bodda Pyne, Louisa Fanny *1901–1911 I*

FRANCIS MACDONALD CORNFORD
Harrison, Jane Ellen *1922–1930*

JAMES SUTHERLAND COTTON
Burton, Isabel *1901 I*; *XXII*
Edwards, Amelia Ann Blanford *1901 II*;
  XXII

WILLIAM PRIDEAUX COURTNEY
Acland, Christian Henrietta Caroline *I*; *I*
Bray, Anna Eliza *VI*; *II*
Davy, Jane *XIV*; *V*
Fanshawe, Catherine Maria *XVIII*; *VI*
Germain, Elizabeth *XXI*; *VII*
Macaulay, Catharine *XXXIV*; *XII*
Miles, Sibella Elizabeth *XXXVII*; *XIII*
Scott, Sarah *LI*; *XVII*
Sellon, Priscilla Lydia *LI*; *XVII*
Vesey, Elizabeth *LVIII*; *XX*
Williams, Anna *LXI*; *XXI*
Wynn, Charlotte Williams *LXIII*; *XXI*

MANDELL CREIGHTON
Blamire, Susanna *V*; *II*
Bowes, Elizabeth *VI*; *II*
Keys, Mary *XXXI*; *XI*

LIONEL HENRY CUST
Carter, Ellen *IX*; *III*
Casali, Andrea *IX*; *III*
Clarke, Harriet Ludlow *X*; *IV*
Gentileschi, Artemisia *XXI*; *VII*
Grace, Mary *XXII*; *VIII*
Kendrick, Emma Eleonora *XXX*; *X*
Kettle, Tilly *XXXI*; *XI*
Knight, Mary Anne *XXXI*; *XI*
Lawrance, Mary *XXXII*; *XI*
Lofthouse, Mary *XXXIV*; *XII*
Montalba, Henrietta Skerrett *XXXVIII*;
  XIII
Morgan, Alice Mary *XXXIX*; *XIII*
Newton, Ann Mary *XL*; *XIV*
Shore, Louisa Catherine *LII*; *XVIII*

JAMES DALTON
Lutyens, Agnes Elisabeth *1981–1985*

WILLIAM AUBREY DARLINGTON
Ashton, Winifred *1961–1970*
Loraine, Violet Mary *1951–1960*
Wyndham, Mary *1931–1940*
Wynyard, Diana *1961–1970*

HENRY DAVEY
Hallé, Wilma Maria Francisca
  1901–1911 II
Lemmens-Sherrington, Helen
  1901–1911 II
Novello, Clara Anastasia *1901–1911 III*
Sterling, Antoinette *1901–1911 III*

GEOFFREY DEARMER
Kennet, Edith Agnes Kathleen *1941–1950*

ALAN DENT
Lawrence, Gertrude *1951–1960*
Millar, Gertie *1951–1960*

EDWARD J. DENT
Baylis, Lilian Mary *1931–1940*

JAMES CAXTON DIBDIN
Powell, Mrs *XLVI*; *XVI*

RICHARD WATSON DIXON
Bulmer, Agnes *VII*; *III*

AUSTIN DOBSON
Beauclerk, Diana *IV*; *II*
Canning, Elizabeth *VIII*; *III*
Charlotte Augusta *X*; *IV*
Greenaway, Kate *1901–1911 II*

WILLIAM DOUGLAS–HOME
Johnson, Celia *1981–1985*

JOHN ANDREW DOYLE
Rowlandson, Mary *XLIX*; *XVII*

VICTOR WILLIAM MICHAEL DRURY
Gillie, Annis Calder *1981–1985*

BARON DUNSANY
Villiers, Margaret Elizabeth Child-
1941–1950

JOHN WOODFALL EBSWORTH
Cresswell, Madam *XIII*; *V*
Ebsworth, Mary Emma *XVI*; *VI*

LIONEL FREDERIC ELLIS
Barnett, Henrietta Octavia Weston
1931–1940

M. EPSTEIN
Goodman, Julia *1901–1911 II*

ST JOHN ERVINE
Kendal, Margaret Shafto *1931–1940*
Tempest, Marie *1941–1950*

ALEXANDER CHARLES EWALD
Albany, Louisa Maximiliana Carolina
Emanuel *I*; *I*

LOUIS ALEXANDER FAGAN
Charretie, Anna Maria *X*; *IV*
Cosway, Maria Cecilia Louisa *XII*; *IV*

CAESAR LITTON FALKINER
Stokes, Margaret M'Nair *1901 III*; *XXII*

KEITH FALKNER
Baillie, Isobel *1981–1985*

HAROLD FERGUSON
Hess, Julia Myra *1961–1970*

CHARLES HARDING FIRTH
Claypoole or Claypole, Elizabeth *XI*; *IV*
Hay, Lucy *XXV*; *IX*
Whorwood, Jane *LXI*; *XXI*

W. H. GRATTAN FLOOD
Holmes, Augusta Mary Anne
1901–1911 II

MICHAEL FOOT
Szabo, Violette Reine Elizabeth
Missing Persons

BRYAN FORBES
Evans, Edith Mary *1971–1980*

PETER JEREMY LEWINTER FRANKL
Werner, Alice *Missing Persons*

ABRAHAM FRYBERG
Kenny, Elizabeth *1951–1960*

GEOFFREY FRYER
Manton, Sidnie Milana *1971–1980*

ROGER FULFORD
Pankhurst, Christabel Harriette *1951–1960*

JAMES GAIRDNER
Anne of Bohemia *I*; *I*
Anne *I*; *I*
Anne *I*; *I*
Anne of Cleves *I*; *I*

Askew, Anne *II*; *I*
Catherine of Aragon *IX*; *III*
Catherine Howard *IX*; *III*
Catherine Parr *IX*; *III*
Elizabeth *XVII*; *VI*
Elizabeth *XVII*; *VI*
Margaret, Duchess of Burgundy *XXXVI*; *XII*
Mary of France *XXXVI*; *XII*
Pole, Margaret *XLVI*; *XVI*

VIVIAN HUNTER GALBRAITH
Clarke, Maude Violet *1931–1940*

SAMUEL RAWSON GARDINER
Arabella Stuart *II*; *I*
Henrietta Maria *XXV*; *IX*

RICHARD GARNETT
Adams, Sarah Flower *I; I*
Blackwell, Elizabeth *V*; *II*
Blind, Mathilde *1901 I*; *XXII*
Cadell, Jessie *VIII*; *III*
Clairmont, Clara Mary Jane *X*; *IV*
Coleridge, Sara *XI*; *IV*
Crowe, Catherine *XIII*; *V*
Darusmont, Frances *XIV*; *V*
Fox, Caroline *XX*; *VII*
Godwin, Catherine Grace *XXII*; *VIII*
Harwood, Isabella *XXV*; *IX*
Hofland, Barbara *XXVII*; *IX*
Jameson, Anna Brownell *XXIX*; *X*
Keary, Annie *XXX*; *X*
Knight, Ellis Cornelia *XXXI*; *XI*
Landon, Letitia Elizabeth *XXXII*; *XI*
Lee, Rachel Fanny Antonia *XXXII*; *XI*
Levy, Amy *XXXIII*; *XI*
Linton, Eliza Lynn *1901 III*; *XXII*
Mulock, Dinah Maria *XXXIX*; *XIII*
Norton, Caroline Elizabeth Sarah *XLI*; *XIV*
Oliphant, Margaret Oliphant *1901 III*; *XXII*
Pfeiffer, Emily Jane *XLV*; *XV*
Radcliffe, Ann *XLVII*; *XVI*
Rossetti, Christina Georgina *XLIX*; *XVII*
Rossetti, Lucy Madox *XLIX*; *XVII*
Shelley, Mary Wollstonecraft *LII*; *XVIII*
Southey, Caroline Anne *LIII*; *XVIII*
Tautphoelus, Baroness von *LV*; *XIX*
Trollope, Frances *LVII*; *XIX*

IAN J. GENTLES
Chidley, Katherine *Missing Persons*

JOHN WESTBY-GIBSON
Adam, Jean *I*; *I*
Calvert, Caroline Louisa Waring *VIII*; *III*

JOHN GIELGUD
Rutherford, Margaret *1971–1980*

VAL HENRY GIELGUD
Neilson, Julia Emilie *1951–1960*

JOHN THOMAS GILBERT
Brooke, Charlotte *VI*; *II*
Grierson, Constantia *XXIII*; *VIII*

HERBERT HARLAKENDEN
GILCHRIST
Gilchrist, Anne *XXI*; *VII*

BENEDICT WILLIAM GINSBURG
Cavell, Edith *1912–1921*

GORDON GOODWIN
Celesia, Dorothea *IX*; *III*
Creed, Elizabeth *XIII*; *V*
Elizabeth *XVII*; *VI*
Fenton, Lavinia *XVIII*; *VI*
Fermor, Henrietta Louise *XVIII*; *VI*
Fitzroy, Mary *XIX*; *VII*
Fletcher, Eliza *XIX*; *VII*
Geddes, Jenny *XXI*; *VII*
Gilbert, Elizabeth Margaretta Maria *XXI*; *VII*
Graham, Janet *XXII*; *VIII*
Gunning, Susannah *XXIII*; *VIII*
Hack, Maria *XXIII*; *VIII*
Hay, Mary Cecil *XXV*; *IX*
Henrietta or Henrietta Anne *XXV*; *IX*
Hesketh, Harriet *XXVI*; *IX*
Hutchinson, Anne *XXVIII*; *X*
Johnstone, Christian Isobel *XXX*; *X*
Lennox, Charlotte *XXXIII*; *XI*
M'Avoy, Margaret *XXXIV*; *XII*
Makin, Bathsua *XXXV*; *XII*
Mary *XXXVI*; *XII*
Murray, Amelia Matilda *XXXIX*; *XIII*
Ogborne, Elizabeth *XLII*; *XIV*

ALEXANDER GORDON
Bache, Sarah *II*; *I*
Barwell, Louisa Mary *III*; *I*
Brightwell, Cecilia Lucy *VI*; *II*
Carpenter, Mary *IX*; *III*
Cobbe, Frances Power *1901–1911 I*
Godiva or Godgifu *XXII*; *VIII*
Hewley, Sarah *XXVI*; *IX*
Magee, Martha Maria *XXXV*; *XII*
Smith, Elizabeth *LIII*; *XVIII*
Smith, Pleasance *LIII*; *XVIII*
Southcott, Joanna *LIII*; *XVIII*
Waring, Anna Letitia *1901–1911 III*

JOHN GORE
Mary *1951–1960*

MARIUS GORING
Robson, Flora *1981–1985*

EDMUND GOSSE
Behn, Afra, Aphra, or Ayfara *IV*; *II*
Brightwen, Eliza *1901–1911 I*
Gosse, Emily *XXII*; *VIII*
Otté, Elise *1901–1911 III*
Pix, Mary *XLV*; *XV*

ARTHUR HENRY GRANT
Alice Maud Mary *I*; *I*
Baillie, Marianne *II*; *I*
Bather, Lucy Elizabeth *III*; *I*

ROBERT EDMUND GRAVES
Beale, Mary *IV*; *II*
Bell, Maria *IV*; *II*
Benwell, Mary *IV*; *II*
Gillies, Margaret *XXI*; *VII*
Mutrie, Martha Darley *XXXIX*; *XIII*
Setchel, Sarah *LI*; *XVII*

DAVID GRAY
Ryan, Elizabeth Montague *1971–1980*

ROBERT GREAVES
Penson, Lillian Margery *1961–1970*

RICHARD GREENE
Clark, Esther *Missing Persons*
Collier, Mary *Missing Persons*
Cristall, Anne Batten *Missing Persons*
Dixon, Sarah *Missing Persons*

Egerton, Sarah Fyge *Missing Persons*
Jones, Mary *Missing Persons*
Kelly, Isabella *Missing Persons*
Wright, Mehetabel Wesley
  Missing Persons

GEORGE GREENFIELD
Blyton, Enid Mary *1961–1970*

WILLIAM ALEXANDER GREENHILL
Kennedy, Grace *XXX*; *X*

HENRY RIVERSDALE GRENFELL
Waldegrave, Frances Elizabeth Anne
  LIX; *XX*

JOHN GRIGG
Astor, Nancy Witcher *1961–1970*

FRANCIS HINDES GROOME
Walkinshaw, Clementina *LIX*; *XX*

ALEXANDER BALLOCH GROSART
Alexander, Helen *I*; *I*
Bacon, Ann *II*; *I*
Baillie, Grizel *II*; *I*
Barnard, Anne *III*; *I*

IVOR GUEST
Rambert, Marie *1981–1985*

WILLEM D. HACKMANN
Ayrton, Hertha *Missing Persons*

JAMES CUTHBERT HADDEN
Cousin, Anne Ross *1901–1911 I*
Hearn, Mary Anne *1901–1911 II*
Inverarity, Elizabeth *XXIX*; *X*
Laidlaw, Anna Robena *1901–1911 II*
Luke, Jemima *1901–1911 II*
Lyon, Agnes *XXXIV*; *XII*
Mackellar, Mary *XXXV*; *XII*
Mara, Gertrude Elizabeth *XXXVI*; *XII*
Masters, Mary *XXXVII*; *XIII*
Nunn, Marianne *XLI*; *XIV*
Parsons, Elizabeth *XLIII*; *XV*
Steele, Anne *LIV*; *XVIII*
White, Alice Mary Meadows *LXI*; *XXI*

WILLIAM HALEY
Bonham Carter, Helen Violet *1961–1970*

**GERALD KENNETH SAVERY
HAMILTON-EDWARDS**
Marina *1961–1970*
Victoria Alexandra Alice Mary *1961–1970*
Victoria Eugénie Julia Ena *1961–1970*

JOHN ANDREW HAMILTON
Long, Amelia *XXXIV*; *XII*
Miller, Lydia Falconer *XXXVII*; *XIII*
Morgan, Sydney *XXXIX*; *XIII*

GEOFFREY COLIN HARCOURT
Robinson, Joan Violet *1981–1985*

BRIAN HARRISON
Butler, Christina Violet *Missing Persons*

ROBERT HARRISON
Harrison, Mary *XXV*; *IX*

LESLIE POLES HARTLEY
Asquith, Emma Alice Margaret *1941–1950*

FREDERICK JOSEPH HARVEY
Bland, Edith *1922–1930*

ROY HENDERSON
Ferrier, Kathleen Mary *1951–1960*

THOMAS FINLAYSON HENDERSON
Buchan or Simpson, Elspeth *VII*; *III*
Cavendish, Christiana *IX*; *III*
Cavendish, Elizabeth *IX*; *III*
Cavendish, Georgiana *IX*; *III*
Cockburn, Alicia or Alison *XI*; *IV*
Douglas, Margaret *XV*; *V*
Dunlop, Frances Anne Wallace *XVI*; *VI*
Halkett, Anne or Anna *XXIV*; *VIII*
Hamilton, Anne *XXIV*; *VIII*
Killigrew, Catherine or Katherine *XXXI*;
  XI
Macdonald, Flora *XXXV*; *XII*
Macfarlane, Mrs *XXXV*; *XII*
Maclehose, Agnes *XXXV*; *XII*
Margaret of Denmark *XXXVI*; *XII*
Mary Queen of Scots *XXXVI*; *XII*
Mary of Gueldres *XXXVI*; *XII*
Stewart-Mackenzie, Maria Elizabeth
  Frederica *LIV*; *XVIII*
Wardlaw, Elizabeth *LIX*; *XX*

DAVID HEY
Fiennes, Celia *Missing Persons*

ALAN G. HILL
Wordsworth, Dorothy *Missing Persons*

THOMAS HODGKIN
Fry, Sara Margery *1951–1960*

HARRY HODGKINSON
Durham, Mary Edith *Missing Persons*

WILLIAM DAVID HOGARTH
Bell, Gertrude Margaret Lowthian
  1922–1930

H. P. HOLLIS
Clerke, Agnes Mary *1901–1911 I*

EMLYN HOOSON
Ashley, Laura *1981–1985*

O. J. R. HOWARTH
Dixie, Florence Caroline *1901–1911 I*

FRANK HOWES
Smyth, Ethel Mary *1941–1950*

CHARLES ERNEST HUGHES
Clarke, Mary Victoria Cowden *1901 II*;
  XII

JOHN TREVOR HUGHES
Russell, Dorothy Stuart *1981–1985*

PAUL HULTON
Hermes, Gertrude Anna Bertha *1981–1985*

CHRISTMAS HUMPHREYS
Leyel, Hilda Winifred Ivy *1951–1960*

WILLIAM HUNT
Ælfgifu *I*; *I*
Ælfgifu *I*; *I*
Ælfthryth *I*; *I*
Ælfthryth, or Elfrida, *I*; *I*
Aldgyth *I*; *I*
Berengaria *IV*; *II*
Bertha *IV*; *II*
Boughton, Joan *VI*; *II*
Chessar, Jane Agnes *X*; *IV*

Chudleigh, Elizabeth *X*; *IV*
Coventry, Maria, Countess *XII*; *IV*
Cuthburh or Cuthburga *XIII*; *V*
Eadburga, Eadburh, Bugga, or Bugge
  XVI; *VI*
Eadburge *XVI*; *VI*
Eanflaed *XVI*; *VI*
Ebba or Æbba *XVI*; *VI*
Edith or Eadgyth *XVI*; *VI*
Edith or Eadgyth *XVI*; *VI*
Eleanor of Castile *XVII*; *VI*
Emma *XVII*; *VI*
Ethelburga or Æthelburh *XVIII*; *VI*
Ethelfleda, Æthelflaed, or Ælfled *XVIII*;
  VI
Frideswide, Fritheswith, or Fredeswitha
  XX; *VII*
Gunning, Elizabeth *XXIII*; *VIII*
Isabella of Angoulême *XXIX*; *X*
Isabella *XXIX*; *X*
Margaret *XXXVI*; *XII*
Margaret, the Maid of Norway *1901 III*;
  XXII
Matilda *XXXVII*; *XIII*
Milburg, Mildburga, or Mildburh
  XXXVII; *XIII*
Mildred or Mildryth *XXXVII*; *XIII*
Nest or Nesta *XL*; *XIV*
Nicholson, Margaret *XLI*; *XIV*
Osyth, Osith, or Osgith *XLII*; *XIV*
Philippa of Hainault *XLV*; *XV*
Sexburga, Seaxburg, or Sexburh *LI*; *XVII*
Sexburga, Saint *LI*; *XVII*
Werburga or Werburh *LX*; *XX*

HUGH ESMOR HUXLEY
Hanson, Emmeline Jean *1971–1980*

ANTHONY HYMAN
Byron, Augusta Ada *Missing Persons*

BENJAMIN DAYDON JACKSON
Banks, Sarah Sophia *III*; *I*

WILLIAM A. W. JARVIS
Sorabji, Cornelia *1951–1960*

AUGUSTUS JESSOPP
Elizabeth *XVII*; *VI*

JAMES JOLL
Wiskemann, Elizabeth Meta *1971–1980*

JAMES JONES
Sharp, Evelyn Adelaide *1981–1985*

REES M. JENKIN JONES
Griffiths, Ann *XXIII*; *VIII*

HENRY REYMOND FITZWALTER
KEATING
Allingham, Margery Louise *1961–1970*
Christie, Agatha Mary Clarissa *1971–1980*
Marsh, Edith Ngaio *1981–1985*

THOMAS EDWARD KEBBEL
Fitzherbert, Maria Anne *XIX*; *VII*

CHARLES KENT
Berry, Mary *IV*; *II*
Blessington, Marguerite *V*; *II*
Kelly, Frances Maria *XXX*; *X*

GEOFFREY KEYNES
Cornford, Frances Crofts *1951–1960*

BRIAN KIMMINS
Kimmins, Grace Thyrza *1951–1960*

CHARLES LETHBRIDGE
KINGSFORD
Grey, Elizabeth *XXIII*; *VIII*
Hensey, Florence *XXVI*; *IX*
Hildilid *XXVI*; *IX*
Joan or Joanna of Acre *XXIX*; *X*
Joan or Joanna of Navarre *XXIX*; *X*
Kempe, Margerie *XXX*; *X*
Perrers, Alice *XLV*; *XV*
Swynford, Catherine *LV*; *XIX*

ARCHIBALD LAURENCE PATRICK
KIRWAN
Caton-Thompson, Gertrude *1981–1985*

AARON KLUG
Franklin, Rosalind Elsie *Missing Persons*

JOSEPH KNIGHT
Baddeley, Sophia *II*; *I*
Barry, Ann Spranger *III*; *I*
Barry, Elizabeth *III*; *I*
Bartley, Sarah *III*; *I*
Becher, Eliza *IV*; *II*
Bellamy, George Anne *IV*; *II*

DAVID MARSHALL LANG
Lister, Anne *Missing Persons*

PHILIP LARKIN
Pym, Barbara Mary Crampton *1971–1980*

JOHN KNOX LAUGHTON
Digby, Lettice *XV*; *V*
Franklin, Eleanor Anne *XX*; *VII*
Franklin, Jane *XX*; *VII*
Hamilton, Emma *XXIV*; *VIII*
Nelson, Frances Herbert *XL*; *XIV*
Wallace, Eglantine *LIX*; *XX*
Williams, Helen Maria *LXI*; *XXI*

W. J. LAWRENCE
Mellon, Sarah Jane *1901–1911 II*
Thompson, Lydia *1901–1911 III*
Vaughan, Kate *1901–1911 III*

EDMUND LEACH
Richards, Audrey Isabel *1981–1985*

SIDNEY LEE
Adela *I*; *I*
Aguilar, Grace *I*; *I*
Armine or Armyne, Mary *II*; *I*
Aust, Sarah *II*; *I*
Ayrton, Matilda Chaplin *;I*
Barton, Elizabeth *III*; *I*
Baynard, Ann *III*; *I*
Bendish, Bridget *IV*; *II*
Bocher, Boucher, or Butcher, Joan *V*; *II*
Bowdler, Henrietta Maria *VI*; *II*
Bowdler, Jane *VI*; *II*
Butler, Eleanor *VIII*; *III*
Callcott, Maria *VIII*; *III*
Catherine of Valois *IX*; *III*
Coventry, Anne *XII*; *IV*
Craigie, Pearl Mary Teresa *1901–1911 I*
Crofts or Croft, Elizabeth *XIII*; *V*
Dilke, Emilia Frances *1901–1911 I*
Dowriche, Anne *XV*; *V*
Dudley, Jane *XVI*; *VI*
Fitton, Mary *XIX*; *VII*
Fitzgerald, Elizabeth *XIX*; *VII*
Harley, Brilliana *XXIV*; *VIII*
Haywood, Eliza *XXV*; *IX*
Herbert, Mary *XXVI*; *IX*
Jane Seymour *XXIX*; *X*
Lisle, Alice *XXXIII*; *XI*

Mary I *XXXVI*; *XII*
Montagu, Elizabeth *XXXVIII*; *XIII*
Rich, Penelope *XLVIII*; *XVI*
Rowe, Elizabeth *XLIX*; *XVII*
Shipton, *LII*; *XVIII*
Victoria *1901 III*; *XXII*
Wroth, Mary *LXIII*; *XXI*

JAMES LEES-MILNE
Jourdain, Emily Margaret *Missing Persons*
Mitford, Nancy Freeman- *1971–1980*

ROBIN HUMPHREY LEGGE
Parepa-Rosa, Euphrosyne Parepa de
    Boyesku *XLIII*; *XV*
Patey, Janet Monach *XLIV*; *XV*
Patti, Carlotta *XLIV*; *XV*
Rainforth, Elizabeth *XLVII*; *XVI*
Titiens, or Tietjens, Teresa Caroline
    Johanna *LVI*; *XIX*

JOHN LEHMANN
Sitwell, Edith Louisa *1961–1970*

ANTHONY LEJEUNE
Thomas, Margaret Haig *1951–1960*

JOHN MEWBURN LEVIEN
Albani, Marie Louise Cécilie Emma
    1922–1930
Butt, Clara Ellen *1931–1940*
Melba, Nellie *1931–1940*

BERNARD LEVIN
West, Rebecca *1981–1985*

SAMUEL ROBINSON LITTLEWOOD
Vanbrugh, Irene *1941–1950*
Vanbrugh, Violet *1941–1950*

B. S. LONG
Chase, Marian Emma *1901–1911 I*
Farmer, Emily *1901–1911 II*

SACKVILLE HATTON HARRINGTON
LOVETT
Besant, Annie *1931–1940*

WILLIAM BOSWELL LOWTHER
Peters, Mary *XLV*; *XV*
Saffery, Maria Grace *L*; *XVII*

CHARLES P. LUCAS
Bishop, Isabella Lucy *1901–1911 I*

JOSEPH HIRST LUPTON
Owen, Alice *XLII*; *XIV*

NORMAN MACCOLL
Chapman, Mary Francis *X*; *IV*
Grant, Anne *XXII*; *VIII*

MICHAEL MACDONAGH
O'Leary, Ellen *XLII*; *XIV*

JAMES RAMSAY MACDONALD
Macleod, Mary *XXXV*; *XII*

JOHN MACDONELL
Austin, Sarah *II*; *I*

JAMES MACGIBBON
Stopes, Marie Charlotte Carmichael
1951–1960

AENEAS JAMES GEORGE MACKAY
Drummond, Annabella *XVI*; *VI*
Graham, Clementina Stirling *XXII*; *VIII*
Jane or Johanna *XXIX*; *X*
Margaret, Saint *XXXVI*; *XII*

ALAN MACLEAN
Johnson, Pamela Hansford *1981–1985*

NORMAN MACLEAN
Balfour, Frances *1931–1940*

WILLIAM DUNN MACRAY
Fitzgerald, Katherine *XIX*; *VII*
Pakington, Dorothy *XLIII*; *XV*

FREDERICK MADDEN
Perham, Margery Freda *1981–1985*

JOHN ALEXANDER FULLER-
MAITLAND
Bates, Sarah *III*; *I*
Colquhoun, Janet *XI*; *IV*
Lind, Johanna Maria *XXXIII*; *XI*

JAMES JOSEPH MALLON
Anderson, Mary Reid *1912–1921*

MAX MALLOWAN
Murray, Margaret Alice *1961–1970*

ALBERT MANSBRIDGE
McMillan, Margaret *1931–1940*

ARTHUR MARSHALL
Brazil, Angela *1941–1950*

EDWARD HENRY MARSHALL
Brassey, Anna or Annie *1901 I*; *XXII*

CHARLES TRICE MARTIN
Carmylyon, Alice or Ellys *IX*; *III*

THEODORE MARTIN
Cibber, Susannah Maria *X*; *IV*
Clive, Catherine *XI*; *IV*

PERCY MARYON-WILSON
Royden, Agnes Maud *1951–1960*

FRANK THOMAS MARZIALS
Rowan, Frederica Maclean *XLIX*; *XVII*

PETER MATHIAS
Carus-Wilson, Eleanora Mary *1971–1980*

GODFREY HUGH LANCELOT
LE MAY
Churchill, Jeanette *Missing Persons*
Hughes, Elizabeth Phillipps *Missing
Persons*

CHARLES HERBERT MAYO
Mayo, Elizabeth *XXXVII*; *XIII*

ROBIN MCDOUALL
Lewis, Rosa *1951–1960*

ALEXANDER HASTIE MILLAR
Hastings, Flora Elizabeth *XXV*; *IX*
Murray, Elizabeth *XXXIX*; *XIII*

ARTHUR MILLER
Boadicea *V*; *II*

PERCY MILLICAN
Norgate, Kate *1931–1940*

RICHARD MILLWARD
Arendrup, Edith *Missing Persons*

JULIAN MITCHELL
Compton-Burnett, Ivy *1961–1970*

JAMES MONAHAN
Genée, Adeline *1961–1970*

WILLIAM COSMO MONKHOUSE
Carpenter, Margaret Sarah *IX*; *III*
Heaton, Mary Margaret *XXV*; *IX*
Landseer, Jessica *XXXII*; *XI*
Linwood, Mary *XXXIII*; *XI*

J. E. G. DE MONTMORENCY
Hill, Rosamund Davenport- *1901–1911 II*
Hubbard, Louisa Maria *1901–1911 II*

NORMAN MOORE
Hasell, Elizabeth Julia *XXV*; *IX*
Leadbeater, Mary *XXXII*; *XI*
MacMoyer, Florence *XXXV*; *XII*
O'Carroll, Margaret *XLI; XIV*
O'Malley, Grace *XLII*; *XIV*

KENNETH O. MORGAN
Lloyd George, Frances Louise *1971–1980*

SHERIDAN MORLEY
Cons, Emma *Missing Persons*
Cooper, Gladys Constance *1971–1980*
Thorndike, Agnes Sybil *1971–1980*

HERBERT STANLEY MORRISON
Lowe, Eveline Mary *1951–1960*

VICTOR MORRISON
Hastings, Anthea Esther *1981–1985*

IVOR NEWTON
Cohen, Harriet *1961–1970*
Fachiri, Adila Adrienne Adalbertina
  Maria *1961–1970*

ALBERT NICHOLSON
Crane, Lucy *XIII*; *V*
Holbrook, Ann Catherine *XXVII*; *IX*
Le Breton, Anna Letitia *XXXII*; *XI*
Longworth, Maria Theresa *XXXIV*; *XII*

EDMUND TOULMIN NICOLLE
Toulmin, Camilla Dufour *LVII*; *XIX*

NIGEL NICOLSON
Bagnold, Enid Algerine *1981–1985*

PIERCE LAURENCE NOLAN
Nagle, Nano or Honora *XL*; *XIV*

GERALD LE GRYS NORGATE
Cook, Eliza *1901 II*; *XXII*
Linskill, Mary *XXXIII*; *XI*
Palmer, Eleanor *XLIII*; *XV*
Peacock, Lucy *XLIV*; *XV*

EDWARD O'BRIEN
Felkin, Ellen Thorneycroft *1922–1930*
Murry, Kathleen *1922–1930*

DAVID JAMES O'DONOGHUE
Ferguson, Mary Catherine *1901–1911 II*
Roche, Regina Maria *XLIX*; *XVII*
Tonna, Charlotte Elizabeth *LVII*; *XIX*

FREEMAN MARIUS O'DONOGHUE
Mee, Anne *XXXVII*; *XIII*
Moser, Mary *XXXIX*; *XIII*
Pope, Clara Maria *XLVI*; *XVI*
Read, Catherine *XLVII*; *XVI*
St Aubyn, Catherine *L*; *XVII*
Sharpe, Louisa *LI*; *XVII*
Wright, Patience *LXIII*; *XXI*

THOMAS OLDEN
Brigit *VI*; *II*
Darlugdach *XIV*; *V*
Modwenna or Moninne *XXXVIII*; *XIII*

BERNARD MICHAEL EDMUND
O'MAHONEY
Vansittart, Henrietta *Missing Persons*

JOHN HENRY OVERTON
Astell, Mary *II*; *I*
Hastings, Elizabeth *XXV*; *IX*
Hastings, Selina *XXV*; *IX*
Hopton, Susanna *XXVII*; *IX*

W. B. OWEN
O'Brien, Charlotte Grace *1901–1911 III*
Rye, Maria Susan *1901–1911 III*

WILLIAM ROBERT OWENS
Beaumont, Agnes *Missing Persons*

HAROLD FREDERICK OXBURY
Mannin, Ethel Edith *1981–1985*
Matthews, Jessie Margaret *1981–1985*

FREDERICK PAGE
Meynell, Alice Christiana Gertrude
1922–1930

WILLIAM GEORGE BERNARD PAGE
Hodson, Margaret *XXVII; IX*

STEPHEN PAGET
Nightingale, Florence *1901–1911 III*

DAVID PAINTING
Dillwyn, Elizabeth Amy *Missing Persons*

JOHN WOOD PALMER
Mathews, Elvira Sibyl Marie Laughton
1951–1960

JOHN PARKER
Farren, Ellen *1901–1911 II*
Horniman, Annie Elizabeth Fredericka
1931–1940
Vezin, Jane Elizabeth *1901–1911 III*

PETER J. PARR
Kenyon, Kathleen Mary *1971–1980*

HENRY PATON
Douglas, Jane *XV; V*
Douglas, Janet *XV; V*

BRIAN PEARCE
Morley, Iris *Missing Persons*

DEREK PEPYS-WHITELEY
Courtneidge, Esmeralda Cicely *1971–1980*

HENRY PHILLIPS
Lloyd, Dorothy Jordan *1941–1950*

SIMON WILTON PHIPPS
Batten, Edith Mary *1981–1985*

HARRY GRIFFITHS PITT
Lehzen, Louise *Missing Persons*

WILLIAM JAMES PLATT
Cable, Alice Mildred *1951–1960*
French, Evangeline Frances *1951–1960*

ALBERT FREDERICK POLLARD
Long, Catharine *XXXIV; XII*
Mozley, Anne *XXXIX; XIII*
Parr, Harriet *1901 III; XXII*
Seymour, Catherine *LI; XVII*
Stanley, Charlotte *LIV; XVIII*

JOHN POLLOCK
Aylward, Gladys May *1961–1970*

WALTER JAMES MACQUEEN POPE
Tilley, Vesta *1951–1960*

D'ARCY POWER
Stewart, Isla *1901–1911 III*

FREDERICK MAURICE POWICKE
Norgate, Kate *1931–1940*

ERNEST RADFORD
Bartholomew, Ann Charlotte *III; I*
Bingham, Margaret *V; II*

WILLIAM FRASER RAE
Sheridan, Caroline Henrietta *LII; XVIII*
Sheridan, Elizabeth Ann *LII; XVIII*
Sheridan, Frances *LII; XVIII*
Sheridan, Helen Selina *LII; XVIII*

MAX REINHARDT
Heyer, Georgette *1971–1980*

JAMES MCMULLEN RIGG
Colville, Elizabeth *XI; IV*
Cowper, Mary *XII; IV*
Crewe, Frances Anne *XIII; V*
Fox, Elizabeth Vassall *XX; VII*
Francis, Anne *XX; VII*
Gordon, Henrietta *XXII; VIII*
Hall, Agnes C. *XXIV; VIII*
Hamilton, Elizabeth *XXIV; VIII*
Howard, Henrietta *XXVIII; X*
Kent, Victoria Mary Louisa, Duchess of
XXXI; XI
Kirkhoven or Kerckhoven, Catherine
XXXI; XI
Knight, Henrietta *XXXI; XI*
Knipp or Knep, Mrs *XXXI; XI*
Lane, Jane *XXXII; XI*
Lee, Ann *XXXII; XI*
Mary, Princess of Hesse *XXXVI; XII*

Mortimer, Mrs Favell Lee *XXXIX*; *XIII*
Wallmoden, Amalie Sophie Marianne
  LIX; *XX*

CHARLES HENRY ROBERTS
Howard, Rosalind Frances *1912–1921*

WILLIAM ROBERTS
Davies, Catherine *XIV*; *V*

GEORGE CROOM ROBERTSON
Grote, Harriet *XXIII*; *VIII*

CHARLES JOHN ROBINSON
Calderwood, Margaret *VIII*; *III*

LENNOX ROBINSON
Gregory, Isabella Augusta *1931–1940*

PAUL JACQUES VICTOR ROLO
Harari, Manya *1961–1970*

KENNETH ROSE
Alice Mary Victoria Augusta Pauline
  1981–1985
Marie Louise *1951–1960*
Ramsay, Victoria Patricia Helena
  Elizabeth *1971–1980*

JOHN HORACE ROUND
Abdy, Maria *I*; *I*
Adeliza *I*; *I*
Adeliza of Louvain *I*; *I*

EDWARD FRANCIS RUSSELL
Somerset, Isabella Caroline *1912–1921*

MICHAEL SADLEIR
Harraden, Beatrice *1931–1940*
Mackay, Mary *1922–1930*
Maxwell, Mary Elizabeth *1912–1921*
Savage, Ethel Mary *1931–1940*

LLOYD CHARLES SANDERS
Frampton, Mary *XX*; *VII*
Leveson–Gower, Harriet Elizabeth
  Georgiana *XXXIII*; *XI*

**HILARY AIDAN ST GEORGE
SAUNDERS**
Houston, Fanny Lucy *1931–1940*

JOHN SAVILLE
Cole, Margaret Isabel *1971–1980*

LARRY J. SCHAAF
Atkins, Anna *Missing Persons*

HAROLD SCOTT
Barker, Lilian Charlotte *1951–1960*

JAMES MOFFAT SCOTT
Hennell, Mary *XXV*; *IX*

THOMAS SECCOMBE
Eastlake, Elizabeth *1901 II*; *XXII*
Hunter, Rachel *XXVIII*; *X*
Kelty, Mary Anne *XXX*; *X*
Kirby, Elizabeth *XXXI*; *XI*
Lacy, Harriette Deborah *XXXI*; *XI*
Latter, Mary *XXXII*; *XI*
Lewson, Jane *XXXIII*; *XI*
Malcolm, Sarah *XXXV*; *XII*
Moore, Ann *XXXVIII*; *XIII*
Myddleton or Middleton, Jane *XXXIX*;
  XIII
Needham, Elizabeth *XL*; *XIV*
Osborne, Ruth *XLII*; *XIV*
Parsons, Elizabeth *XLIII*; *XV*
Phillips, Catherine *XLV*; *XV*
Phillips, Teresia Constantia *XLV*; *XV*
Pilkington, Laetitia *XLV*; *XV*
Sedley, Catharine *LI*; *XVII*
Snell, Hannah *LIII*; *XVIII*
Stanhope, Hester Lucy *LIV*; *XVIII*
Stuart or Stewart, Frances Teresa *LV*;
  XIX
Taglioni, Marie *LV*; *XIX*
Talbot, Elizabeth *LV*; *XIX*
Talbot, Mary Anne *LV*; *XIX*
Taylor, Jane *LV*; *XIX*
Thomas, Elizabeth *LVI*; *XIX*
Thomson, Katharine *LVI*; *XIX*
Toft or Tofts, Mary *LVI*; *XIX*
Trench, Melesina *LVII*; *XIX*
Trollope, Theodosia *LVII*; *XIX*
Tussaud, Marie *LVII*; *XIX*
Unwin, Mary *LVIII*; *XX*
Vane, Frances Anne *LVIII*; *XX*
Villiers, Barbara *LVIII*; *XX*
Villiers, Elizabeth *LVIII*; *XX*
Walter, Lucy *LIX*; *XX*
Wenham, Jane *LX*; *XX*

Wentworth, Henrietta Maria *LX*; *XX*
Wharton, Anne *LX*; *XX*
Wilson, Harriette *LXII*; *XXI*
Wilson, Margaret *LXII*; *XXI*
Wood, Ellen *LXII*; *XXI*

EDWARD SEYMOUR
Victoria Alexandra Olga Mary *1931–1940*

ROBERT M. SHACKLETON
Watson, Janet Vida *1981–1985*

ROBERT FARQUHARSON SHARP
Hudson, Mary *XXVIII*; *X*

JAMES BYAM SHAW
Dodgson, Frances Catharine *1951–1960*

DESMOND SHAWE–TAYLOR
Teyte, Margaret *1971–1980*

NED SHERRIN
Brahms, Caryl *1981–1985*

EVELYN SHIRLEY SHUCKBURGH
Boothby, Miss Hill *V*; *II*
Churchill, Arabella *X*; *IV*
Clare, Elizabeth de *X*; *IV*

HUGH MACDONALD SINCLAIR
Chick, Harriette *1971–1980*

PAUL SLACK
Hoby, Margaret *Missing Persons*

GEORGE BARNETT SMITH
Baillie, Joanna *II*; *I*

JOHN GEORGE SMYTH
Chambers, Dorothea Katharine *1951–1960*
Sterry, Charlotte *1961–1970*

DONALD SOPER
Stocks, Mary Danvers *1971–1980*

WILLIAM BARCLAY SQUIRE
Anderson, Lucy *I*; *I*
Arne, Cecilia *II*; *I*
Barnard, Charlotte Alington *III*; *I*
Bewick, Jane *V*; *II*
Bishop, Ann *V*; *II*

Bland, Maria Theresa *V*; *II*
Brent, Charlotte *VI*; *II*
Caradori-Allan, Maria Caterina Rosalbina
 IX; *III*
Crouch, Anna Maria *XIII*; *V*
Davies, Cecilia *XIV*; *V*
Davies, Marianne *XIV*; *V*
Dickons, Maria *XV*; *V*
Dussek, Sophia *XVI*; *VI*

DONALD STEEL
Smith, Frances *1971–1980*

LESLIE STEPHEN
Arblay, Frances d' *II*; *I*
Austen, Jane II; *I*
Blandy, Mary *V*; *II*
Brontë, Charlotte *VI*; *II*
Cockburn, Catharine *XI*; *IV*
Cross, Mary Ann *XIII*; *V*
Damer, Anne Seymour *XIII*; *V*
Delany, Mary *XIV*; *V*
Edgeworth, Maria *XVI*; *VI*
Elstob, Elizabeth *XVII*; *VI*
Ferrier, Susan Edmondstone *XVIII*; *VI*
Fielding, Sarah *XVIII*; *VI*
Fleming, Margaret *XIX*; *VII*
Gethin, Grace *XXI*; *VII*
Gisborne, Maria *XXI*; *VII*
Godolphin, Margaret *XXII*; *VIII*
Godwin, Mary Wollstonecraft *XXII*; *VIII*
Martineau, Harriet *XXXVI*; *XII*
Montagu, Mary Wortley *XXXVIII*; *XIII*
More, Hannah *XXXVIII*; *XIII*
North, Marianne *XLI*; *XIV*
Piozzi, Hester Lynch *XLV*; *XV*

HENRY MORSE STEPHENS
Clarke, Mary Anne *X*; *IV*

**JOHN INNES MACKINTOSH
STEWART**
Sayers, Dorothy Leigh *1951–1960*

OLIVER STEWART
Bailey, Mary *1951–1960*

OWEN STINCHCOMBE
Malleson, Elizabeth *Missing Persons*

REYNOLDS STONE
Raverat, Gwendolen Mary *1951–1960*

GEORGE STRONACH
Kincaid, Jean *XXXI*; *XI*
Wallace, Grace *LIX*; *XX*

ROY STRONG
Teerlinc, Levina *Missing Persons*

PETER SUTCLIFFE
Gérin, Winifred Eveleen *1981–1985*

CHARLES WILLIAM SUTTON
Becker, Lydia Ernestine *1901 I*; *XXII*
Crewdson, Jane *XIII*; *V*
Dobson, Susannah *XV*; *V*
Green, Eliza S. Craven *XXIII*; *VIII*
Hemans, Felicia Dorothea *XXV*; *IX*
Jevons, Mary Anne *XXIX*; *X*
Jewsbury, Geraldine Endsor *XXIX*; *X*
Jewsbury, Maria Jane *XXIX*; *X*
Mangnall, *XXXVI*; *XII*
Meteyard, Eliza *XXXVII*; *XIII*
Raffald, Elizabeth *XLVII*; *XVI*

CHRISTOPHER SYKES
Mann, Cathleen Sabine *1951–1960*

JAMES TAIT
Joan *XXIX*; *X*
Joan *XXIX*; *X*
Margaret *XXXVI*; *XII*
Margaret Tudor *XXXVI*; *XII*
Mary of Guise *XXXVI*; *XII*

CHARLES HOLWELL TALBOT
Christina of Markyate *Missing Persons*

RICHARD HENRY TAWNEY
Postan, Eileen Edna le Poer *1931–1940*

HENRY RICHARD TEDDER
Cornelys, Theresa *XII*; *IV*
Currer, Frances Mary Richardson *XIII*; *V*

DANIEL LLEUFER THOMAS
Puddicombe, Anne Adalisa *1901–1911 III*
Williams, Jane *LXI*; *XXI*

HUGH HAMSHAW THOMAS
Arber, Agnes *1951–1960*

GEORGE THORN-DRURY
Philips, Katherine *XLV*; *XV*

ANTHONY THWAITE
Plath, Sylvia *Missing Persons*

HENRY AVRAY TIPPING
Beaufort, Margaret *IV*; *II*

THOMAS FREDERICK TOUT
Catherine of Braganza *IX*; *III*
Christina *X*; *IV*
Isabella of France *XXIX*; *X*
Isabella of France *XXIX*; *X*
Margaret *XXXVI*; *XII*
Margaret of Anjou *XXXVI*; *XII*

JOSEPH BURNEY TRAPP
Yates, Frances Amelia *1981–1985*

WALTER HAWKEN TREGELLAS
Arundell, Mary *II*; *I*
Bonaventure, Thomasine *V*; *II*

JOHN COURTENAY TREWIN
Campbell, Beatrice Stella *1931–1940*
Collins, Josephine *1951–1960*
Compton, Fay *1971–1980*
McCarthy, Lillah *1951–1960*
Trevelyan, Hilda *1951–1960*

WILFRED ROBERT TROTTER
Nevill, Dorothy Fanny *Missing Persons*

MARK TULLY
Gandhi, Indira Priyadarshani *1981–1985*

ERNEST UNDERWOOD
Johnson, Amy *1941–1950*

EDMUND VENABLES
Cameron, Lucy Lyttelton *VIII*; *III*
Etheldreda, *XVIII*; *VI*
Fiennes or Fienes, Anne *XVIII*; *VI*
Hilda or Hild *XXVI*; *IX*
Honywood, Mary *XXVII*; *IX*
Ostrith or Osthryth *XLII*; *XIV*

ALSAGER VIAN
Davies, Christian *XIV*; *V*
Dawson, Nancy *XIV*; *V*
Dormer, Jane *XV*; *V*
Drummond, Margaret *XVI*; *VI*
Dunbar, Agnes *XVI*; *VI*
Fenning, Elizabeth *XVIII*; *VI*
Frankland, Jocosa or Joyce *XX*; *VII*

Greene, Anne *XXIII*; *VIII*
Griffith, Elizabeth *XXIII*; *VIII*
Grimston or Grymeston, Elizabeth *XXIII*;
 VIII
Hatfield, Martha *XXV*; *IX*
Hayes, Catharine *XXV*; *IX*

ROBERT WALLACE
Ormerod, Eleanor Anne *1901–1911 III*

PATRICK GERARD WALSH
Waddell, Helen Jane *1961–1970*

ADOLPHUS WILLIAM WARD
Anne of Denmark *I*; *I*
Anne *I*; *I*
Caroline *IX*; *III*
Caroline Mathilda *IX*; *III*
Charlotte Augusta Matilda *X*; *IV*
Elizabeth *XVII*; *VI*
Gaskell, Elizabeth Cleghorn *XXI*; *VII*
Hyde, Anne *XXVIII*; *X*
Hyde, Jane *XXVIII*; *X*
Keroualle, Louise Renée de *XXXI*; *XI*
Mary II *XXXVI*; *XII*
Mary of Modena *XXXVI*; *XII*
Rathbone, Hannah Mary *XLVII*; *XVI*
Schulenburg, Ehrengard Melusina
 von der *L*; *XVII*
Wood, Mary Anne Everett *LXII*; *XXI*

ROBERT AVERY WARD
Umphelby, Fanny *LVIII*; *XX*

PAUL WATERHOUSE
Baxter, Lucy *1901–1911 I*

MORGAN GEORGE WATKINS
Berners, Bernes, or Barnes, Juliana *IV*; *II*
Catchpole, Margaret *IX*; *III*
Harrison, Susannah *XXV*; *IX*
Lee, Sarah *XXXII*; *XI*
Pigot, Elizabeth Bridget *XLV*; *XV*

COLIN WATSON
Cripps, Isobel *1971–1980*

FRANCIS WATT
Charlotte Sophia *X*; *IV*
Harding, Anne Raikes *XXIV*; *VIII*
Hardy, Elizabeth *XXIV*; *VIII*
Harvey, Margaret *XXV*; *IX*

PETER WAYMARK
Dors, Diana *1981–1985*

GEOFFREY WEBB
Esdaile, Katharine Ada *1941–1950*

DAVID HENRY WEINGLASS
Riddell, Maria Woodley *Missing Persons*

CHARLES WELCH
James, Eleanor *XXIX*; *X*

JOHN WHEELER–BENNETT
Alexandra Victoria Alberta Edwina Louise
 Duff *1951–1960*

STEPHEN WHEELER
Roberts, Emma *XLVIII*; *XVI*

CHARLES HAROLD EVELYN WHITE
Martin, Sarah *XXXVI*; *XII*

JAMES WHITE
Hone, Evie *1951–1960*

FRED T. WILLEY
Summerskill, Edith Clara *1971–1980*

BERTRAM COGHILL ALAN WINDLE
Martin, Violet Florence *1912–1921*

BARON WINDLESHAM
Isaacs, Stella *1971–1980*

HUGH WONTNER
D'Oyly Carte, Bridget *1981–1985*

G. S. WOODS
Thurston, Katherine Cecil *1901–1911 III*
Victoria Adelaide Mary Louise *1901–1911*
 III

BERNARD BARHAM WOODWARD
Anning, Mary *1901 I*; *XXII*
Pratt, Anne *XLVI*; *XVI*

HUGH EVELYN WORTHAM
Helena Victoria *1941–1950*

Part 4

OCCUPATION INDEX

Subjects may have more than one entry

Art, design, patrons, photographers, architecture

Sharpe, Louisa *LI*; *XVII*
Sheridan, Clare Consuelo *1961–1970*
Siddal, Elizabeth Eleanor *Missing Persons*
Soyer, Elizabeth Emma *LIII*; *XVIII*
Spry, Constance *1951–1960*
Stillman or Spartali, Marie *Missing Persons*

Teerlinc, Levina *Missing Persons*
Thornycroft, Mary *LVI*; *XIX*
Tussaud, Marie *LVII*; *XIX*
Walker, Ethel *1951–1960*
Wright, Patience *LXIII*; *XXI*

Authors, historians, scholars, librarians, journalists

Abdy, Maria *I*; *I*
Acton, Eliza *I*; *I*
Adam, Jean *I*; *I*
Adams, Mary Grace Agnes *1981–1985*
Aguilar, Grace *I*; *I*
Aikin, Lucy *I*; *I*
Allingham, Margery Louise *1961–1970*
Anderson, Stella 1931–1940
Anning, Mary *1901 I*; *XXII*
Anspach, Elizabeth, Margravine of *II*; *I*
Arblay, Frances, Madame d' *II*; *I*
Arbuthnot, Harriet *Missing Persons*
Armitage, Ella Sophia *Missing Persons*
Arundell, Mary *II*; *I*
Ashford, Margaret Mary Julia *1971–1980*
Ashton, Winifred *1961–1970*
Asquith, Cynthia Mary Evelyn *1951–1960*
Astell, Mary *II*; *I*
Aust, Sarah *II*; *I*
Austen, Jane *II*; *I*
Austin, Sarah *II*; *I*
Bagnold, Enid Algerine *1981–1985*
Baillie, Grizel *II*; *I*
Baillie, Joanna *II*; *I*
Baillie, Marianne *II*; *I*
Baker, Anne Elizabeth *III*; *I*
Balfour, Clara Lucas *III*; *I*
Balfour, Frances *1931–1940*
Banks, Isabella *1901 I*; *XXII*
Bannerman, Anne *III*; *I*
Barbauld, Anna Letitia *III*; *I*
Barber, Mary *III*; *I*
Barker, Jane *Missing Persons*
Barnard, Anne *III*; *I*
Bartholomew, Ann Charlotte *III*; *I*
Barwell, Louisa Mary *III*; *I*
Bateson, Mary *1901–1911 I*
Bather, Lucy Elizabeth *III*; *I*
Baxter, Lucy *1901–1911 I*
Bayly, Ada Ellen *1901–1911 I*
Baynard, Ann *III*; *I*
Beaumont, Agnes *Missing Persons*

Beeton, Isabella Mary *Missing Persons*
Behn, Afra, Aphra, or Ayfara *IV*; *II*
Bell, Gertrude Margaret Lowthian *1922–1930*
Benger, Elizabeth Ogilvy *IV*; *II*
Bennett, Agnes Maria *IV*; *II*
Bentley, Phyllis Eleanor *1971–1980*
Berkeley, Eliza *IV*; *II*
Berners, Bernes, or Barnes, Juliana *IV*; *II*
Berry, Mary *IV*; *II*
Besant, Annie *1931–1940*
Betham, Mary Matilda *IV*; *II*
Bing, Gertrud *1961–1970*
Bishop, Isabella Lucy *1901–1911 I*
Black, Clementina Maria *Missing Persons*
Blamire, Susanna *V*; *II*
Bland, Edith *1922–1930*
Bland, Elizabeth *V*; *II*
Blessington, Marguerite *V*; *II*
Blind, Mathilde *1901 I*; *XXII*
Bloomfield, Georgiana *1901–1911 I*
Blount, Martha *V*; *II*
Blyton, Enid Mary *1961–1970*
Bonhote, Elizabeth *V*; *II*
Boothby, Miss Hill *V*; *II*
Bowdler, Henrietta Maria *VI*; *II*
Bowdler, Jane *VI*; *II*
Bowen, Elizabeth Dorothea Cole *1971–1980*
Bowes, Mary Eleanor *VI*; *II*
Bradstreet, Anne *VI*; *II*
Brahms, Caryl *1981–1985*
Brand, Barbarina *VI*; *II*
Brand, Hannah *VI*; *II*
Brassey, Anna or Annie *1901 I*; *XXII*
Bray, Anna Eliza *VI*; *II*
Bray, Caroline *1901–1911 I*
Brazil, Angela *1941–1950*
Brightwell, Cecilia Lucy *VI*; *II*
Brittain, Vera Mary *1961–1970*
Broderip, Frances Freeling *VI*; *II*
Brontë, Charlotte *VI*; *II*

Davies, Catherine *XIV*; *V*
Davies, Lucy Clementina *XIV*; *V*
Davys, Mary *XIV*; *V*
Delany, Mary *XIV*; *V*
De la Ramée, Marie Louise *1901–1911 I*
Dick, Anne *XV*; *V*
Dilke, Emilia Frances *1901–1911 I*
Dillwyn, Elizabeth Amy *Missing Persons*
Dixie, Florence Caroline *1901–1911 I*
Dixon, Sarah *Missing Persons*
Dobson, Susannah *XV*; *V*
Dorset, Catherine Anne *XV*; *V*
Dowriche, Anne *XV*; *V*
Drake, Judith *Missing Persons*
Drane, Augusta Theodosia *1901 II*; *XXII*
Du Bois, Dorothea *XVI*; *VI*
Dudley, Jane *XVI*; *VI*
Duncombe, Susanna *XVI*; *VI*
Dunlop, Frances Anne Wallace *XVI*; *VI*
Durham, Mary Edith *Missing Persons*
Eastlake, Elizabeth *1901 II*; *XXII*
Eden, Emily *XVI*; *VI*
Edgeworth, Maria *XVI*; *VI*
Edwards, Amelia Ann Blanford *1901 II*; *XXII*
Edwards, Matilda Barbara Betham- *1912–1921*
Egerton, Sarah Fyge *Missing Persons*
Ellerman, Annie Winifred *1981–1985*
Elliot, Jane or Jean *XVII*; *VI*
Elphinstone, Hester Maria *XVII*; *VI*
Elstob, Elizabeth *XVII*; *VI*
Esdaile, Katharine Ada *1941–1950*
Ewing, Juliana Horaria *XVIII*; *VI*
Fane, Priscilla Anne *XVIII*; *VI*
Fanshawe, Catherine Maria *XVIII*; *VI*
Farjeon, Eleanor *1961–1970*
Felkin, Ellen Thorneycroft *1922–1930*
Fenwick, Eliza *Missing Persons*
Ferguson, Mary Catherine *1901–1911 II*
Fermor, Henrietta Louise *XVIII*; *VI*
Ferrier, Susan Edmondstone *XVIII*; *VI*
Fielding, Sarah *XVIII*; *VI*
Fiennes, Celia *Missing Persons*
Finch, Anne *XIX*; *VII*
Fleming, Margaret *XIX*; *VII*
Fletcher, Eliza *XIX*; *VII*
Forbes, Joan Rosita *1961–1970*
Fothergill, Jessie *1901 II*; *XXII*
Fox, Caroline *XX*; *VII*
Frampton, Mary *XX*; *VII*

Francis, Anne *XX*; *VII*
Franklin, Eleanor Anne *XX*; *VII*
Frere, Mary Eliza Isabella *1901–1911 II*
Fullerton, Georgiana Charlotte *XX*; *VII*
Fyleman, Rose Amy *1951–1960*
Gardner, Mrs *XX*; *VII*
Garnett, Constance Clara *1941–1950*
Garrod, Dorothy Anne Elizabeth *Missing Persons*
Gaskell, Elizabeth Cleghorn *XXI*; *VII*
Gatty, Margaret *XXI*; *VII*
Gerard, Jane Emily *1901–1911 II*
Gérin, Winifred Eveleen *1981–1985*
Germain, Elizabeth *XXI*; *VII*
Gethin, Grace *XXI*; *VII*
Gilbert, Ann *XXI*; *VII*
Gilchrist, Anne *XXI*; *VII*
Gisborne, Maria *XXI*; *VII*
Glasse, Hannah *XXI*; *VII*
Glover, Jean *XXII*; *VIII*
Glyn, Elinor *1941–1950*
Godolphin, Margaret *XXII*; *VIII*
Godwin, Catherine Grace *XXII*; *VIII*
Godwin, Mary Wollstonecraft *XXII*; *VIII*
Gordon, Lucie or Lucy *XXII*; *VIII*
Gore, Catherine Grace Frances *XXII*; *VIII*
Gore-Booth, Eva Selina *Missing Persons*
Gosse, Emily *XXII*; *VIII*
Goudge, Elizabeth de Beauchamp *1981–1985*
Graham, Clementina Stirling *XXII*; *VIII*
Graham, Janet *XXII*; *VIII*
Grant, Anne *XXII*; *VIII*
Grant, Elizabeth *XXII*; *VIII*
Green, Alice Sophia Amelia *1922–1930*
Green, Eliza S. Craven *XXIII*; *VIII*
Greenwell, Dora *XXIII*; *VIII*
Gregory, Isabella Augusta *1931–1940*
Grey, Elizabeth *XXIII*; *VIII*
Grierson, Constantia *XXIII*; *VIII*
Griffith, Elizabeth *XXIII*; *VIII*
Grimston or Grymeston, Elizabeth *XXIII*; *VIII*
Grote, Harriet *XXIII*; *VIII*
Gunning, Elizabeth *XXIII*; *VIII*
Gunning, Susannah *XXIII*; *VIII*
Gurney, Anna *XXIII*; *VIII*
Hack, Maria *XXIII*; *VIII*
Halkett, Anne or Anna *XXIV*; *VIII*
Hall, Agnes C. *XXIV*; *VIII*
Hall, Anna Maria *XXIV*; *VIII*

Southey, Caroline Anne *LIII*; *XVIII*
Spence, Elizabeth Isabella *LIII*; *XVIII*
Spender, Lily *LIII*; *XVIII*
Stannard, Henrietta Eliza Vaughan *1901–1911 III*
Starke, Mariana *LIV*; *XVIII*
Stebbing, Lizzie Susan *1941–1950*
Steel, Flora Annie *1922–1930*
Stenton, Doris Mary *1971–1980*
Stepney, Catherine *LIV*; *XVIII*
Stewart-Mackenzie, Maria Elizabeth Frederica *LIV*; *XVIII*
Stokes, Margaret M'Nair *1901 III*; *XXII*
Strickland, Agnes *LV*; *XIX*
Strong, Eugénie *1941–1950*
Stuart-Wortley, Emmeline Charlotte Elizabeth *LV*; *XIX*
Sutherland, Lucie Stuart *1971–1980*
Swanwick, Anna *1901 III*; *XXII*
Talbot, Catherine *LV*; *XIX*
Tautphoelus, Baroness von *LV*; *XIX*
Taylor, Eva Germaine Rimington *1961–1970*
Taylor, Harriet Hardy *Missing Persons*
Taylor, Jane *LV*; *XIX*
Thicknesse, Ann *LVI*; *XIX*
Thirkell, Angela Margaret *1961–1970*
Thomas, Elizabeth *LVI*; *XIX*
Thomas, Margaret Haig *1951–1960*
Thompson, Flora Jane *Missing Persons*
Thomson, Katharine *LVI*; *XIX*
Thornton, Alice *Missing Persons*
Thurston, Katherine Cecil *1901–1911 III*
Tighe, Mary *LVI*; *XIX*
Tollett, Elizabeth *LVI*; *XIX*
Tonna, Charlotte Elizabeth *LVII*; *XIX*
Toulmin, Camilla Dufour *LVII*; *XIX*
Trench, Melesina *LVII*; *XIX*
Trimmer, Sarah *LVII*; *XIX*
Trollope, Frances *LVII*; *XIX*
Trollope, Theodosia *LVII*; *XIX*
Tucker, Charlotte Maria *LVII*; *XIX*
Umphelby, Fanny *LVIII*; *XX*
Underhill, Evelyn *1941–1950*
Unwin, Mary *LVIII*; *XX*
Uttley, Alice Jane *1971–1980*

Veley, Margaret *LVIII*; *XX*
Verney, Margaret Maria *1922–1930*
Vesey, Elizabeth *LVIII*; *XX*
Volusene, Florence *LVIII*; *XX*
Waddell, Helen Jane *1961–1970*
Wakefield, Priscilla *LVIII*; *XX*
Waldie, Charlotte Ann *LIX*; *XX*
Wallace, Eglantine *LIX*; *XX*
Wallace, Grace *LIX*; *XX*
Ward, Barbara Mary *1981–1985*
Ward, Ida Caroline *1941–1950*
Ward, Mary Augusta *1912–1921*
Wardlaw, Elizabeth *LIX*; *XX*
Warner, Sylvia Townsend *1971–1980*
Watts, Susanna *Missing Persons*
Webb, Mary Gladys *1922–1930*
Webster, Augusta *LX*; *XX*
Wellesley, Dorothy Violet *1951–1960*
Werner, Alice *Missing Persons*
West, Jane *LX*; *XX*
West, Rebecca *1981–1985*
Weston, Elizabeth Jane *LX*; *XX*
Wharton, Anne *LX*; *XX*
Williams, Anna *LXI*; *XXI*
Williams, Ella Gwendolen Rees *1971–1980*
Williams, Helen Maria *LXI*; *XXI*
Williams, Jane *LXI*; *XXI*
Wilson, Caroline *LXII*; *XXI*
Wilson, Mrs Cornwall Baron, Margaret *LXII*; *XXI*
Winkworth, Catherine *LXII*; *XXI*
Wiskemann, Elizabeth Meta *1971–1980*
Wood, Ellen *LXII*; *XXI*
Wood, Mary Anne Everett *LXII*; *XXI*
Woodroffe, Anne *LXII*; *XXI*
Woolf, Adeline Virginia *1941–1950*
Woolley or Wolley, Hannah *LXII*; *XXI*
Worboise, Emma Jane *LXII*; *XXI*
Wordsworth, Dorothy *Missing Persons*
Wright, Mehetabel Wesley *Missing Persons*
Wroth, Mary *LXIII*; *XXI*
Wynn, Charlotte Williams *LXIII*; *XXI*
Yates, Frances Amelia *1981–1985*
Yearsley, Ann *LXIII*; *XXI*
Yonge, Charlotte Mary *1901–1911 III*

Botany, gardening, conservation

Arber, Agnes *1951–1960*
Atkins, Anna *Missing Persons*

Blackburne, Anna *V*; *II*
Blackwell, Elizabeth *V*; *II*

Brightwen, Eliza *1901–1911 I*
Burges, Mary Anne *VII*; *III*
Gwynne-Vaughan, Helen Charlotte
 Isabella *1961–1970*
Howard, Louise Ernestine *Missing Persons*
Ibbetson, Agnes *XXVIII*; *X*
Jekyll, Gertrude *Missing Persons*
Long, Amelia *XXXIV*; *XII*

Loudon, Jane *XXXIV*; *XII*
Nevill, Dorothy Fanny *Missing Persons*
Pratt, Anne *XLVI*; *XVI*
Sackville-West, Victoria Mary *1961–1970*
Sargant, Ethel *Missing Persons*
Saunders, Edith Rebecca *Missing Persons*
Spry, Constance *1951–1960*

Business, industry, finance, printing, publishing

Atkins, Anna *Missing Persons*
Dillwyn, Elizabeth Amy *Missing Persons*
James, Eleanor *XXIX*; *X*

Lewis, Rosa *1951–1960*
Peacock, Lucy *XLIV*; *XV*

Diplomats, public and social service, administrators, philanthropists, secret service

Anderson, Adelaide Mary *Missing Persons*
Armine or Armyne, Mary *II*; *I*
Batten, Edith Mary *1981–1985*
Bell, Gertrude Margaret Lowthian
 1922–1930
Bosanquet, Helen *Missing Persons*
Bovey or Boevey, Catharina *VI*; *II*
Burdett-Coutts, Angela Georgina
 1901–1911 I
Carpenter, Mary *IX*; *III*
Chandler, Johanna *X*; *IV*
Cobbe, Frances Power *1901–1911 I*
Cons, Emma *Missing Persons*
Creed, Elizabeth *XIII*; *V*
Darusmont, Frances *XIV*; *V*
Denman, Gertrude Mary *1951–1960*
Dickson, Elizabeth *XV*; *V*
Fiennes or Fienes, Anne *XVIII*; *VI*
Frankland, Jocosa or Joyce *XX*; *VII*
Fullerton, Georgiana Charlotte *XX*; *VII*
Gilbert, Elizabeth Margaretta Maria *XXI*;
 VII
Gore-Booth, Eva Selina *Missing Persons*
Hadow, Grace Eleanor *1931–1940*
Hanbury, Elizabeth *1901–1911 II*

Hastings, Elizabeth *XXV*; *IX*
Hewley, Sarah *XXVI*; *IX*
Hill, Octavia *1912–1921*
Hollond, Ellen Julia *XXVII*; *IX*
Houston, Fanny Lucy *1931–1940*
Howard, Louise Ernestine *Missing Persons*
Isaacs, Stella *1971–1980*
Jebb, Eglantyne *1922–1930*
Markham, Violet Rosa *1951–1960*
Martindale, Hilda *1951–1960*
Owen, Alice *XLII*; *XIV*
Paget, Muriel Evelyn Vernon *1931–1940*
Pattison, Dorothy Wyndlow *XLIV*; *XV*
Pye, Edith Mary *Missing Persons*
Salt, Barbara *1971–1980*
Sharp, Evelyn Adelaide *1981–1985*
Stewart-Murray, Katharine Marjory
 1951–1960
Sumner, Mary Elizabeth *Missing Persons*
Sutherland, Lucie Stuart *1971–1980*
Szabo, Violette Reine Elizabeth
 Missing Persons
Tuckwell, Gertrude Mary *1951–1960*
Wakefield, Priscilla *LVIII*; *XX*
Watt, Margaret Rose *1941–1950*

Domestic servants, shop keepers

Greene, Anne *XXIII*; *VIII*
Jeffery, Dorothy *XXIX*; *X*

Nicholson, Margaret *XLI*; *XIV*
Raffald, Elizabeth *XLVII*; *XVI*

Education

Anderson, Kitty *1971–1980*
Bacon, Ann *II*; *I*

Batten, Edith Mary *1981–1985*
Beale, Dorothea *1901–1911 I*

Besant, Annie *1931–1940*
Bodichon, Barbara Leigh Smith *1901 I*;
  XXII
Bryan, Margaret *VII*; *III*
Bryant, Sophie *Missing Persons*
Burrows, Christine Mary Elizabeth
  1951–1960
Buss, Frances Mary *Missing Persons*
Chessar, Jane Agnes *X*; *IV*
Clare, Elizabeth de *X*; *IV*
Clough, Anne Jemima *1901 II*; *XXII*
Darbishire, Helen *1961–1970*
Davies, Sarah Emily *1912–1921*
Dove, Jane Frances *1941–1950*
Grey, Maria Georgina *1901–1911 II*
Hill, Rosamund Davenport- *1901–1911 II*
Hughes, Elizabeth Phillipps *Missing
  Persons*
Johnson, Bertha Jane *Missing Persons*
Kirkhoven or Kerckhoven, Catherine
  XXXI; *XI*
Malleson, Elizabeth *Missing Persons*
McMillan, Margaret *1931–1940*

Magee, Martha Maria *XXXV*; *XII*
Maitland, Agnes Catherine *1901–1911 II*
Mangnall, Richmal *XXXVI*; *XII*
Mason, Charlotte Maria Shaw
  Missing Persons
Mayo, Elizabeth *XXXVII*; *XIII*
Newall, Bertha Surtees *1931–1940*
Palmer, Charlotte *XLIII*; *XV*
Penrose, Emily *1941–1950*
Pole, Margaret *XLVI*; *XVI*
Postan, Eileen Edna le Poer *1931–1940*
Raisin, Catherine Alice *Missing Persons*
Reid, Elisabeth Jesser *Missing Persons*
Rogers, Annie Mary Anne Henley
  1931–1940
Saunders, Edith Rebecca *Missing Persons*
Shirreff, Emily Anne Eliza *LII*; *XVIII*
Sidgwick, Eleanor Mildred *1931–1940*
Somerville, Mary *1961–1970*
Stansfeld, Margaret *1951–1960*
Stocks, Mary Danvers *1971–1980*
Wordsworth, Elizabeth *1931–1940*

Engineering, instrument making, printers

Coade, Eleanor *Missing Persons*
Faithfull, Emily *Missing Persons*
Glasse, Hannah *XXI*; *VII*

Haslett, Caroline Harriet *1951–1960*
Vansittart, Henrietta *Missing Persons*

Law, lawyers, police, prisons, victims, criminals, impostors, witches, gamblers

Barker, Lilian Charlotte *1951–1960*
Blandy, Mary *V*; *II*
Brownrigg, Elizabeth, *VII*; *III*
Canning, Elizabeth *VIII*; *III*
Carleton, Mary *IX*; *III*
Catchpole, Margaret *IX*; *III*
Crofts or Croft, Elizabeth *XIII*; *V*
Dawes or Daw, Sophia *XIV*; *V*
Douglas, Janet *XV*; *V*
Fenning, Elizabeth *XVIII*; *VI*
Frith, Mary *XX*; *VII*
Hayes, Catharine *XXV*; *IX*
Hensey, Florence *XXVI*; *IX*
Kettle or Kyteler, Alice *XXXI*; *XI*
Kincaid, Jean *XXXI*; *XI*
Lisle, Alice *XXXIII*; *XI*

Macfarlane, Mrs *XXXV*; *XII*
Malcolm, Sarah *XXXV*; *XII*
Manning, Marie *XXXVI*; *XII*
Needham, Elizabeth *XL*; *XIV*
Nicholson, Margaret *XLI*; *XIV*
Orme, Eliza *Missing Persons*
Osborne, Ruth *XLII*; *XIV*
Parsons, Elizabeth *XLIII*; *XV*
Pilkington, Laetitia *XLV*; *XV*
Rich, Penelope *XLVIII*; *XVI*
Sorabji, Cornelia *1951–1960*
Toft or Tofts, Mary *LVI*; *XIX*
Vane, Frances Anne *LVIII*; *XX*
Wenham, Jane *LX*; *XX*
Williams, Ivy *1961–1970*

Lloyd George, Megan *1961–1970*
Lowe, Eveline Mary *1951–1960*
Lytton, Constance Georgina
  Missing Persons
Martin, Sarah *XXXVI*; *XII*
Miller, Florence Fenwick *Missing Persons*
O'Brien, Charlotte Grace *1901–1911 III*
Orme, Eliza *Missing Persons*
Paget, Mary Rosalind *1941–1950*
Pankhurst, Christabel Harriette *1951–1960*
Pankhurst, Emmeline *1922–1930*
Pankhurst, Estelle Sylvia *Missing Persons*
Paterson, Emma Anne *XLIV*; *XV*
Pethick-Lawrence, Emmeline
  Missing Persons
Phillips, Marion *Missing Persons*
Rathbone, Eleanor Florence *1941–1950*
Reid, Elisabeth Jesser *Missing Persons*
Robins, Elizabeth *Missing Persons*

Rye, Maria Susan *1901–1911 III*
Sanger, Sophy *Missing Persons*
Sharp, Evelyn *Missing Persons*
Smyth, Ethel Mary *1941–1950*
Sorabji, Cornelia *1951–1960*
Stopes, Marie Charlotte Carmichael
  1951–1960
Strachey, Rachel Conn *Missing Persons*
Summerskill, Edith Clara *1971–1980*
Swanwick, Helena Maria Lucy
  Missing Persons
Taylor, Harriet Hardy *Missing Persons*
Taylor, Helen *1901–1911 III*
Twining, Louisa *Missing Persons*
Weston, Agnes Elizabeth *1912–1921*
Whorwood, Jane *LXI*; *XXI*
Wilkinson, Ellen Cicely *1941–1950*

Religion, saints, martyrs, hymn writers, fanatics, recluses, missionaries

Aikenhead, Mary *I*; *I*
Askew, Anne *II*; *I*
Aylward, Gladys May *1961–1970*
Bache, Sarah *II*; *I*
Balfour, Frances *1931–1940*
Ball, Frances *III*; *I*
Ball, Hannah *III*; *I*
Barton, Elizabeth *III*; *I*
Blaugdone, Barbara *Missing Persons*
Bocher, Boucher, or Butcher, Joan *V*; *II*
Booth, Catherine *1901 I*; *XXII*
Boughton, Joan *VI*; *II*
Bowes, Elizabeth *VI*; *II*
Brettargh, Katharine *VI*; *II*
Brigit *VI*; *II*
Buchan or Simpson, Elspeth *VII*; *III*
Burnet, Margaret *VII*; *III*
Burton, Catharine *VIII*; *III*
Bury, Elizabeth *VIII*; *III*
Butler, Eleanor *VIII*; *III*
Cable, Alice Mildred *1951–1960*
Camm, Anne *VIII*; *III*
Campbell, Willielma *VIII*; *III*
Cannera or Cainner *VIII*; *III*
Chidley, Katherine *Missing Persons*
Christina *X*; *IV*
Christina of Markyate *Missing Persons*
Clitherow, Margaret *XI*; *IV*
Cons, Emma *Missing Persons*

Cousin, Anne Ross *1901–1911 I*
Cuthburh or Cuthburga *XIII*; *V*
Darlugdach *XIV*; *V*
Eadburga, Eadburh, Bugga, or Bugge
  XVI; *VI*
Ebba or Æbba *XVI*; *VI*
Edith or Eadgyth *XVI*; *VI*
Elliott, Charlotte *XVII*; *VI*
Ethelburga or Æthelburh *XVIII*; *VI*
Etheldreda, *XVIII*; *VI*
Fell, Margaret *XVIII*; *VI*
Fisher, Mary *XIX*; *VII*
Follows, Ruth *XIX*; *VII*
French, Evangeline Frances *1951–1960*
Frideswide, Fritheswith, or Fredeswitha
  XX; *VII*
Gaunt, Elizabeth *XXI*; *VII*
Girling, Mary Anne *XXI*; *VII*
Griffiths, Ann *XXIII*; *VIII*
Gundrada de Warenne *XXIII*; *VIII*
Hallahan, Margaret Mary *XXIV*; *VIII*
Hatfield, Martha *XXV*; *IX*
Havergal, Frances Ridley *XXV*; *IX*
Hearn, Mary Anne *1901–1911 II*
Hilda or Hild *XXVI*; *IX*
Hildilid *XXVI*; *IX*
Hooten, Elizabeth *XXVII*; *IX*
Hutchinson, Anne *XXVIII*; *X*
Juliana *XXX*; *X*

Royalty, titled aristocrats, courtiers

Sciences, geology, geography, life sciences, physics, meteorology, chemistry, metallurgy, mathematics

Social sciences, sociology, anthropology, economics, psychology

Society women, mistresses, prostitutes, famous beauties, heiresses, eccentrics

Lee, Rachel Fanny Antonia *XXXII*; *XI*
Lewson, Jane *XXXIII*; *XI*
Mohl, Madame Mary *XXXVIII*; *XIII*
Murphy, Marie Louise *XXXIX*; *XIII*
Murray, Elizabeth *XXXIX*; *XIII*
Myddleton or Middleton, Jane *XXXIX*; *XIII*
Nest or Nesta *XL*; *XIV*
Nevill, Dorothy Fanny *Missing Persons*
O'Carroll, Margaret *XLI*; *XIV*
Palmer, Eleanor *XLIII*; *XV*
Pearl, Cora *XLIV*; *XV*
Perrers, Alice *XLV*; *XV*
Phillips, Teresia Constantia *XLV*; *XV*
Robinson, Mary *XLIX*; *XVII*
Schulenburg, Ehrengard Melusina von der *L*; *XVII*
Sedley, Catharine *LI*; *XVII*
Shore, Jane *LII*; *XVIII*
Spencer, Dorothy *LIII*; *XVIII*
Stanhope, Hester Lucy *LIV*; *XVIII*
Stuart or Stewart, Frances Teresa *LV*; *XIX*
Swynford, Catherine *LV*; *XIX*
Villiers, Barbara *LVIII*; *XX*
Villiers, Elizabeth *LVIII*; *XX*
Walkinshaw, Clementina *LIX*; *XX*
Wallmoden, Amalie Sophie Marianne *LIX*; *XX*
Walter, Lucy *LIX*; *XX*
Wentworth, Henrietta Maria *LX*; *XX*
Wilson, Harriette *LXII*; *XXI*

Sport, exploration, travel

Baden-Powell, Olave St Clair *1971–1980*
Baillie, Marianne *II*; *I*
Bell, Gertrude Margaret Lowthian *1922–1930*
Bishop, Isabella Lucy *1901–1911 I*
Brassey, Anna or Annie *1901 I*; *XXII*
Burton, Isabel *1901 I*; *XXII*
Callcott, Maria *VIII*; *III*
Chambers, Dorothea Katharine *1951–1960*
Dixie, Florence Caroline *1901–1911 I*
Dod, Charlotte *Missing Persons*
Durham, Mary Edith *Missing Persons*
Eden, Emily *XVI*; *VI*
Fiennes, Celia *Missing Persons*
Forbes, Joan Rosita *1961–1970*
Franklin, Jane *XX*; *VII*
Gleitze, Mercedes *Missing Persons*
Hardy, Mary Anne *1901 II*; *XXII*
Johnson, Amy *1941–1950*
Kingsley, Mary Henrietta *1901 III*; *XXII*
Leitch, Charlotte Cecilia Pitcairn *1971–1980*
Lister, Anne *Missing Persons*
Ryan, Elizabeth Montague *1971–1980*
Smith, Frances *1971–1980*
Stansfeld, Margaret *1951–1960*
Sterry, Charlotte *1961–1970*

Theatre, cinema, dance, music, song, broadcasting

Abington, Frances *I*; *I*
Addison, Laura *I*; *I*
Albani, Marie Louise Cécilie Emma *1922–1930*
Albertazzi, Emma *I*; *I*
Anderson, Lucy *I*; *I*
Arne, Cecilia *II*; *I*
Ashwell, Lena Margaret *1951–1960*
Baddeley, Sophia *II*; *I*
Baillie, Isobel *1981–1985*
Banks, Sarah Sophia *III*; *I*
Barnard, Charlotte Alington *III*; *I*
Barry, Ann Spranger *III*; *I*
Barry, Elizabeth *III*; *I*
Bartley, Sarah *III*; *I*
Barwell, Louisa Mary *III*; *I*
Bates, Sarah *III*; *I*
Baylis, Lilian Mary *1931–1940*
Becher, Eliza *IV*; *II*
Bellamy, George Anne *IV*; *II*
Bewick, Jane *IV*; *II*
Bicknell, M. [Margaret?] *V*; *II*
Billington, Elizabeth *V*; *II*
Bishop, Ann *V*; *II*
Bland, Maria Theresa *V*; *II*
Bodda Pyne, Louisa Fanny *1901–1911 I*
Booth, Sarah *V*; *II*
Boutel, Mrs *VI*; *II*
Bracegirdle, Anne *VI*; *II*
Bradshaw, Ann Maria *VI*; *II*

Kemble, Elizabeth *XXX*; *X*
Kemble, Frances Anne *1901 III*; *XXII*
Kemble, Maria Theresa or Marie Therése *XXX*; *X*
Kemble, Priscilla *XXX*; *X*
Kendal, Margaret Shafto *1931–1940*
Kennedy or Farrell, Mrs *XXX*; *X*
Knipp or Knep, Mrs *XXXI*; *XI*
Lacy, Harriette Deborah *XXXI*; *XI*
Laidlaw, Anna Robena *1901–1911 II*
Langtry, Emily Charlotte *Missing Persons*
Lawrence, Gertrude *1951–1960*
Leclercq, Carlotta *1901 III*; *XXII*
Leigh, Vivien *1961–1970*
Lejeune, Caroline Alice *1971–1980*
Lemmens-Sherrington, Helen *1901–1911 II*
Lind, Johanna Maria *XXXIII*; *XI*
Linley, Mary *XXXIII*; *XI*
Linwood, Mary *XXXIII*; *XI*
Litchfield, Mrs Harriet *XXXIII*; *XI*
Litton, Marie *XXXIII*; *XI*
Lopokova, Lydia Vasilievna *1981–1985*
Loraine, Violet Mary *1951–1960*
Lutyens, Agnes Elisabeth *1981–1985*
McCarthy, Lillah *1951–1960*
Mara, Gertrude Elizabeth *XXXVI*; *XII*
Marsh, Edith Ngaio *1981–1985*
Mathews, Lucia Elizabeth or Elizabetta *XXXVII*; *XIII*
Matthews, Jessie Margaret *1981–1985*
Mattocks, Isabella *XXXVII*; *XIII*
Melba, Nellie *1931–1940*
Mellon, Harriet *XXXVII*; *XIII*
Mellon, Sarah Jane *1901–1911 II*
Menken, Adah Isaacs *XXXVII*; *XIII*
Millar, Gertie *1951–1960*
Moore, Eleanora *XXXVIII*; *XIII*
Mountain, Rosoman *XXXIX*; *XIII*
Neilson, Julia Emilie *1951–1960*
Neilson, Lilian Adelaide *XL*; *XIV*
Nicol, Mrs *XLI*; *XIV*
Nicol, Emma *XLI*; *XIV*
Nisbett, Louisa Cranstoun *XLI*; *XIV*
Novello, Clara Anastasia *1901–1911 III*
Oldfield, Anne *XLII*; *XIV*
Oliver, Martha Cranmer *XLII*; *XIV*
Orger, Mary Ann *XLII*; *XIV*
Parepa-Rosa, Euphrosyne Parepa de Boyesku *XLIII*; *XV*
Patey, Janet Monach *XLIV*; *XV*
Paton, Mary Ann *XLIV*; *XV*

Patti, Carlotta *XLIV*; *XV*
Paul, Isabella Howard *XLIV*; *XV*
Pavlova, Anna *Missing Persons*
Pitt, Ann *XLV*; *XV*
Pope, Elizabeth *XLVI*; *XVI*
Pope, Jane *XLVI*; *XVI*
Pope, Maria Ann *XLVI*; *XVI*
Porter, Mary *XLVI*; *XVI*
Powell, Mrs *XLVI*; *XVI*
Pritchard, Hannah *XLVI*; *XVI*
Rainforth, Elizabeth *XLVII*; *XVI*
Rambert, Marie *1981–1985*
Robins, Elizabeth *Missing Persons*
Robinson, Anastasia *XLIX*; *XVII*
Robinson, Mary *XLIX*; *XVII*
Robson, Flora *1981–1985*
Romer, Emma *XLIX*; *XVII*
Rousby, Clara Marion Jessie *XLIX*; *XVII*
Rowson, Susanna *XLIX*; *XVII*
Rutherford, Margaret *1971–1980*
Salmon, Eliza *L*; *XVII*
Saunders, Margaret *L*; *XVII*
Sedgwick, Amy *1901 III*; *XXII*
Seymour, Mrs *LI*; *XVII*
Shaw, Mary *LI*; *XVII*
Sheridan, Elizabeth Ann *LII*; *XVIII*
Sheridan, Helen Selina *LII*; *XVIII*
Siddons, Sarah *LII*; *XVIII*
Slingsby, Mary *LII*; *XVIII*
Smithson, Harriet Constance *LIII*; *XVIII*
Smyth, Ethel Mary *1941–1950*
Stephens, Catherine *LIV*; *XVIII*
Stephens, Jane *LIV*; *XVIII*
Sterling, Antoinette *1901–1911 III*
Stirling, Mary Anne *LIV*; *XVIII*
Stocks, Mary Danvers *1971–1980*
Storace, Anna, or Ann Selina *LIV*; *XVIII*
Taglioni, Marie *LV*; *XIX*
Tempest, Marie *1941–1950*
Terry, Alice Ellen *1922–1930*
Teyte, Margaret *1971–1980*
Thicknesse, Ann *LVI*; *XIX*
Thompson, Lydia *1901–1911 III*
Thorndike, Agnes Sybil *1971–1980*
Thurmond, Mrs *LVI*; *XIX*
Tilley, Vesta *1951–1960*
Titiens, or Tietjens, Teresa Caroline Johanna *LVI*; *XIX*
Tofts, Katherine *LVI*; *XIX*
Trevelyan, Hilda *1951–1960*
Vanbrugh, Irene *1941–1950*

Warfare, army, navy, air force, heroines